SHARED AUTHORITY

This important new book advances a fresh philosophical account of the relationship between the legislature and courts, opposing the common conception of law, in which it is legislatures that primarily create the law, and courts that primarily apply it. This conception has eclectic affinities with legal positivism, and although it may have been a helpful intellectual tool in the past, it now increasingly generates more problems than it solves. For this reason, the author argues, legal philosophers are better off abandoning it. At the same time they are asked to dismantle the philosophical and doctrinal infrastructure that has been based on it and which has been hitherto largely unquestioned. In its place the book offers an alternative framework for understanding the role of courts and the legislature; a framework which is distinctly anti-positivist and which builds on Ronald Dworkin's interpretive theory of law. But, contrary to Dworkin, it insists that legal duty is sensitive to the position one occupies in the project of governing; legal interpretation is not the solitary task of one super-judge, but a collaborative task structured by principles of institutional morality such as separation of powers which impose a moral duty on participants to respect each other's contributions. Moreover this collaborative task will often involve citizens taking an active role in their interaction with the law.

Volume 7 in the series Law and Practical Reason

Law and Practical Reason

The intention of this series is that it should encompass monographs and collections of essays that address the fundamental issues in legal philosophy. The foci are conceptual and normative in character, not empirical. Studies addressing the idea of law as a species of practical reason are especially welcome. Recognising that there is no occasion sharply to distinguish analytic and systematic work in the field from historico-critical research, the editors also welcome studies in the history of legal philosophy. Contributions to the series, inevitably crossing disciplinary lines, will be of interest to students and professionals in moral, political, and legal philosophy.

General Editor

Prof George Pavlakos (Antwerp and Glasgow)

Advisory Board

Prof Robert Alexy (Kiel)
Prof Samantha Besson (Fribourg, CH)
Prof Emilios Christodoulidis (Glasgow)
Prof Sean Coyle (Birmingham)
Prof Mattias Kumm (New York and Berlin)
Prof Stanley Paulson (St Louis and Kiel)
Prof Joseph Raz (Columbia Law School)
Prof Arthur Ripstein (Toronto)
Prof Scott Shapiro (Yale Law School)
Prof Victor Tadros (Warwick)

Editorial Assistant

Triantafyllos Gouvas (Antwerp)

Recent titles in the series

Shared Authority

Courts and Legislatures in Legal Theory

Dimitrios Kyritsis

·HART·
PUBLISHING

OXFORD AND PORTLAND, OREGON
2017

Hart Publishing
An imprint of Bloomsbury Publishing Plc

Hart Publishing Ltd	Bloomsbury Publishing Plc
Kemp House	50 Bedford Square
Chawley Park	London
Cumnor Hill	WC1B 3DP
Oxford OX2 9PH	UK
UK	

www.hartpub.co.uk
www.bloomsbury.com

Published in North America (US and Canada) by
Hart Publishing
c/o International Specialized Book Services
920 NE 58th Avenue, Suite 300
Portland, OR 97213-3786
USA

www.isbs.com

**HART PUBLISHING, the Hart/Stag logo, BLOOMSBURY and the
Diana logo are trademarks of Bloomsbury Publishing Plc**

First published in hardback, 2015
Paperback edition, 2017

British Library Cataloguing-in-Publication Data
A catalogue record for this book is available from the British Library.

ISBN: PB: 978-1-50991-379-4
HB: 978-1-84946-389-8

Typeset by Compuscript Ltd, Shannon

To find out more about our authors and books visit www.hartpublishing.co.uk. Here you will
find extracts, author information, details of forthcoming events and the option to sign up for our
newsletters.

To my mother and in memory of my father

Acknowledgments

This book develops some of the main claims and arguments of my DPhil thesis, which I completed at the University of Oxford under the supervision of Nicos Stavropoulos. It is to him that I owe the greatest debt for being a tireless mentor and a constant source of inspiration, during and after my studies.

My views on the issues I explore in this book have evolved significantly since my viva. I am grateful to audiences at New York University, the University of Antwerp, the Legal Research Institute of the National Autonomous University of Mexico (UNAM), the University of Hull, University College London, University of Glasgow, Athens Law School and the University of Oxford, as well as working groups at the International Association for the Philosophy of Law and Social Philosophy (IVR) conference in Granada, Spain, and at the McMaster Conference in the Philosophy of Law, to whom I presented earlier versions of the claims defended here. Nick Barber, Matyas Bodig, Julie Dickson, Luis Duarte d'Almeida, Erik Encarnacion, John Gardner, Juan Vega Gomez, Antony Hatzistavrou, Mike Giudice, Tria Gkouvas, Marco Goldoni, Les Green, Peter Jaffey, Mattias Kumm, Stuart Lakin, Claudio Michelon, Liam Murphy, Konstantinos Papageorgiou, Haris Papadopoulos, George Pavlakos, Giorgio Pino, David Plunkett, Danny Priel, Massimo Renzo, Prince Saprai, Stefan Sciaraffa, Pavlos Sourlas, John Stanton-Ife, Mark Taylor, Stavros Tsakyrakis, Philippos Vasilogiannis and Vasilis Voutsakis read and commented on earlier drafts, saved me from many mistakes, and stimulated and challenged my thinking. I am indebted to them all. A special thanks goes to George Letsas, together with whom I have been thinking about these issues for as long as I can remember. In the last two years or so I have been fortunate to work closely with Dimitris Tsarapatsanis. Our countless discussions provided both an impetus and a necessary check, as the argument of the book was progressing.

In order to complete my DPhil thesis I received a Scholarship from the Arts and Humanities Research Board and a Graduate Assistance Fund Award from the Faculty of Law, University of Oxford. I am grateful to these two institutions for their financial assistance. In addition, I am indebted to Reading Law School, which provided funding to help me complete the manuscript.

Parts of this book have appeared as separate articles: chapter two is an extended version of 'The Persistent Significance of Jurisdiction' (2012) 25 *Ratio Juris* 343, chapters one, three and four include segments of 'The Normativity of The Practice of Officials' in S Bertea and G Pavlakos (eds), *New Essays on the Normativity of Law* (Oxford, Hart Publishing, 2011) 177, and 'Law's Province in the Domain of Value' (forthcoming *Jurisprudence*). I am grateful to Wiley-Blackwell and Hart Publishing for permission to reprint this material.

George Pavlakos, editor of the Law and Practical Reason series, has supported this project in more ways than I can count. His confidence in it and his invaluable guidance have galvanised me at every turn. I also want to thank Richard Hart, Rachel Turner, Emma Swinden, Mel Hamill, Tom Adams and Charlotte Austin of Hart Publishing for their help and professionalism throughout the process, and Tori Crawford for the editorial assistance she provided.

Last but not least, I am grateful to Denise Shields. Her devotion, patience and (sometimes) sheer endurance have given me strength over the years and spurred me on.

I dedicate this book to my parents, Eftyhia and Elias Kyritsis, without whose unfailing encouragement and selfless support I would not have realised my dream of pursuing an academic career; in fact, I would likely not have discovered the joy and value of intellectual inquiry in the first place.

Contents

1

In Praise of Particular Jurisprudence

I. INTRODUCTION

'THOSE WERE THE days'. Understandably perhaps, outsiders may be tempted to assume such a nostalgic posture with regard to the state of contemporary jurisprudential debate. Indeed, in recent years analytical jurisprudence seems to have been stuck in the preliminaries. Instead of focusing on whether, for example, Nazi Germany or apartheid South Africa had law or not (a locus of the intellectual wars of old)[1] or engaging in other similarly urgent issues at the intersection of law and politics, much writing in legal theory nowadays is devoted to housekeeping concerns such as clarifying theoretical positions, and dispelling misunderstandings.[2]

What has not changed much since the days of Hart and Fuller is the geography of the debate. Like then, legal positivists and anti-positivists still occupy the opposite poles arguing over the relationship between law and morality. That is not to say that the debate is stagnant. In the past decades, as each side engaged with the criticisms and proposals of the other, the dialectic between positivism and anti-positivism produced ever more sophisticated philosophical theories as well as an ever more nuanced understanding of the problems that these theories must resolve. What has come to be known as the Hart-Dworkin debate is a case in point. Ronald Dworkin's famous criticism of Hart's doctrine of the rule of recognition as the ultimate foundation of law paved the way for philosophically robust explanations of the normativity of the practice of officials and of judicial duty by Hart's followers. What is more, Dworkin's focus on disagreement in law spawned a vigorous interest in the methodology of jurisprudence and its connection with legal practice. Dworkin's anti-positivism was replicated at the methodological level in the view that law is an interpretive concept:

---

[1] See the classic exchange between HLA Hart and Lon Fuller in the *Harvard Law Review*: HLA Hart, 'Positivism and the Separation of Law and Morals' (1958) 71 *Harvard Law Review* 593; and L Fuller, 'Positivism and Fidelity to Law: A Reply to Professor Hart' (1958) *Harvard Law Review* 630.

[2] Two characteristic examples of this trend are J Gardner, '5 1/2 Positivist Myths' (2001) 46 *American Journal of Jurisprudence* 199; and N Stavropoulos, 'Interpretivist Theories of Law' in E Zalta (ed), *Stanford Encyclopedia of Philosophy (Winter 2003)* available at http://plato.stanford.edu/archives/win2003/entries/law-interpretivist.

jurisprudential positions, he argued, are continuous with – though much more abstract from – substantive legal claims, so they have the same aim and draw on the same resources, including moral arguments. To counter the challenge, his opponents developed intricate accounts of conceptual analysis that insulate the theory of law from the committed and normative theories put forward by practitioners in support of their substantive legal claims. On those accounts, the theory of law merely reports and organises the latter, and can thus remain neutral and descriptive.

There are signs, however, that the Hart-Dworkin debate is exhausting its momentum. For one thing, it is widely felt that competing theories have done all that is needed to incorporate the philosophical lessons from it. So for instance, some especially influential versions of legal positivism have downplayed the importance of the rule of recognition, seeing it as an existence condition of law but lacking in explanatory power; along with it they dodge the problems that Dworkin argued beset it. And to neutralise the sting of disagreement in law, legal positivists of today have drawn a distinction, about which I will have a lot to say in this book, between adjudication and the theory of law. Disagreement is pervasive in adjudication, they say, but the theory of law studies the deeper agreement, which alone makes legal disagreement possible and meaningful. The same distinction has been employed to block the connection Dworkin's interpretive methodology seeks to establish between jurisprudence and first-order legal argumentation. All sorts of arguments may be relevant in adjudication, given its purpose, but they do not carry through to the upstream investigation into the essential features of all legal practice.

It goes without saying that the jury is out about the cogency of any of those responses,[3] and it is impossible to evaluate them all in one book. I give this brief overview of the state of play because it appears to confirm a pattern that should be familiar from other fields of knowledge. The introduction of a new idea or a new discovery fundamentally disrupts established ways of thinking and path-dependencies. This propels the discipline forward, which adjusts so as to absorb the shock. Because the disruption reaches to core elements of the orthodoxy, the adjustment may be drastic. Old theories are discredited and abandoned, and novel theories take their place. Boundaries between disciplines are re-drawn. Then, some kind of equilibrium is once again established, and the attention of participants moves to more concrete issues that take as a given some general framework, as this has been re-shaped by this process.

What could be the next iteration in this dialectic? In order to have a similarly rejuvenating effect, the impetus cannot come from an idea that merely repeats

---

[3] Dworkin himself was rather sceptical and at times dismissive of the positivist rejoinders to his criticism. He referred to one contemporary variant of legal positivism as 'Pickwickian' and to another as 'Ptolemaic'. See R Dworkin, *Justice in Robes* (Cambridge MA, Harvard University Press, 2006).

an already entrenched position or loads the dice. This can be avoided in a number of ways. To begin with, it may be useful for competing theories to look across the aisle and find some common ground. Clearly, not all of the good work in the theory of law is done with the aim of vindicating one camp against the other, and neither are all the insights of individual theories tainted by their commitment to positivism or anti-positivism.[4] But of course some disagreement cannot and should not be bypassed. If the debate between positivism and anti-positivism tracks some fundamental philosophical concerns about the nature of law, their differences must interest us as much as their commonalities. Still, it would be more productive to find new ways of engagement between the two views, since the old ones have now led to a stalemate. At the very least it is imperative, when framing the problem, to be prepared to take seriously the insights, concerns and objections of the other side. This is what I attempt to do in this book.

In this introductory chapter my aim is to offer a map of the entire argument. Due to the fact that the approach I adopt is different in several respects from that to be found in much contemporary jurisprudential writing, I take special care to make explicit the philosophical motivation behind it. In so doing, I engage in current debates about the methodology of jurisprudence. In particular, I try to indicate how this approach can help us make progress in the debate between positivism and anti-positivism. I begin by introducing the notion of a legal system with courts and a legislature. I go on to explain the philosophical motivation for my choice of focus.

II. COURTS AND LEGISLATURES IN LEGAL THEORY

The legal systems that we are familiar with are equipped with legal officials of various sorts. We can say that these officials administer the law or, more generally, run the legal system. In fact, it is doubtful that there can ever be a legal system without them.[5] But whether the presence of legal officials is a necessary feature of all law or not, their importance where they are to be found is undeniable. Hence, it is no surprise that they have provided a point of focus for much of our thinking about the nature of law.

Obviously, legal philosophers do not take a biographical interest in legal officials. Legal officials are of philosophical interest because of the roles they

---

[4] I have pursued this 'conciliatory' strategy in D Kyritsis, 'What is Good about Legal Conventionalism?' (2008) 14 *Legal Theory* 135. There I sought to show that the notion of a joint practice of officials, which has been elaborated within legal conventionalism, a strand of jurisprudential thought that starts with HLA Hart, can be appropriated by a robust natural law theory.

[5] HLA Hart, *The Concept of Law*, 2nd edn with a new Postscript (Oxford, Oxford University Press, 1994). J Raz, 'The Institutional Nature of Law' (1975) 38 *Modern Law Review* 489, 491.

occupy. In advanced legal systems, these roles tend to be fixed and stable over time. Some of them are particularly salient and important. They correspond to the various familiar legal institutions such as the head of state, the courts, the police etc. Individual judges may come and go, but the institution of a court, if one exists, does not change with every change in its membership.[6] In fact, when we refer to legal officials what we typically have in mind are the legal institutions in whose name these officials act. What grounds this continuity are, as Joseph Raz has put it, 'the norms which establish these institutions'.[7] These norms determine what counts as an exercise of institutional power as opposed to usurpation, delineate the jurisdiction of this or that institution and so forth.[8]

Now, in the legal systems that we are familiar with, legal institutions share two very general features. The first feature is that their role (or jurisdiction) is not unlimited. I do not wish to deny at this point what some theorists have asserted, namely that legal systems as a whole claim to have comprehensive jurisdiction, in the sense that any matter may be legally regulated within a certain territory. Even so, the various legal institutions that belong to a legal system are conferred certain powers only, such as the power to regulate certain matters and not others or to regulate them in one way rather than another. The second feature is that in any given legal system there are different types of legal institutions. Perhaps legal systems exist or are possible that have only one institution, but this is not the type of legal system that we are familiar with. In those there are no 'jacks of all trades'. The two features, though conceptually distinct, are closely connected. Two different institutions are also likely to have different and therefore limited jurisdictions – otherwise why have two of them? And their limited character strongly suggests the possibility of their plurality. Clearly, if a legal system has comprehensive jurisdiction, and one institution that belongs to it is authorised to regulate only some of the matters that fall within it, we should expect that there is another institution that takes care of the rest.

[6] The term 'institution' is also used in a broader sense, which encompasses the institution of contract or marriage. See relatedly N MacCormick, *Institutions of Law: An Essay in Legal Theory* (Oxford, Oxford University Press, 2007). I use the term to refer to those institutions which function as agents of governance. Courts and legislatures are this sort of institution.

[7] Raz, 'The Institutional Nature of Law' (n 5) 492.

[8] Given the tight connection between institutions and officials, I shall henceforth speak of institutions such as courts and legislatures and officials such as judges and legislators interchangeably. Needless to say, this terminological choice glosses over the fact that many courts – including the most important ones – and all legislatures are collegiate bodies. Their acts are constituted by a combination of acts performed by their members. As a result there is an important distance between the norms that determine the duties and powers of, say, an individual judge and the court of which he is a member. Though the distinction is important, it does not directly bear on the argument of this book. I shall therefore ignore it. The literature on the moral, deliberative, and strategic ramifications of decision-making by collegiate bodies is vast. See among others L Kornhauser and L Sager, 'The Many as One: Integrity and Group Choice in Paradoxical Cases' (2004) 32 *Philosophy and Public Affairs* 249.

This book seeks to draw some philosophical lessons from the workings of institutions that exhibit the two aforementioned features. To this effect, it examines the relationship between two legal institutions, courts and the legislature. For the sake of brevity I shall call it the C-L relationship, and I shall call legal systems that have both of these institutions C-L legal systems. C-L legal systems exemplify both of the features listed above. First, they comprise more than one institutional role. Secondly, these institutional roles are limited. As common wisdom has it, legislators are there to pass statutes and judges to decide cases. There is, of course, nothing prima facie incoherent, say, about expanding the role of the legislator to encompass the adjudication of private disputes. But the piece of common wisdom illustrates the limited nature of the institutional roles that legal officials perform, as well as their plurality. Adherents to the common wisdom believe that, as things stand, it is not the legislators' job to decide private disputes; we have a different kind of legal official to do that, whom we call judges.

In addition, I discuss C-L legal systems because judges and legislators are usual suspects in contemporary theorising about the nature of law, and in this sense the jurisprudential analysis undertaken here is continuous with current jurisprudential trends. Judges, it is fair to say, have attracted the attention of legal theorists more frequently than legislators.[9] Their attitudes, practices, duties and powers have provided the basis for the extrapolation of more general philosophical lessons about the nature of law. But legislatures are never too far off the picture. As a matter of fact, recent years have witnessed a flurry of philosophical interest in legislatures.[10]

III. MUST WE BE ESSENTIALIST ABOUT INSTITUTIONS?

I said above that the focus of this book is the C-L relationship. It should be noted, however, that I do not intend to offer a complete account of it or of C-L legal systems as a whole. So, for one thing, I readily concede that C-L legal systems may well have other institutions speaking and acting in their name.[11] Neither do I contend that the existence of courts and legislatures is the most important thing about these legal systems. More importantly, I do not give a detailed upfront explanation of what I take the essential features of each institution to be.

---

[9] J Waldron, *Law and Disagreement* (Oxford, Oxford University Press, 1999) 44–45.
[10] A good recent example is R Ekins, *The Nature of Legislative Intent* (Oxford, Oxford University Press, 2012). The philosophical study of legislation now has a dedicated journal, too, entitled *The Theory and Practice of Legislation*.
[11] On legal theory's relative neglect of the executive, see P Cane, 'Public Law in *The Concept of Law*' (2013) 33 *Oxford Journal of Legal Studies* 649.

This last form of reticence may come as a surprise. How can we ever hope to make any philosophical progress in this topic, unless we have more closely identified the two parties in the C-L relationship? Without such knowledge, so the objection goes, we can never be sure that we are studying the relationship between courts and the legislature as opposed to that, say, between courts and the executive. There is a further reason to doubt the plausibility of the project I am embarking on, namely that the characteristics of actual courts and legislatures in the legal systems that we are familiar with are rather varied and contingent. Although it is likely that some basic features of courts and the legislature stay the same across legal systems, there are several features that are unique to some or are not shared by all. In addition, some courts may for whatever reason come to perform tasks that we would tend to associate with the legislature and vice versa.

A sceptic would draw from this the conclusion that it is a fallacy to believe in courts and legislatures having an essential nature at all. He would contend perhaps that the concepts of courts and legislatures are nothing but sociological generalisations. All that they do is collect together roughly similar institutions. That is not to deny there may be a good reason why such institutions are so common, but there is no conceptual necessity that things should be thus. The sceptical challenge may be said to gain support from the fact that as a historical matter the contemporary distinction between courts and the legislature is a relatively recent development. In the not too distant past, the distinction, if it existed at all, was a blurry one.[12] Arguably, the fact that it has hardened now does not preclude that it may change yet again in the future.

Even if we are inclined to say that the nature of a court or a legislature does not change whenever the same public body is empowered to act as both, we still have to reckon with the risk of generalising from peculiarities of this or that legal system. If in my legal system courts are assigned an exotic power, say, they can veto the election of the head of state, what is stopping me from thinking that this is part of their very nature, a feature any body must possess to count as a court? Unless we first define what a court and a legislature necessarily are we cannot adequately check this risk.

This book does little to address this sceptical challenge. It draws on the fact that courts and legislatures are so ubiquitous and entrenched in advanced legal systems that we all have an intuitive understanding of what makes a public body one or the other or something else completely, and largely relies on this intuitive understanding. Although I shall flesh out this intuitive understanding a bit more in the rest of this chapter, I shall do so primarily for the purpose of specifying

---

[12] For a useful historical account of the evolution of courts and Parliament as two distinct institutions in the UK, see among others N Duxbury, *Elements of Legislation* (Cambridge, Cambridge University Press, 2012).

the philosophical motivation for my interest in the C-L relationship. My non-committal attitude on this issue has to do with the dialectical structure of the argument. In the following chapters I shall compare and evaluate the way two prominent philosophical theories of law have cashed out the C-L relationship. I start with Raz's influential theory of legal authority. Although Raz has expressed doubts about the aptness of the label 'legal positivism' being attached to his theory, he can reasonably be classed as a legal positivist in the sense that he thinks valid law is identifiable without reference to moral considerations, solely by appeal to a directive's provenance from a source that is recognised as authoritative. I then go on to examine Dworkin's brand of anti-positivism. Contrary to theorists like Raz, Dworkin contends that all legal duty is necessarily also grounded in moral considerations. As we will see, both of these theories draw for their own reasons a distinction between courts and the legislature; thus they are relevant to this inquiry. However, their understanding of the two bodies is heavily dependent on their starkly different overall views of the nature of law. Hence, to defend as a preliminary matter a particular understanding of their nature would likely beg important questions.

A further reason for my reticence is that it is not my immediate purpose to show that one or the other theory gives a more adequate portrayal of the two bodies. What I chiefly want to assess is how, given their understanding of the two bodies, they explicate their relationship. I focus on a specific aspect of it, namely the courts' dependence on the doings and sayings of the legislature. By this I mean the fact that judges decide cases before them taking into account (in a sense to be further specified) the doings and sayings of the legislature, and in particular its decisions, which are typically enshrined in the texts of statutes. There is broad agreement on this feature of the C-L relationship, but its philosophical basis is still elusive and contested. It is by reference to this issue that I want to compare the two theories. I argue that, while Raz's theory comes up against significant difficulties in trying to furnish such a basis, Dworkin's theory, properly elaborated, provides a superior solution. Now, you may think that the dependence of judicial decision-making on legislative decisions is something novel, historically speaking, or ephemeral. For instance, you may think that it is lacking in legal systems without the legislative production that is so characteristic of the ones that we are familiar with. But if it is present in *our* C-L legal systems, then for the reasons I sketch in the next section it makes sense to study it no matter what the sceptic says.

IV. SHARED AUTHORITY

It is undeniable that C-L legal systems are very common, as is the dependence of courts on the doings and sayings of the legislature. But this by itself does not explain why they deserve our philosophical attention. So let me offer some reasons for choosing to study the C-L relationship.

First of all, this relationship dramatises a classic jurisprudential quandary. As a general matter, legal duty is thought to be determined by social facts about the doings and sayings of political institutions, especially the decisions they make. Legal positivists and anti-positivists alike take this desideratum to be their starting point. Thus, John Gardner has said that all legal positivism is committed to the proposition that

> a norm is valid as a norm of [a given legal system] in virtue of the fact that at some relevant time and place some relevant agent or agents announced it, practiced it, invoked it, enforced it, endorsed it, or otherwise engaged with it . . . Conversely, if it was never engaged with by any relevant agents, then it does not count as a law even though it may be an excellent norm that all the relevant agents should have engaged with it unreservedly.[13]

On the other side of the fence, interpretivism, as summarised by Nicos Stavropoulos, accepts the same thesis:

> It is uncontroversial that the question whether gratuitous promises bind in law is partly dependent upon political decisions and practices. It is further widely accepted that such decisions and practices crucially include what officials said and did in the past, conceived simply in terms of the texts and utterances they issued and their settled practice of behaving in a certain way, all of which at least in part make propositions of law true. For example, it is widely accepted that the text of a statute that reads 'gratuitous promises shall not be enforced', or the fact that judges, as a matter of settled practice, are disposed not to enforce gratuitous promises, would go a long way towards explaining why such promises are not enforceable.[14]

What is a matter of controversy between the two camps is why this should be so. More specifically, why and under what conditions does the fact that someone has decided that I ought to do *y* make it the case that I now ought to do *y*? The quandary is more often discussed by reference to legal duties addressed to citizens, and indeed it is in this context that speaking of legal duty seems most intuitive. This marks a difference from the present inquiry. The C-L relationship is one that holds between legal institutions, not legal institutions and citizens. Still, the similarities cannot be overlooked. As in the latter case, in the context of the C-L relationship we think that what one institution may and may not do is systematically determined by the doings and sayings of the other. Earlier I wrote that courts depend on legislative decisions. It may, of course, be that they also depend on the doings and sayings of other institutions. But that does not change the fact that the legislature is one of the bodies – perhaps the most important body – whose decisions judges *qua* legal officials further. This is

---

[13] Gardner, '5 1/2 Positivist Myths' (n 2) 200.
[14] Stavropoulos, 'Interpretivist Theories' (n 2).

not meant as a factual statement about what some or most judges do, but as a normative statement about their official responsibilities. Courts just are the type of institution, whose job description crucially includes the furthering of legislative decisions. It would be wrong of judges to decide cases coming before them *qua* judges on the basis of what by their own lights is the best course of action. In fact, we are inclined to say that judges have a *legal* duty to further legislative decisions and not to decide cases *de novo*; that it would be *legally* wrong of them to do otherwise. Clearly, it is too soon to make up our minds about the soundness of this aspect of ordinary usage. Nevertheless, we cannot fail to note that there are instances where failure of a judge to further a legislative decision that is relevant to a case before her brings legal sanction such as that her judgment may be quashed on appeal. This provides evidence – albeit not conclusive – that what we are dealing with here is a *legal* duty.

This is not a novel claim. Jeremy Waldron has theorised the structural similarities between what he calls inter-institutional authority or authority for officials and law's authority over citizens.[15] He argues that the mark of authority is not necessarily compliance. To be sure, compliance is the typical response expected from citizens in the face of authority. But we think that an authority properly elicits a range of further responses that include the respect different cooperating officials owe one another. This type of respect, Waldron argues, is triggered, whenever an *institutional settlement* has occurred, whereby a question of common concern has been decided one way or another in accordance with arrangements that are put in place to provide such settlement. Respect then takes the form of '[playing] one's part in the social processes that are necessary to sustain and implement such decision as a settlement'.[16] More specifically, when an institutional decision demands respect as having settled an issue of common concern, other officials undertake not to treat this issue as open for as long as the settlement is binding, even if they think the specific settlement is suboptimal. In this sense we can say that officials can have authority over each other – *qua* officials – as much as they do over citizens.

Thus understood, the C-L relationship exhibits all the elements of the classic quandary. The same kind of social fact, primarily the decisions of some legal officials, is thought to give rise to duties (possibly legal duties) not only on the part of citizens but also other legal officials. In addition, it appears that this is so not circumstantially but systemically. It is not just that the decision of a legal official, say, a legislator, happens to change the moral calculation of judges, as would the fact that I have chanced upon a person drowning in a pond on my way to fulfil a promise to a friend. Rather, the decision has this effect for a special

[15] J Waldron, 'Authority for Officials' in L Meyer, S Paulson and T Pogge (eds), *Rights, Culture and the Law: Themes from the Legal and Political Philosophy of Joseph Raz* (Oxford, Oxford University Press, 2003) 45.

[16] ibid 56.

reason, namely because the legislator possesses some kind of authority over judges. Just as in the case of citizens, the question arises by virtue of what he has that authority. Predictably, anti-positivists contend that the dependence of the judicial role on the doings and sayings of the legislature is a function of certain moral values, just as in the case of ordinary citizens. Can legal positivists maintain their austere position that such values never figure in the explanation of that dependence or that they do not necessarily figure in it? Or is the anti-positivist account more convincing?

The preceding remarks suggest that the C-L relationship could serve as a battleground for the long-standing dispute between legal positivists and anti-positivists to play out. However, the C-L relationship is not just another battleground. Testing the way the two jurisprudential traditions explicate it promises significant philosophical gains. To begin with, an inquiry into the C-L relationship allows us to probe and challenge an assumption that is fairly common among legal philosophers. When they refer to the legislature and the courts, many of them take it for granted that a legislature is essentially a rule-creating institution and courts are essentially rule-applying ones. According to this assumption, legislative decisions create rules, which it is the duty of the courts to apply. Not because and insofar as it is a good thing that it should be so, but solely out of a conceptual necessity (that it is part of the very concepts of the legislative and judicial functions) matched with the contingent social fact that courts have a practice of treating the rules coming from *this* legislature as authoritative. Thus Hart takes it to be a matter of 'common knowledge'[17] that courts 'determine what the rules are and when they have been broken'[18] and legislatures 'make new rules and abolish old ones'.[19]

There is a two-fold problem with assuming from the outset that legislatures create rules and courts apply them. First, we cannot easily – or at any rate self-evidently – fit into this simple picture a pervasive feature of many modern C-L legal systems, namely judicial review of legislation for its conformity with higher-order norms, typically of constitutional status. In legal systems with such a practice what we might call the courts' receptive attitude towards the legislature is combined with an active supervisory stance and a readiness to withhold assistance on the basis of what is essentially an independent moral judgement. By virtue of what can a rule-applying institution wield this power? In order to answer this question, we must inevitably look beyond the simple picture of courts as rule-applying institutions and the legislature as a rule-creating one.

In addition, the simple picture carries the risk of rigging the game in favour of legal positivism. If it is granted that conceptual necessity dictates that one institution creates rules that are valid rules of the system (provided that the other

[17] Hart, *The Concept of Law* (n 5) 3.
[18] ibid.
[19] ibid.

applies them as such), then the stage of moral evaluation of those rules envisaged by anti-positivist theories appears largely redundant, a mere add-on to an already complete account of law.[20] If anything, the further stage tells us that something is good law. But we need to know that something is the law before we can judge whether it is good or bad.[21] In that first stage, we do not need to have any recourse to moral considerations.

This assumption, and its connection with positivism, is evinced in a recurring criticism of Dworkin's theory. Dworkin famously argues that the content of the law is determined by the principles that offer the best interpretation of institutional history. According to a popular rendition of Dworkin's theory, when we interpret, we single out at a pre-interpretive stage the political decisions that comprise institutional history. Next, we identify which principles of political morality best fit and justify those decisions. Some critics have protested that Dworkinian interpretation, thus understood, presupposes legal positivism; at best, it merely fills in the gaps or adds a moral gloss over the extant law. How can we identify which political decisions our interpretation must be directed at, unless we have an independent criterion that classifies them as part of the law? If you believe that the job of the legislature is to create rules, then you are particularly prone to this rendition of Dworkin's theory. You will think that what the pre-interpretive stage does is to select those rules. There are other rules, say, the rules that govern the life of a specific religion or the rules that make up my daily writing routine, and it is the function of the pre-interpretive stage to filter them out. Still, the legislature's rules are already part of the law independently of interpretation – interpretation takes them as a given.

With his focus on courts, Dworkin appears to invite this rendition of his theory. Recall that in *Law's Empire* as well as in his earlier work Dworkin explicates legal interpretation from the point of view of an ideal judge, Hercules.[22] When faced with hard cases whose correct legal resolution is a subject of controversy among legal experts, Hercules must interpretively unearth the principles that underpin legal practice, thus laying bare the determinants of the content of the law in easy cases as well. However, this strategy has its disadvantages. From the

[20] As is well known, inclusive legal positivists contend that in some legal systems the criteria of legal validity may include moral principles. Consequently, in those legal systems the rules coming from the legislature must additionally satisfy moral criteria, in order to count as valid law. This does not necessarily mean that inclusive positivists are immune to the assumption mentioned in the text. After all, they are still positivists, insofar as they insist that there may be legal systems where no moral principle figures among the criteria of validity. See J Coleman, 'Negative and Positive Positivism' (1982) 11 *Journal of Legal Studies* 139.

[21] The theory of law encapsulated in the maxim '*lex iniusta non est lex*' may be thought to be vulnerable to this objection. Thus, one may argue that it takes as given a body of '*leges*', which it then sifts by reference to justice. Although only standards that pass the moral test deserve to be called law in the strict sense, those that fail are still '*leges*', albeit in a 'watered down', 'peripheral' sense.

[22] R Dworkin, *Law's Empire* (Oxford, Hart Publishing, 1998) ch 9.

point of view of the judge the very fact of the dependence of his task on the political decisions of the legislature is so obvious that it is almost never argued for. Hence, a strategy that adopts that viewpoint seems to confirm the assumption described in the previous paragraph, namely that it must presuppose the identification and relevance of legal rules, such as those enacted by the legislature, in the task of working out what are our concrete legal rights and duties.

It could be argued, then, that Dworkin's theory is really not so different from legal positivism. Rather than challenging legal positivism, it confirms its truth. At best, it is offering a theory of adjudication. It tells us what judges ought to do when, for instance, the legislature has enacted immoral rules or when no pre-existing rule speaks to the case before them. It may be that in such cases they ought to follow Dworkin's prescription. That is, they ought to look at legal practice as a whole in order to identify moral principles that show it in its best light and apply those principles so as to cancel or temper the immorality of the legislative rule or resolve the unanticipated legal issue. This is no doubt an important task that legal philosophers can and should undertake, but it is not in conflict with legal positivism. Legal positivism answers the prior question whether some standard is valid law.[23] It has nothing to say about what judges must combine valid law with in order to reach a decision.

Being so firmly embedded, this assumption obstructs progress in the debate between legal positivists and anti-positivists. It is thus necessary to isolate and problematise it. In fact, Dworkin is not forced to accept it. As will be shown in chapter three, we can explain the role of courts and the legislature in a different way, more congenial to the Dworkinian position. These two institutions, it will be argued, participate in a joint institutional project aimed at governing. They *share* the authority to govern. But their relationship is truly one of *shared authority* only to the extent that it is structured in a way that serves the point of the joint project; for this to be the case, it is necessary – though not sufficient – that the project accord with principles of political morality regarding the proper allocation of government power.[24] It is these principles and not any conceptual necessity that determine what (limited) role each institution performs, and what rights and duties it has vis-à-vis the other, at least to a significant extent.[25] By this I mean that the acts of courts and the legislature have the normative significance that they do in determining the content of the law because and insofar as such principles dictate.[26] Accordingly, these principles are a necessary part of legal

[23] See Gardner (n 2); W Waluchow, *Inclusive Legal Positivism* (Oxford, Oxford University Press, 1994) 42–46.

[24] This is a necessary but not a sufficient condition; the content of the rights and duties they impose on citizens with their decisions must also meet certain moral conditions.

[25] We should not exclude the possibility that some of their rights and duties are unrelated to the project of governing. But it is unlikely that this will be the case with regard to the most important ones.

[26] Subject also to other conditions relating to the content of the law.

interpretation. For an interpreter like a judge to decide how much moral weight, if any, to assign to the sayings and doings of the legislature, he must decide what role the legislature has in the institutional division of labour. Its sayings and doings have weight in accordance with that division of labour.

Equipped with this account we can resist the view that the courts' dependence on legislative decisions is grounded in a conceptual truth that the former are rule-applying institutions, whereas the latter are rule-creating institutions. We can say instead that the respect courts owe legislative decisions is a function of the structure of the joint project of governing they are involved in, in virtue of the considerations of institutional design that underpin it. This understanding of the role of courts vis-à-vis the legislature accounts for the phenomena that are commonly treated as instances of rule-application: in a few words, courts have a receptive role vis-à-vis the legislature because it is appropriate that they do so by virtue of, for example, the democratic credentials of the legislature or its ability to secure coordination, on the one hand, and the fact that the court is well positioned to give effect to the decisions of the legislature in individual cases, on the other.

In the same spirit we can approach other aspects of the C-L relationship. In particular, we can attempt to reconcile the receptive aspect of the role of courts towards the legislature with the more active aspects of that role, say, in legal systems that follow a practice of constitutional review of legislation for its conformity with higher-order legal standards. Both aspects can be accounted for, if at all, in light of the point of the joint institutional project of governing and the principles that structure it. The analysis will place special emphasis on the notion of separation of powers. It will be suggested that this idea can be understood to collect together many of the principles that grant the C-L relationship shared authority. Among those is the principle of checks and balances, namely the political imperative that we keep the exercise of power by state agents in check. Although it must be balanced against other separation of powers considerations, this principle exerts its own independent influence, recommending institutional arrangements that allow for one legal institution to control the other. Practices of constitutional review are such arrangements. Thus, constitutional review is not at odds with the view that courts and the legislature participate in a joint institutional project. The C-L relationship goes well, as far as its point is concerned, if it includes a robust checks and balances element, and this can sometimes be achieved by having courts ensure that the legislature does its assigned job properly.

No doubt, we will come across legal systems where the relationship between courts and the legislature falls short of separation of powers standards. Interpretivists will not look at legal systems of this sort through rose-tinted glasses. Rather, they will contend that in the measure of their moral deficiency such legal systems do not affect our legal rights and duties. In this respect, the claim that the courts and the legislature are engaged in a joint project differs from the seemingly similar claim made by some legal positivists who have come to be known as legal conventionalists. Legal conventionalists also claim that legal officials are engaged in a joint activity which provides the foundation of legal obligation. What according to them sustains the joint activity is either a set of beliefs on the part of participants that it is proper to coordinate their conduct with that of their fellow-participants or a set of interlocking intentions to act in a way that is responsive to the action of other participants. In this picture, the existence of those beliefs and intentions is independent of their moral merit. Even morally wicked intentions can interlock in the requisite way. For legal conventionalists, then, there can be law where the practice of legal officials suffers from much more fundamental flaws than that it flouts separation of powers. The difference from the account defended here is striking. Being anti-positivistic, the latter takes it that we have a legal duty provided it is morally justified in the relevant sense that we have it. With this as our starting point, the task of legal philosophy becomes that of explicating the appropriate moral justification, which is bound to be complex. This book contends that that complex structure also involves recourse to separation of powers standards. For an actual practice of officials to generate legal rights and duties it must also satisfy such standards.

Not only does a focus on the C-L relationship challenge a common misperception of Dworkin's interpretive legal philosophy, it also helps elaborate and develop that philosophy. Anti-positivist theories are commonly attacked for allegedly failing to pay sufficient attention to the dynamic character of law. The content of the law, it is argued, is subject to deliberate change. In this respect, law is different from morality, which, if it evolves at all, does not evolve by means of deliberate human action, that is, human action intended to bring about this evolution. In fact, one of the main driving forces behind legal positivism is to explain this aspect of the law. Its claim that social facts determine the law is supposed to account for it. The social facts that legal positivists single out for this role, like the fact that the legislature said or did something, are precisely facts about officials charged with deliberately changing the law acting on their intention to change it. (This, as we shall see in chapter two, is at the heart of Raz's theory of law.) Interpretivists claim that our rights and duties are determined by principles of political morality, albeit those that best explain and justify past political history. They thus shift the emphasis away from social facts of the type mentioned above. But that, so the argument goes, would be to put the cart before the horse. In Waldron's terminology, legislative decisions are meant to settle an issue of common concern. A judge who must consult his moral judgement to determine the relevance of that decision for the content of the law allegedly fails to respect the fact of settlement. He shows himself willing to re-open the issue of common concern and decide it by his own moral lights. The connection between this charge and the assumption discussed in previous paragraphs should be obvious. Those who argue that Dworkin cannot but presuppose the existence of legal rules at the pre-interpretive stage typically do so because they believe that these rules reflect the dynamic character of law; they are created by decisions that are intended to affect our rights and duties and are made by an institution that has the role of creating rules with its decisions.

By making clear how interpretivism explicates the dependence of courts on legislative decisions, the book goes some way towards deflecting this attack. By the same token, it brings interpretivism closer to its adversary inasmuch as it explicitly aims to incorporate the latter's core intuition within the interpretivist framework. When a judge interprets, he ought not to appeal only to principles of political morality concerning what rights and duties we would have in a perfectly just society. He should also consult principles about the proper allocation of power between participants in the joint project of governing, including himself. These, too, should be counted among the principles that best explain and justify past political history, since that history crucially involves the cooperation between institutions for the purpose of governing well. The latter principles will direct the judge to give weight to the decisions of other institutions that participate in the project of governing. Because their normative force is independent of that of principles of substantive justice, they may give the judge reason to further a decision that is sub-optimal from the point of view of substantive justice. In a nutshell, we can say that judicial duty – as all official duty – is a combination of principles of substantive justice and institutional design. Hence, the account advocated here explains why institutional say-so matters, but does so within an anti-positivist framework, where legal duty is necessarily determined by moral principles.

Though the account offered here reasserts interpretivism's anti-positivist credentials, it does not leave it unaltered. In particular, it casts in doubt Dworkin's court-centric understanding of the theory of law. Dworkin has argued that the content of the law is the set of judicially enforceable moral rights. The basis of the limitation is that judicial enforceability is for Dworkin the mark of legality, the value that law distinctively serves. Jeremy Waldron has made a trenchant critique of this tendency, which he detects in analytical legal philosophers of all stripes.[27] His concern, of course, is that by focusing on judges we neglect legislatures. He argues that legislatures perform a function that is closely connected with what he takes to be the moral point of law, namely its ability, when it goes well, to settle societal disputes about what ought to be done. Waldron contends that the legislature discharges this function, when, after due deliberation that takes into account the various interests and perspectives across society, it enacts a law which is understood to be binding on the whole community. This fact

---

[27] Waldron, 'Law and Disagreement' (n 9) ch 2.

eludes us as long as we do not go beyond the observation that the legislature is a source of law and thus refrain from examining its design and structure. Waldron accuses contemporary legal philosophers of precisely this failure.

> Though . . . positivist jurisprudence defines law in terms of its sources, the property of *being a source of law* is for the positivist the most interesting that can be said about a person or institution . . . That is the remarkable thing; and any *other* features that the body may possess – including the features that actually enable it to have this jurisgenerative quality – pale into philosophical insignificance by comparison.[28]

Perhaps, something similar can be said about Dworkin. Of course, unlike legal positivism, it is far from obvious that Dworkinian interpretivism neglects 'the features that actually enable [an institution] to have this jurisgenerative quality'. For in the interpretivist story it is such features and their moral relevance that determine whether the say-so of an institution bears on legal duty and, if so, how it does. All the same, by closely identifying the point of law with adjudication in the way indicated in the previous paragraph, Dworkin may still be guilty of overly narrowing the scope of the theory of law. This is the position that I defend in this book. Building on and generalising Waldron's insight, I contend that Dworkin's court-centrism delivers an impoverished conception of legality. Instead, I argue that legality has a systemic as well as an adjudicative dimension. In its systemic dimension, it requires that government as a whole is structured in a way that guarantees that public power will be exercised properly. Accordingly, for a legal system to exhibit the value of legality, it is not sufficient that its judges direct the use of state coercion under certain conditions and not others. Additionally, it must be the case that the joint project of governing accords with a scheme of division of labour and checks and balances that is geared towards justice. For this purpose, we must care about efficiency and the prevention of abuse as much as we do about judicial enforceability. Not all of the requirements of legality, thus understood, are judicially enforceable, but that does not make them any less important for understanding what it means for a legal system to go well. Hence, it is a mistake for theories of law to zoom in on the determinants of the rights and duties that are judicially enforceable. They risk missing out on the systemic dimension of legality.

The expansive conception of legality I argue for is motivated by the same spirit as Dworkin's, notwithstanding the fact that I reach a different conclusion. In *Law's Empire* Dworkin sought to connect the theory of law with the theory of political legitimacy. He argued that a legal system that adheres to legality is also morally legitimate. That's because when judges of that system only enforce the rights and duties that flow from the principles of political morality that explain and justify past political history, as legality demands, they maintain the *integrity* of their political community, and integrity in adjudication gives a convincing

[28] ibid 44.

answer to the problem of political legitimacy in societies fraught by moral disagreement. I agree with Dworkin that anti-positivists stand to gain from reflecting on political legitimacy. But I claim that he goes amiss in focusing on integrity
in adjudication. I suggest, instead, that we should view adjudication as just one
component, albeit an important one, of an institutional structure that collectively aims to govern well. In order to understand the role of courts and the
political values that govern them, we need to place them in that structure. Again,
the reason for zooming out in this manner comes from the theory of political
legitimacy. Legitimacy is not merely a retail thing. Crucially, a political community is also legitimate when it has established standing guarantees for the
proper exercise of power because these guarantees can convince the losing side
in a political contest to submit to a policy to which it objects. We commonly
group this form of guarantees under another classic political concept, namely
separation of powers. This, I argue, is a concept our theories of law must be
made sensitive to.

Apart from the positive case for a revised interpretivism, the book, as already
noted, has a critical component as well. It takes issue with Raz's theory of law.
According to Raz's sources thesis, the existence and content of authoritative
directives must be identifiable by resort to the social fact of their provenance
from a de facto authority, without regard to any of the normative considerations
that the authority in question is supposed to rely on in its judgement. In the next
chapter I argue that the sources thesis fails to account for the role of jurisdictional considerations (namely considerations about the scope of the power of
legal authorities such as courts and legislatures) in the identification of valid law.
To this effect, I focus on a C-L legal system, where courts have a practice of
reviewing legislation for its conformity with fundamental rights. In such a legal
system, I will show, the special normative status of (at least some) directives
made by a legal authority depends on respect for jurisdiction. But assessing that
an authority has stayed intra vires involves recourse to the normative considerations that are the authority's job to weigh up. Thus, by engaging in this exercise,
we vitiate the sources thesis. We show that in order to identify a legal standard
we cannot look at social facts only.

My criticism of the sources thesis highlights the importance of incorporating
jurisdiction in our philosophical accounts of legal authority. So it springs from
the same insight that drives the entire argument of the book, namely that we do
well to think of institutions that participate in the joint project of governing and
of their contributions to that project not in isolation but in the context of that
project. This also means attending to the fact that their power is limited, inasmuch as it is shared with their fellow-participants. To this effect, we need to have
a proper appreciation of the moral principles that govern power-sharing of this
sort. These will ultimately select which social facts are relevant and determine
(at least in part) how they bear on the content of the law. Through the notion of

jurisdiction, the criticism teaches us that even a positivist theory like Raz's must make room for them. At the same time it prepares the ground for the discussion of Dworkin's theory in chapters 3 and 4, where I connect jurisdiction with the broader notion of separation of powers and I thus bring the moral principles underlying it into full view.

V. META-THEORETICAL RESERVATIONS

Although the dependence of courts on the legislature is a central issue of the theory of law, we ought not to overstate the ambition of the claim made in this book. Being focused on one specific issue, the strategy adopted here leaves a number of routes open. So, for instance, it is not the case that, if one of the theories I compare proves to be problematic, the other must be true. Conversely, even if, as I am going to argue, it turns out that Dworkin's theory does a better job of explaining the relationship between courts and the legislature, this does not entail that it is all things considered preferable over Raz's, as it may be deficient on other counts. Furthermore, it is possible that Raz's theory can be improved upon to accommodate the critique. Although my diagnosis will be that the difficulties of Raz's theory are connected with some of its core elements, I do not preclude that a way out can be navigated. Finally, being limited in its scope, my strategy allows that a completely different theory may actually fare better than both of the options examined. Even the sceptic who denies that courts and legislatures have essential features can agree with my critique of Raz and also accept some of the positive claims I make in defence of Dworkin, while maintaining that his account of C-L legal systems is optimal. Of course, the sceptic will insist that it is a mistake to think there is a philosophically interesting distinction between the two institutions that are the focus of my inquiry and between them and other institutions such as the ones we refer to using the label 'executive'. There are, he will argue, elements of what is traditionally called 'legislation' and 'adjudication' in the job description of all these institutions. He will conclude that while the explanation of the C-L relationship may be correct, the focus on it is misplaced. It is mistaking a sociological regularity for a conceptual necessity and glossing over many contingencies along the way.

The possibilities I have listed possibly sound rather remote and vague. Is my inquiry as modest and unassuming as the previous paragraph seems to suggest? It could be objected that, in fact, it loads the dice from the get-go. It does so because its structure assumes that the two theories operate on a level playing field and are thus amenable to a comparison. This, the argument would go, ignores that the two theories are pursuing radically different philosophical projects. The one, Raz's, is analysing what the law is, while the other, Dworkin's, is prescribing what it ought to be. Accordingly, one is descriptive, shunning any moral commitments, while the other is normative. Dworkin says that legislative decisions ought to have a certain role in the determination of judicial duty because it is a morally good thing that they do so. This is not at all the spirit of Raz's enterprise. Raz claims that his account of the law is a philosophical elaboration of law but makes no judgement on whether law is a good thing to have. He may have views about the latter issue too. However, these are separate from his understanding of the nature of law. Clearly, if this distinction is sound, my inquiry is guilty of comparing the incomparable.

The objection evokes the more recent dividing line between positivists and anti-positivists, this time at the level of meta-theory. According to most positivists including Raz, jurisprudential inquiry must stay away from making moral evaluations. It must explain the essential features of law as it finds it. Of course, law plays a very important role in moral discourse. So, it is the kind of thing of which it is sensible to ask whether it is morally good or not. In fact, it is often a matter of the greatest urgency that it is good. But you have to first identify what it is before you can then ask those moral questions about it. Anti-positivists, on the other hand, maintain that jurisprudence cannot but incorporate substantive moral commitments. Dworkin, for instance, contends that law is a social practice which is to be understood in the light of its moral point. This, for Dworkin, is the justification of the use of coercion by the state. So, to analyse what law is you must take sides on moral questions, just as you would in order to determine what justice is.

Given the state of play, it would seem that my inquiry does not even take off the ground. It would seem that I first have to resolve the methodological issue, so as to address the aforementioned objection. It may turn out that one or the other theory is misguided at the level of methodology, well before we get to the issue that is the point of focus of my inquiry. If Dworkin has the best view about the proper methodology of jurisprudence, then Raz is tying his hand behind his back by not making explicit reference to moral values. If, on the contrary, Raz's methodology is the right one, then Dworkin is at best engaging in the second-stage prescriptive project that his detractors attribute to him. But, even if there is no easy or compelling case to be made in favour of one or the other methodology, it might be thought that the divergence of the two theories precludes a meaningful comparison.

The meta-theoretical debate in jurisprudence has helped bring out important further nuances in our main theories of the nature of law and has made jurisprudes themselves more self-reflective. But we should not allow our methodological preoccupations to blind us to the potential for fruitful comparison between theories of law that otherwise differ on both the substantive and the meta-theoretical level, especially when they examine the same aspect of legal practice. Surely, if certain principles of political morality are peculiarly relevant to the evaluation of the C-L relationship (in the sense that they provide a standard to which it is appropriate to hold the relationship or a standard that the relationship aims at), it is at least useful for an analytic legal positivist studying that relationship to bear them in mind. More importantly and controversially, there is a way to bypass the methodological obstacle altogether. Instead of vindicating one or the other theory *in toto*, we focus on evaluating its solution to a philosophical problem, which, when described at the appropriate level of abstraction, is common to both. This is the metaphysical problem about the determination of the content of the law. Mark Greenberg has argued that both positivists and anti-positivists strive to identify the determinants of legal duty, with one side claiming that only social facts count as such determinants – or are the ultimate necessary determinants of the content of the law –, and the other countering that value facts necessarily also figure among such determinants.[29] Greenberg maintains that facts about the doings and sayings of institutions leave the content of the law radically indeterminate and gives us a number of reasons in support of the view that value facts are a good candidate to make these social facts yield determinate legal duties. This book adopts Greenberg's strategy. It takes a set of putative legal rights and duties, those concerning the scope of official power in the C-L relationship, and queries what could be their determinants. Its critical part confirms Greenberg's diagnosis that social facts – at least within the Razian framework – cannot be the sole determinant of these duties. It then proceeds to apply the Dworkinian theory to the C-L relationship as a way of testing whether a combination of moral and social facts is better suited to the task.

It goes without saying that, given their different answers to the problem of metaphysical determination, positivist and anti-positivist accounts of the extension of legal duty will not map on each other. Legal positivists accept the existence of valid law that is deeply immoral, and anti-positivists include in the extension of the content of the law duties that no institution has explicitly decreed, just by virtue of the fact it is morally justified that we have them. We should expect that the present inquiry will confirm this divergence. Anti-positivists are likely to accept limits to judicial power in the context of the C-L relationship, which legal positivists will reject, and vice versa. But it would be counter-productive, because question-begging, to argue on this basis that comparison between the two theories cannot be meaningful. Two lawyers who argue opposite sides in a legal dispute can meaningfully engage with each other. They needn't agree all the way down. In fact, their disagreement can be far from marginal. It is likely that each of them stresses different precedents and discards or narrowly interprets others. The same can be said about competing theories of law. The fact that they disagree about the extension of the content of the law does not necessarily mean that they are answering different ques-

---

[29] M Greenberg, 'How Facts Make Law' (2004) 10 *Legal Theory* 157.

tions. Besides, as we have seen, there is a description of the philosophical problem which both can be said to be dealing with.

VI. WORKING FROM THE PARTICULAR

Philosophical theories of law seek to articulate essential truths about law. Legal philosophers tend to go about this task by abstracting from specific legal systems and peeling back their peculiarities, so as to arrive at conclusions that are true of all of them. Conversely, they criticise competing theories for failing to account for this or that legal system, actual or possible. In other words, legal theorists operate under what Raz has called the 'assumption of universality'. According to it:

> it is a criterion of adequacy of a legal theory that it is true of all the intuitively clear instances of municipal legal systems. Since a legal theory must be true of all legal systems, the identifying features by which it characterizes them must of necessity be very general and abstract.[30]

'Legal philosophy', Raz concludes, 'must be content with those few features which all legal systems necessarily possess'.[31] The assumption of universality has acquired renewed potency today, as emerging and unfamiliar 'law-like social'[32] phenomena at the international (eg global administrative law) and supranational level (eg EU integration) test our theories of law and arguably expose their bias towards municipal legal systems. Alongside the optimists who think that our traditional theoretical tools can be adjusted to account for these phenomena, there are the pessimists who doubt that law has any essential properties. Unable to find any common ground in those phenomena, many theorists are thus left to report the various social practices that the term law is used to describe.[33] This book goes against the tide. It consciously narrows its scope by focusing on a subset of legal systems, namely those that have courts and a legislature. This methodological approach faces the formidable challenge that it does not apply (at least not readily) to law in general, for instance, to those legal systems without one or both of these institutions, if there are any.[34] If so, the universality and therefore the philosophical interest of my conclusions are undermined.

[30] Raz (n 5) 490.
[31] ibid 491.
[32] K Culver and M Giudice, *Legality's Borders: An Essay in General Jurisprudence* (Oxford, Oxford University Press, 2010) xvi.
[33] eg Brian Tamanaha builds his 'socio-legal positivist' account of law from 'whatever people identify and treat through their social practices as law'. B Tamanaha, *A General Jurisprudence of Law and Society* (Oxford, Oxford University Press, 2001) 166. This includes customary law, religious law etc.
[34] In his early work Joseph Raz argues that there can be legal systems without a legislature. See J Raz, *The Concept of a Legal System* (Oxford, Oxford University Press, 1975) 190–91.

How can we respond to the challenge of parochialism? We could, of course, attempt to establish that the existence of both institutions is a universal feature of all law. This is not the route I am going to take. For the sake of argument I assume that there may be legal systems that are not C-L legal systems. I thus wear my parochialism on my sleeve. In other words, I engage in what has aptly been called *particular* jurisprudence. Particular jurisprudence is to be contrasted to general jurisprudence. As Waldron, one of its proponents has put it, particular jurisprudence aims to 'show how some of the elements and theorems that are emphasised in the general analytic study of law come to life' in the particular legal system or type of legal system that the theorist has chosen as his point of focus.[35] What we achieve in this way is that 'we can see the point of them in that context, whereas they seem rather mysterious abstractions in the context of the most general jurisprudential inquiry'.[36] Not only that, but increased conceptual abstraction may also involve important loss in depth of understanding.[37]

Waldron's case in favour of particular jurisprudence applies to the present inquiry. As I have explained above, although C-L legal systems may just be a common type of legal system, here they serve to dramatise a central philosophical concern about law, namely how legal rights and duties depend on the sayings and doings of legal officials. I illustrate this concern by focusing on the interdependence of two institutions whose roles in legal systems are limited and different. We think that their interdependence affects their official *duty*. Because of each other's sayings and doings, they, no less than other legal participants, are said to be under a legal duty to do certain things and not others in their official capacity.

Insofar as the concern I have identified is one that pertains to the nature of all law and not of just one type of legal systems, I hope that what I say about C-L legal systems will not be parochial. Conversely, for the challenge of parochialism to stick, it is not enough to point out that there are legal systems that are different from C-L legal systems. Additionally, the objection must identify a philosophically relevant difference between the two types of legal system. Is it perhaps that, in that other type of legal system, legal institutions do not have a legally limited role? Why is this difference relevant for explaining how legal rights and duties depend on the doings and sayings of legal officials? This is not an extravagant theoretical demand. Many theorists casually draw conclusions from the relationship between courts and the legislature based on the implicit assumption that, despite superficial differences, these conclusions hold in legal systems that depart from the paradigmatic type. It falls on those who challenge them to point out in what sense the feature identified has limited scope.

---

[35] See relatedly J Waldron, 'Can There Be a Democratic Jurisprudence?' (2009) 58 *Emory Law Journal* 675, 679.

[36] ibid.

[37] cp A Halpin, 'The Methodology of Jurisprudence: Thirty Years Off the Point' (2006) 19 *Canadian Journal of Law and Jurisprudence* 67.

In this sense, particular jurisprudence of the sort I engage in is different from the non-essentialist jurisprudence advanced by Fred Schauer.[38] Schauer criticises the tendency of analytical jurisprudence to focus only on essential features of all law and to neglect those aspects that are pervasive and of great importance to understanding the operation of the legal systems, where they are to be found. His example is coercion. Schauer agrees with many positivists that there may be law without coercion. However, he thinks it plainly obvious that actual legal systems rely heavily on coercive means for their effectiveness, and it is crucial for jurisprudes to ask what precise function coercion fulfils in them and how it fulfils it. Accordingly, they should not be deterred by the fact that coercion is a parochial rather than a necessary feature of law. Analogously, he maintains, although the capacity to fly is not an essential feature of birds, we learn something important about them by explaining what bestows this capacity on so many birds.[39] Whatever the merits of non-essentialist jurisprudence, its course is parallel to the one taken in this book. Particular jurisprudence seeks to elucidate the essential by examining how it is instantiated in a specific context.

Besides, it may be that the philosophical programme I have outlined yields critical gains, in the sense that it exposes the difficulties that influential theories of law have explaining the relationship between courts and legislatures in C-L legal systems. In such a case, the philosophical merit of the theory in question will be seriously undercut, however well it fares in explaining the working of legal systems that are unlike C-L legal systems.[40] Conversely, to the extent that the positive proposal put forward here helps us understand the nature of the C-L relationship, it is theoretically interesting even if it is shown not to apply to all possible legal systems. Although we can envisage legal systems without courts and legislatures, our theoretical interest in such systems seems to be diminished the more they differ from this paradigmatic case of law.

VII. LEGAL AND CONSTITUTIONAL THEORY

As the preceding summary makes clear, the argument of the book is motivated by the conviction that the theory of law ought to draw on constitutional theory.[41] It suggests that by studying public law concepts like jurisdiction and

---

[38] See F Schauer, 'The Best Laid Plans' (2010) 120 *Yale Law Journal* 586.

[39] ibid.

[40] In fact, some so-called non-essentialist jurisprudence primarily serves this critical function. It elaborates important characteristics of actual legal systems with the aim of finding counterexamples to theories about the nature of law. In this sense, it is also driven by an essentialist commitment. See eg Cane, 'Public Law in *The Concept of Law*' (n 11).

[41] In the same vein, Peter Cane has recently used public law to stress test Hart's theory of law. He summarises his argument as follows: '[P]aying careful attention to standard accounts of public law and to differences between those accounts and the image of public law embedded in Hart's

separation of powers we can gain valuable insights into the nature of legal authority; furthermore, that we can make progress in our thinking about political legitimacy by factoring into it the role that the web of legal institutions can play in securing citizens' allegiance. In turn, it warns that if we neglect this kind of concept we risk confusion and misunderstanding. Not just in our public law theorising but in our theorising about the nature of law. The difficulties I shall argue Raz and Dworkin run into are evidence of that. The close link between public law and legal theory is something we should expect. If it is a central element of law that it involves institutions functioning together to affect the rights and duties of citizens, constitutional law has a lot to teach us about the content and limits of their power.[42]

The influence works the other way as well. Despite being pitched at a high level of abstraction the main claims of this book are at the same time meant to echo the concerns of public lawyers. For one thing, they pertain to a legal phenomenon of special interest to them, namely the C-L relationship, especially as this is reconfigured in a legal system with a practice of constitutional review. The question to what extent courts have the power to interfere with legislative decisions when they review them for their constitutionality is one of the fixed points of constitutional scholarship. This book does not engage in the difficult normative issues that surround the question but it addresses a philosophical quandary that is at its heart: How can one official have authority over another, when the latter is charged to supervise the former's decisions?

Besides, whether one believes in the self-contained nature of the theory of law or not, it is rather uncontroversial that modes of thought which are hatched there tend to catch on. This is all the more common in constitutional law, where black-letter solutions to doctrinal disputes are few and far between. As a result, constitutional lawyers often advance 'conceptual' arguments – alongside the more conventional ones of text and precedent – in support of their claims. Hence, a clearer philosophical understanding of the C-L relationship is going to have important ramifications in our approach to specific constitutional law questions. Whilst I do not explicitly explore this avenue in this book, I discuss a number of philosophical views that have obvious counterparts in constitutional theory. The theoretical puzzles that I associate with them are likely to reappear further downstream.

---

theory can tell us something theoretically significant not only (tautologically) about the nature of *public* law in modern, common law legal systems, but also about the nature of *law*, full stop, in such systems'. (ibid 655) Whereas this book focuses on the relationship between courts and the legislature, Cane places emphasis on the jurisprudential potential of another perennial topic of public law, the role of the executive in modern legal systems.

[42] For a recent attempt to cross-fertilise the two disciplines, see M Addler and K Himma, *The Rule of Recognition and the US Constitution* (Oxford, Oxford University Press, 2009).

2

The Persistent Significance of Jurisdiction

I. INTRODUCTION

ONTEMPORARY LEGAL POSITIVISM is a broad church. It comprises a diverse range of theories that speak to a wide array of jurisprudential topics. As a result, it is very difficult to come up with a set of theses that all of them would subscribe to. Of course, there is no shortage of anodyne and not particularly informative formulations that can be said to loosely capture a positivist ethos. For instance, it is often said that all legal positivists champion the separation of law and morality.[1] But because they are anodyne and uninformative, such formulations cannot form the basis of a systematic examination of the merits of legal positivism as a whole. Scratch their surface a little and you will encounter a host of conflicting interpretations, divergent starting points and influences as well as philosophical motivations. The idea of separation of law and morality itself has often been discredited, precisely on the ground that it obfuscates crucial differences and nuances.[2]

Rather than look for a common denominator, some anti-positivists have attempted to bypass the aforementioned problem by identifying some salient themes or tenets, which they take to constitute an interesting and distinctive jurisprudential position that is reasonably attributable to most legal positivists.[3] An obvious difficulty with this approach is that it leaves it open to self-identified positivists to disavow the position, thus necessitating a closer engagement with specific theories. But that is exactly the kind of engagement that the approach seeks to avoid by focusing on a stipulated position. Although the aforementioned difficulty does not provide a knockdown argument against the approach, I am going to opt for a more straightforward methodology. I shall focus on one

---

[1] See the classic defence of this thesis in HLA Hart, 'Positivism and the Separation of Law and Morals' (1958) 71 *Harvard Law Review* 593.

[2] See eg J Raz, 'About Morality and the Nature of Law' (2003) 48 *American Journal of Jurisprudence* 1; L Green, 'Positivism and the Inseparability of Law and Morals' (2008) 83 *New York University Law Review* 1035.

[3] This is the methodology employed by Ronald Dworkin in R Dworkin, *Taking Rights Seriously* (London, Duckworth, 1978) ch 2; and Mark Greenberg in M Greenberg, 'The Standard Picture and Its Discontents' in L Green and B Leiter (eds), *Oxford Studies in Philosophy of Law: Volume 1* (Oxford, Oxford University Press, 2011) 39.

theory, Joseph Raz's, which is widely regarded as offering a powerful and influential defence of some crucial aspects of the positivist credo. In particular, it elaborates an intuition that is the motivating force for much positivist thinking. The intuition is that our legal rights and duties depend on social facts about the decisions and other acts of institutions charged with affecting our rights and duties. As is well known, Raz accounts for the intuition by appeal to the notion of practical authority.

This intuition is crucial for the overall argument of the book. Courts and legislatures are characteristically institutions with the aforementioned power. We want to know whether we can explicate their relationship, and especially the dependence of judicial duty on legislative decisions, in terms of that power. Raz also claims we can do so without appeal to considerations about what would be morally justified for the two institutions to do. In this sense, if he succeeds in providing such an explanation, he will have given us a strong reason to prefer legal positivism.[4] Although it is not the only dimension along which we can distinguish legal positivism and anti-positivism, the dependence of legal duty – including judicial duty – on moral merit is one of the central issues that divide the two camps.

In this chapter I shall advance an argument against the Razian account. I shall show that it overlooks a feature of legal practice whose import cannot be fully understood without reference to moral considerations. In this sense, whilst this chapter looks only at one theory, it aims to make a point that casts doubt over the entire legal positivist edifice. I cannot exclude that a different version of legal positivism will do a better job at accounting for the feature in question, but if I am right about its connection with moral considerations, then achieving this is going to be a tall order indeed.

The leitmotif of my critique will be the notion of jurisdiction. That jurisdiction is a concept of great significance will hardly come as news to a legal audience. Granted, its importance may be conceded with a certain degree of exasperation by public lawyers. For decades, they have grappled with the concept of jurisdiction in the context of judicial review of administrative action. They have sought, for instance, to draw a line between issues that may properly be regarded as jurisdictional and those that pertain to the substance of a tribunal's decision. In this task they have been driven by a desire to mark out the scope of judicial review of administrative action. Yet, jurisdiction has proved notoriously difficult to pin down. We cannot do away with it, but we are unclear what it is we cannot do away with.

I have to warn frustrated public lawyers that it is not the aim of this chapter to explain away the puzzle of jurisdiction, but instead to further entrench it. Far

---

[4] The reason will not be conclusive, however. It may be for instance that the Razian account fails to explain other important aspects of legal practice or that there is an equally satisfactory anti-positivist explanation of the C-L relationship, which produces a tie.

from being merely an eccentric feature of administrative law, I shall suggest, the concept of jurisdiction has an important role to play in philosophical reflection on law. So, if there is a puzzle about the concept of jurisdiction, it is one that must concern legal philosophers at least as much as administrative lawyers. Still, I do not intend to offer a full-blown, self-standing argument for the jurisprudential significance of jurisdiction. My task here is critically to reconstruct the place of jurisdiction in Raz's theory of law. As a result, for the purposes of this chapter I shall take for granted the broad parameters of the Razian framework.

The chapter will have the following structure. I shall start by identifying an exegetical problem concerning the role Raz assigns jurisdictional considerations in his account of law. I shall then focus on one solution to this problem. According to this solution, the identification of valid law never requires recourse to jurisdictional considerations. The main argument of this chapter is directed against this solution. It consists of a critical examination of three articulations of Raz's theory of law that aim to vindicate it. It concludes that none of them succeeds. It then proceeds to examine a set of recent arguments by John Gardner and Timothy Endicott that are relevant to my critique and may be construed to undercut its force. Last, I bring the threads of the argument together. The failure of the Razian account is an instructive one and allows us to draw some more general conclusions which furnish a springboard for the ensuing analysis.

II. THE PUZZLE

A. Practical Authorities

Raz's theory of practical authority needs little by way of introduction, so here I shall limit myself to a short summary. According to Raz, practical authorities play a discrete role in our practical lives. Their purpose is to facilitate their subjects' compliance with reasons that apply to them, which Raz calls dependent reasons (dependence thesis). Typically, someone is an authority over me, if I am more likely to comply with the reasons that apply to me by following her directives than by trying to comply with those reasons on my own (normal justification thesis). Hence, authorities are there to mediate between their subjects and dependent reasons, in the sense that they have to take into account the dependent reasons (or a subset thereof) and sum them up in the directives they issue (this includes discounting some of them).

However, authoritative directives are not recommendations merely to be borne in mind by authority-subjects; nor are they supposed just to be added to the dependent reasons. Rather, on top of creating new reasons to perform or abstain from some act, authoritative directives pre-empt their addressees from acting on the dependent reasons that these directives are meant to adjudicate on (pre-emption thesis). They give us reasons that are equipped with what Raz calls exclusionary force.[5] Take the following example. Suppose you and I have a dispute due to a clash of interest and we decide to turn to an arbitrator. We do not expect the arbitrator simply to give us a piece of advice and then leave us to deal with the dispute ourselves.[6] Quite the contrary, we expect her to adjudicate the dispute, so that we do not have to deal with it ourselves. It is implicit in our decision to bring the matter before her that we will treat her dictate as in some way binding. For, by hypothesis if we are left to our own devices, it is very likely that the disagreement will persist. Generalising from this type of example Raz contends that it would be incompatible with authoritative guidance if authority-subjects were to act on the same reasons that the authoritative directive is supposed to be based on.[7] Were we to do that, we would be, as Raz puts it, guilty of counting the dependent reasons twice, once by independently acting on them and once by acting on the authoritative directive.[8]

The same idea can be presented in a slightly different way. On the Razian understanding the purpose of authoritative guidance is to replace our judgement of the right course of action in a set of circumstances for the judgement of someone else who is bound to decide on the reasons that apply to us. Hence, the fact that an authority has issued a directive expressing her judgement in the exercise of her role must make a difference to the practical reasoning of authority-subjects. Yet, claims Raz, it would eliminate the significance of the authority's intervention, its *practical difference*, if in order to identify what the authority has told them to do its subjects had to identify and weigh up the underlying reasons again. It would defeat the purpose of having an authority in the first place.

B. Legal Authority

From the preceding account of the function of authority Raz derives the sources thesis, which sets out the conditions for the authoritative bindingness of a directive:

---

[5] Raz labels reasons with this dual nature *protected* reasons. Apart from authoritative directives, examples of protected reasons are promises and agreements. See J Raz, *Practical Reason and Norms*, 2nd edn with new postscript (Oxford, Oxford University Press, 1990); and J Raz, 'Reasoning with Rules' (2001) *Current Legal Problems* 1, reprinted as J Raz, *Between Authority and Interpretation* (Oxford, Oxford University Press, 2009) ch 7.

[6] Of course some advice may be authoritative. See J Raz, *The Morality of Freedom* (Oxford, Clarendon Press, 1986) 54. In that case the person whose advice we seek will not leave us to deal with the dispute ourselves, properly speaking.

[7] See J Raz, *Ethics in the Public Domain* (Oxford, Oxford University Press, 1994) 211–15.

[8] Raz, *Morality of Freedom* (n 6) 57ff.

First, a directive can be authoritatively binding only if it is, or is at least presented as, someone's view of how its subjects ought to behave. Second, it must be possible to identify the directive as being issued by the alleged authority without relying on reasons or considerations on which [the] directive purports to adjudicate.[9]

Notice that both conditions are non-moral. So, it is a matter of social fact whether the directive is presented as someone's view about what the directive's addressees ought to do as per the first condition. The second condition is non-moral in the sense that it requires that the existence and content of authoritative directives must be identifiable by resort to the social fact of their provenance from a source that claims authority or is perceived as being one (de facto authority), without regard to any of the normative considerations that the authority in question is supposed to rely on in its judgement.[10] To identify the existence and content of legal directives it suffices to establish 'that the enactment took place, and what it says. To do this one needs little more than knowledge of English (including technical legal English), and of the events which took place in Parliament on a few occasions'.[11] If one had to rely on the normative considerations with regard to which the law claims authority in order to identify the law, she would be vitiating law's authority. As much, it seems, follows from the pre-emption thesis.

Now, law for Raz necessarily claims authority whether or not it has it.[12] This presupposes that the law is the sort of thing that *can* have authority. For, it would not make sense for someone to claim authority unless she was capable of having it. In turn, for law to be capable of having authority, it must be the case that legal directives typically operate in the same way that the arbitrator's decision works. They must express law's judgement of what is to be done in certain circumstances; a judgement that purports to reflect the proper balance of reasons that bear on those circumstances. And they must also have exclusionary (or preemptive) force. So, the sources thesis applies to legal rules as well. To be vested with law's authority is to satisfy its conditions.

Directives that meet the two conditions of the sources thesis are legally valid. Validity is a special normative status that is not to be confused with moral bindingness. Of course, directives stemming from a legitimate authority are valid. For Raz, someone is a legitimate authority if she satisfies the normal justification thesis. In such a case, her directives will be both valid and morally binding. But Raz claims that we do not only talk of valid directives in cases of legitimate

---

[9] Raz, *Ethics* (n 7) 218.

[10] ibid. Henceforth, when I refer to the sources thesis in this chapter I shall have in mind only its second limb.

[11] ibid 221.

[12] ibid 210–37. For a more general exposition of Raz's account, see Raz, *Practical Reason and Norms* (n 5) 35–48, 58–85 and J Raz, *The Authority of Law: Essays on Law and Morality* (Oxford, Oxford University Press, 1979) 146–53. For criticism, see KE Himma 'Law's Claim to Legitimate Authority' in J Coleman (ed), *Hart's Postscript* (Oxford, Oxford University Press, 2001) 271.

exercise of authority, but also in the case of de facto authority. A de facto authority 'either claims to be legitimate or is believed to be so and is effective in imposing its will on many over whom it claims authority, perhaps because its claim to legitimacy is recognised by many of its subjects'.[13] So, assuming for a moment that the efficacy condition of the definition obtains, we can say that someone is a de facto authority over somebody else just in case either it claims authoritatively to adjudicate on a set of reasons that apply to its alleged subjects or because the de facto authority's directives are generally believed by the alleged subjects to do so. The directives of a de facto authority are also valid; they are valid directives of a de facto system of authoritative guidance. But of course they need not be morally binding. It may be true even of a very evil regime like apartheid South Africa that it claims authority. Hence, validity may be bestowed on a directive solely by virtue of the directive's membership in a de facto system of authoritative guidance; in turn, according to the sources thesis, that membership is determined in a way that does not involve appeal to the normative considerations that the law claims to adjudicate on. These considerations resurface when we come to address the separate question whether the law has in this or that instance done a good job *qua* authority.[14] But this question arises at an analytically later stage that presupposes valid directives.

For Raz, then, a directive's validity is independent of the moral merit of its content.[15] Note though that validity does not compete with moral bindingness. Validity cannot provide us with a reason to do what morality prohibits for example. Validity is just the mode of existence of directives created by a de facto authority from the point of view of someone who accepts, whether genuinely or disingenuously, its claim to legitimate authority. This point of view can be taken up by others. The fact that there exists such and such a legal rule in the UK can

---

[13] Raz, *Ethics* (n 7) 211. Elsewhere in Raz's work it appears that the conditions of de facto authority are stricter. Thus in *The Morality of Freedom* Raz writes that de facto authority 'implies not only actual power over people but, in the normal case, *both* that the person exercising that power claims to have legitimate authority and that he is acknowledged to have it by some people'. See Raz, *Morality of Freedom* (n 6) 65. To harmonise the two definitions we can take the second to be stating not the necessary and sufficient condition of de facto authority but an empirical generalisation, whereby when a de facto authority is also effective, eg it has 'actual power' over people, some of them are bound to acquire the corresponding belief.

[14] There may of course be cases where, even though this condition is satisfied, we still have no duty to follow the directive. For instance, a reason that it was not the job of the authority to consider may override the duty to follow the directive. Or it may be that disregarding a directive in a certain instance does not compromise the values that the directive is meant to serve.

[15] Paul Markwick has challenged the view that legal reasons have a distinctive property, namely content-independence. See P Markwick, 'Law and Content-Independent Reasons' (2000) 20 *Oxford Journal of Legal Studies* 579. Though very illuminating in many respects, his analysis does not affect my argument or Raz's. All I am claiming is that it is an implication of Raz's conception of authority that the validity of authoritative directives – and hence the reasons they create – is independent of the moral merit or demerit of their content, not that this independence is what makes them legal.

be reported by an American law professor, who does not treat what the Queen in Parliament enacts as authoritatively binding or over whom UK law does not claim authority. In fact, even an anarchist who thinks that no authority is ever legitimate can make the same statement. His statement will be relative to those who hold what the Queen in Parliament enacts as authoritative or over whom UK law claims authority.[16]

C. The Qualification

The sources thesis, we have seen, states that valid directives must be identifiable without resort to the dependent reasons. A more complicated picture, however, emerges from the following passage from the *Morality of Freedom*:

> The pre-emption thesis depends on a distinction between jurisdictional and other mistakes. Most, if not all, authorities have limited powers. Mistakes which they make about factors which determine the limits of their jurisdiction render their decisions void. They are not binding as authoritative directives, though the circumstances of the case may require giving them some weight if, for example, others innocently have relied on them. Other mistakes do not affect the binding force of the directives. *The pre-emption thesis claims that the factors about which the authority was wrong, and which are not jurisdictional factors, are pre-empted by the directive.* The thesis would be pointless if most mistakes are jurisdictional or if in most cases it was particularly controversial or difficult to establish which are and which are not.[17]

If, as the above qualification suggests, jurisdictional mistakes render a decision void, it would seem that the identification of the existence of an authoritative directive requires determining that the directive is intra vires as well as that it comes from a recognised legal source.

What are we to make of the relation between the sources thesis and the qualification? Of course, we can decide to abandon the qualification and stick to the sources thesis or amend the sources thesis to include the qualification. But in this chapter I shall not directly deal with either of these routes. Instead, I shall evaluate the following suggestion, namely that there is something about legal authority in particular that makes jurisdiction irrelevant to the identification of the existence of legal directives. On this suggestion, respect for jurisdiction is never necessary for the identification of legal directives, because law claims 'unlimited authority'.[18] Raz dubs this feature of law its comprehensiveness.

---

[16] Raz, *Authority of Law* (n 12) 153–57. There, Raz makes a distinction between statements from the internal point of view and detached statements. The first kind are the ones employed by those who regard someone as an authority over them and the second are exemplified by the anarchist or the law professor.

[17] Raz, *Morality of Freedom* (n 6) 62.

[18] ibid 76.

Other normative systems differ from law in this respect. About them Raz writes:

> These normally institute and govern the activities of organizations tied to some purpose or other. Sport associations, commercial companies, cultural organizations, political parties etc., are all established in order to achieve certain limited goals and each claims authority over behavior relevant to that goal only. Not so with legal systems. They do not acknowledge any limitation of the spheres of behavior, which they claim authority to regulate. If legal systems are established for a definite purpose it is a purpose which does not entail a limitation over their claimed scope of competence.[19]

The suggestion is that, since law's claim to authority admits of no limitation, it would make no sense to make that claim subject to a jurisdictional condition, as it would, perhaps, in the case of other, more 'local' practical authorities. So, the stand-alone sources thesis may not be a component of the theory of all practical authority, but it forms part of the theory of *legal* authority.

Let's call this the *Solution*. Against the Solution, I shall give an example of a legal system where the identification of authoritative directives as such cannot but include recourse to the test of jurisdiction.[20] Note also that in very Razian spirit I shall not be talking about the authority that law in that legal system actually has but only the authority it claims to have, whether or not it has it. The test of jurisdiction, I shall argue, is part of that claim.[21] More specifically, I shall take a legal system with a legislature and courts and a practice of constitutional review of legislation by the courts for its conformity with fundamental rights.[22] I do not mean to say that this is the simplest or most common type of legal system. But it is a type of legal system that best illustrates the point I shall be trying to make, since it brings into sharp relief the issue of division of labour between the two state institutions. And of course it is a type of legal system Raz claims his theory applies to. About this legal system I shall ask: How does law claim authority? Does its claim to authority vindicate the sources thesis? I shall argue that it does not and that the special normative status of (at least some) authoritative directives in this legal system presupposes respect for jurisdiction.

At this point however a preliminary objection may be raised. It may be argued that, if my interest is with the nature of the authority law claims, I should focus not on the C-L relationship but on the relationship between legal institutions in

---

[19] Raz, *Authority of Law* (n 12) 117.

[20] Heidi Hurd has also used jurisdiction to criticise the pre-emption thesis. See H Hurd, 'Challenging Authority' (1991) 100 *Yale Law Journal* 1611, 1629–35.

[21] Needless to say, my argument is equally directed at those who prefer to scrap the qualification altogether and insist on the strict reading of the sources thesis. If there is one authoritative system where directives are not identifiable by recourse to social facts alone, then the sources thesis is false.

[22] Note that when I refer to courts and legislatures, I shall, for the sake of the argument, rely on what I take to be Raz's understanding of those institutions.

general and legal subjects, since it is to the latter that law's claim to authority is addressed. However, the strategy followed here is supported by Raz's understanding of the institutional role of courts. According to Raz, courts are the institutions whose job crucially includes a duty to evaluate the behaviour of individuals not by their own lights but on the basis of existing standards through which law claims authority to regulate the behaviour of legal subjects. In other words courts ought to apply the standards that the law has dictated should govern the behaviour of legal subjects. Also, the nature of that duty seems to be no different from the duty of the legal subjects to follow authoritative directives. Courts are bound to apply existing legal standards 'to the exclusion of all other conflicting reasons',[23] except in cases where 'the exclusion is not total in scope'.[24] Thus, Raz claims that legal standards have exclusionary force for courts as much as for legal subjects.

D. Jurisdiction: Some Preliminaries

Before I proceed, let me say a few words about what I shall take jurisdiction to mean for the purposes of this chapter. As my aim is to assess the place of jurisdiction within the Razian framework, I shall use an understanding of jurisdiction that can be related to that framework. To wit, I shall assume that jurisdiction is the remit of an authority in terms of the dependent reasons that the authority may adjudicate on – call them j-reasons and call the reasons outside the authority's remit non-j reasons.

Thus understood, the test of jurisdiction *involves an appeal to the dependent reasons*. For analytical purposes we can divide the test of jurisdiction into two parts. First, the test of jurisdiction requires the identification of the j-reasons. Clearly, this part of the test of jurisdiction is likely to involve appeal to the dependent reasons. In many – if not all – cases such an appeal is needed to establish which power it is appropriate to entrust to an institution and which purposes it can legitimately be called upon to serve. In light of these judgements, it will then be determined which reasons it should adjudicate on. That being said, it is certainly open to Raz to claim that the first part of the test of jurisdiction does not militate against the sources thesis. The sources thesis, recall, refers to the identification of the directives of an *already established de facto authority*. It takes no view about the considerations that go into establishing someone's authority in the first place.

But, apart from establishing someone's authority over a certain range of reasons, the test of jurisdiction includes the determination of whether a directive

[23] Raz, *Practical Reason* (n 5) 143.
[24] ibid 144.

in question adjudicates on reasons that fall within or without a de facto author-ity's remit. Directives, to use a familiar analogy, do not have tags on them. So answering this question requires an appreciation of j-reasons and non-j reasons and of how they bear on the content of the directive. In other words, it requires recourse to the same considerations that the authority adjudicates on.[25]

It may be objected at this point that my characterisation of the test of juris-diction ignores a different possibility. Often, so the objection goes, the reasoning process outlined in the previous paragraph will be redundant. These are cases where the scope of the authority's power has been settled by a previous author-itative directive. When the authority in question has what lawyers call 'inherent' jurisdiction, the directive determining its jurisdiction will be one that has been issued by that same person or institution. When the authority in question has 'delegated' jurisdiction, the authoritative directive that delimits the scope of its power has been issued by some other institution; that is, the institution, from which the authority in question draws its own power. In such cases, the test of jurisdiction reduces to the application of the power-conferring directive. Hence, the objection concludes, these are cases where the determination of jurisdiction is not a matter of recourse to the dependent reasons, but a matter of appeal to some further social fact, the fact that the relevant power-conferring directive has been issued.

No doubt, these are very common cases, especially in law and other highly institutionalised normative systems. However, even in the presence of such power-conferring provisions, recourse to the dependent reasons is not eviscer-ated. To begin with, power-conferring provisions will typically employ abstract formulations like 'The club committee may only decide on issues pertaining to the life of the club'. Applying this criterion to each particular decision issued by the committee involves making more concrete judgements about which issues the regulation of the life of the club extends to. Furthermore, to assess that an authority has stayed intra vires, one must ascertain whether the reasons a par-ticular directive adjudicates fall into the category of j-reasons or non-j reasons.

But the claim of the chapter may be said to lack edge in a more fundamental sense. On Raz's view, the argument goes, authoritative directives pre-empt legal subjects from determining which course of action the dependent reasons sup-port. But it does not pre-empt them from merely *considering* those reasons. The

---

[25] Very often the second stage of the test of jurisdiction will direct us back to the first stage. Take the example of a club committee that has the power to regulate the life of the club. Suppose further that the question arises whether 'regulating the life of the club' extends to regulating the photos hanging in one's locker. In order to decide this, we need to arrive at a better understanding of the purposes of the club and of what the committee is there to accomplish. Whereas I think that a full account of jurisdiction must tell a story about this type of case, it is crucial to note that my present argument is not so much concerned with these moments of crisis, as it were. There is nothing exceptional or dramatic about the second stage of the test of jurisdiction, as I have described it. It applies to all authoritative directives.

'classificatory' exercise involved in the test of jurisdiction cannot count as the former. When we establish an authority's jurisdiction, we are not interested in determining whether the authority has dictated the right course of action. Perhaps, then, the test of jurisdiction is a form of considering the dependent reasons. Thus, it does not militate against the pre-emption thesis.

For present purposes, I do not wish to challenge the premise of the aforementioned objection. In other words, I assume that the test of jurisdiction is essentially a classificatory exercise that is different from and weaker than acting on a reason.[26] But even if it does not do damage to the pre-emption thesis, it lies in tension with the sources thesis, as commonly understood, and it is this tension that the chapter explores. Besides, if the claim of this chapter holds water, the test of jurisdiction cannot be equated with idle consideration of the dependent reasons. It is part of what makes a directive valid law. It thus invites us to reflect more carefully on how the concept of jurisdiction can be situated in our accounts of law.

After these preliminary remarks, it is time to turn to the main argument. How is law's claim to authority distributed between the courts and the legislature in a C-L system with a practice of constitutional review of legislation? I shall examine three possible Razian answers to this question: 1) the legislature-only reading, 2) the division-of-labour reading; and 3) the dualistic reading. In each case, I shall assess whether these readings can plausibly be said to vindicate the Solution.

III. MAKING ROOM FOR THE COURTS

A. The Legislature-only Reading

Raz maintains that the law claims practical authority. Of course the law is a normative order, not a person. So any claim to authority we attribute to it must be made by someone who speaks and acts in the name of the law.[27] In C-L legal systems two candidates present themselves: the legislature and courts.[28] According to one view, the law claims authority exclusively through legislative

---

[26] In this sense, my claim differs from Hurd's. She maintains that in order to apply the test of jurisdiction, 'one must oneself balance the antecedently existing reasons for action in each case in which those laws apply so as to ensure that in extending its authority to that case, the government has not exceeded the bounds of its jurisdiction'. See Hurd, 'Challenging Authority' (n 20) 1634.

[27] See also L Green, *The Authority of the State* (Oxford, Oxford University Press, 1988) 66. For criticism of this sort of personification, see R Dworkin, *Justice in Robes* (Cambridge MA, Harvard University Press, 2006) 198–201.

[28] As I noted in chapter 1 C-L legal systems do not comprise *only* courts and a legislature. I focus on them here not because no other institution can conceivably make claims on law's behalf but because their relationship exemplifies the philosophical issue I am interested in.

edicts. Let's call this view the legislature-only reading of Raz's theory. The legislature-only reading reflects an understandable tendency to associate law's claim to authority exclusively with legislatures. This is especially so in a democracy, where the legislature is the forum of the elected representatives of the sovereign people. Clearly, the legislature-only reading insulates law's claim to authority from jurisdictional concerns. If only the legislature speaks on law's behalf and if law's claim to authority is unlimited, then it seems only natural to conclude that the special normative status of legal directives does not necessarily depend on any kind of jurisdictional condition. It is sufficient that they emanate from the legislature.

What would the relationship between courts and the legislature have to look like for it to be the case that legislative edicts are all there is to law's claim to authority? There is an easy and seemingly straightforward answer to this question: by their very nature legislatures are law-making institutions, whereas courts have a primarily law-applying function.[29] The job of the latter is authoritatively to determine what the law commands in the case before them. This consists in applying pre-existing law. A crucial part of pre-existing law is the law that the legislature has made. The courts' duty to apply pre-existing law flows from the exclusionary force of authoritative directives. The fact that the legislature has dictated p on a certain issue pre-empts courts from deciding the case before them on their own view of the merits of the case.[30] Now, if Raz accepted such a sharp contrast between law-making and law-applying institutions, whereby courts were mere recipients and conveyor belts of legislative decisions, it would make sense to infer that law claims authority solely through legislative edicts.

However, an exclusive focus on the law-applying function of courts would seriously distort Raz's account of them. For one thing, a court differs from ordinary legal subjects in that its determinations of the law are authoritative. Legal subjects also deliberate about their rights and duties under the law, but their judgements are not binding on anyone. A judicial decision is binding at least for the parties in the dispute. Here, though, arises a paradox. Applicative determinations, as Raz calls them, are either correct or incorrect. In exercising its law-applying function, a court either correctly applies pre-existing law or it does not. Only of creative determinations can we say that they are binding. But when

[29] Raz, *Practical Reason* (n 5) 141–46.

[30] Of course in many legal systems pre-existing law also comprises rules of precedent and customary law. But since I am interested in the relationship between courts and the legislature, not courts and other courts or social practices, I shall ignore this complication. Furthermore, courts are not the only law-applying institutions in Raz's theory. Apart from them, tribunals and other officials, like police officers, are under a duty to apply pre-existing law. In the following discussion I focus solely on courts for the purpose of simplicity. Whatever I say about courts, also applies to other law-applying bodies in Raz's sense. It should be borne in mind that I am using the distinction between law-creating and law-applying functions for the sake of the argument.

courts are applying the law, they do not make new law. So in what sense are their decisions binding? Raz solves the paradox as follows: '[Norm-applying organs like courts] are institutions with power to determine the normative situation of specified individuals, which are required to exercise these powers by applying existing norms, but whose decisions are binding even when wrong'.[31] I shall have more to say about this paradox later on. For the time being it suffices to bear it in mind, since it implies that in a sense courts also assume the role of an authority, even when they apply pre-existing law.

Secondly, for Raz judges typically have the power authoritatively to settle disputes for which pre-existing law does not dictate an outcome. This is the famous positivistic doctrine of judicial discretion. Raz writes:

> Because of the vagueness, open texture, and incompleteness of all legal systems, there are many disputes for which the system does not provide a correct answer. Even if it rules out certain solutions as wrong, there are others which are neither wrong nor right in law. If the system requires, with respect to some such cases, as all legal systems in fact do, that the courts should not refuse to settle the dispute but should render judgment in it, then they are thereby required to determine the case in accordance with their own perception of what is right. Needless to say, even in such cases their discretion can be limited by general legal principles, but they will not eliminate the element of personal judgment of the merits.[32]

Importantly, judges are directed to exercise discretion in cases where pre-existing law has made the legal determination of a case dependent on moral principles as when it dictates that unfair agreements are invalid. In these cases pre-existing law does not play the mediating role that is characteristic of the Razian notion of authority since it refers back to (some of) the reasons it was supposed to take into account and replace. It is up to the courts to spell out what the standard of fairness implies and make new law that truly mediates between legal subjects and the reasons that apply to them. Judicial discretion, then, is another aspect of Raz's theory that assigns limited law-making powers to courts. It does this, though, in a way that is easily reconcilable with their law-applying function. It is only after pre-existing law has run out that judges are called upon to exercise their discretionary powers.

Finally, the exclusionary force of legislative edicts vis-à-vis judges is often qualified. In other words, the fact that there is a pre-existing norm that commands *p* does not exclude for courts all reasons that count in favour of and against *p*. In many legal systems, courts are empowered to disregard or even change a valid norm of the system if they think that some specified reason counts against it. This special power, Raz maintains, is not at odds with their

---

[31] Raz, *Authority of Law* (n 12) 109–10.
[32] ibid 113.

law-applying function, since courts are not at 'complete' liberty to disregard pre-existing legal rules, that is, disregard it for just any reason.

> They may change them only for certain kinds of reasons ... But if the court finds that they are not the best rules because of some other reason, not included in the permissible list, it is nevertheless bound to follow the rules.[33]

Raz uses the example of a court's power to overrule established precedent to illustrate the qualified exclusionary force that he thinks pre-existing law has on judges. But another example is more illuminating for our purposes, since it pits courts against the legislature. Raz has argued that the constitution derives its authority from a self-validating judicial convention, at least after the authority of its drafters has lapsed. At a minimum, its authority is distinct from that of the ordinary legislative body.[34] The power Raz assigns courts in constitutional matters is not to be underestimated. Interpretation of the constitution, claims Raz, includes both conserving and innovative elements. More specifically, it involves balancing the need to provide a stable and continuous institutional framework on the one hand and the need to develop it and make it more just or adapt it to novel circumstances on the other.[35] Since for Raz the implementation of the constitution is in the hands of the courts, it follows that constitutional law makes ample room for judicial creativity.

Judicial authority in constitutional matters typically gives the courts the power to disregard or change ordinary legislation that they find in contravention of constitutional precepts. In these cases, therefore, recourse to constitutional precepts is not excluded by ordinary legislation. As a consequence, in deciding whether they ought to apply pre-existing law, courts are not pre-empted from considering if it has due regard to these precepts and may refuse to apply it if they think it does not. In short, the key for Raz's explanation of constitutional review is the scope of reasons excluded by legislative edicts. Some reasons it is the courts' institutional duty to consider afresh even in the presence of a legislative decision. With regard to those reasons, then, courts are not mere law-applying organs, with the sole task of furthering the will of the legislature. Rather, they become themselves law-making organs with the power to alter the legal rights and duties of legal subjects.

It would be worth highlighting two implications of this qualification. First, this qualification introduces an interesting asymmetry between the attitudes of courts and legal subjects toward legislative edicts. Take the example of a legal system where courts have the authority to interpret a constitutional bill of rights. It seems to me to follow from the aforementioned qualification that the reasons

---

[33] ibid 14.
[34] J Raz, 'On the Authority and Interpretation of Constitutions' in L Alexander (ed), *Constitutionalism: Philosophical Preliminaries* (Cambridge, Cambridge University Press, 1998) 152–94.
[35] ibid 180–83.

excluded by a legislative edict for courts in that system are more limited in scope than the reasons excluded for legal subjects. Here is how. On the one hand, it would vitiate the authoritative status of legislative edicts for legal subjects if they second-guessed the legislator's decision regarding the bearing of constitutional rights. On the other, such recourse to considerations of constitutional rights on the part of the courts would be compatible with the authoritative status of legislative edicts vis-à-vis the courts.[36]

Secondly, and related to the previous point, this qualification gives rise to an ambiguity in Raz's understanding of the exclusionary force of legislative edicts. We have a relatively clear-cut sense of what he takes to be the ground for the exclusionary force of authoritative directives, as it applies to legal subjects: authoritative directives such as legislative edicts are supposed to adjudicate on the reasons that legal subjects have (or a set thereof). These are the reasons that legal subjects are pre-empted from acting on, once the directive has been issued. But it is not so clear why the courts' duty to apply these edicts should have only 'qualified' pre-emptive force. If their duty to apply legislative edicts is the duty to apply those standards that would be binding from the legal subjects' point of view, it is difficult to find a motivation for the asymmetry in the scope of the reasons excluded that we pinpointed in the previous paragraph. Presumably, from the legal subjects' point of view legislative edicts exclude *all* the reasons that the legislature was supposed to base its decision on. Neither can the ground for the 'qualified' exclusionary force of legislative edicts vis-à-vis the courts be that toward judges, unlike other legal subjects, the law claims authority to adjudicate on a different, more limited, class of reasons. First, such a statement would contradict the comprehensiveness that Raz attributes to law's claim to authority. More importantly, whether or not we are inclined to think that the law claims more limited authority over judges, this would hardly affect the nature of judicial duty. For, this duty falls on judges not *qua* authority-subjects but *qua* officials. In this capacity, judges have a duty to consider the reasons that apply to other authority-subjects.[37]

The general lesson to be learnt from the more detailed exposition of Raz's views rehearsed above may be formulated as follows: even if the distinction between law-creating and law-applying functions is maintained, courts themselves do not come out as merely law-applying institutions. To some extent they have the power to develop the law. The two tasks coexist. Indeed, it is sometimes

---

[36] Thus, when Raz writes that '[r]eferences to moral considerations in constitutions are typically not cases of the incorporation of morality but blocks to its exclusion or modification by ordinary legislation', I take him to mean that the exclusion or modification is blocked for judges, not authority subjects. See J Raz, 'Incorporation by Law' (2004) 10 *Legal Theory* 1, 10.

[37] Jeremy Waldron has explored some implications of this point. See J Waldron, 'Authority for Officials' in L Meyer, S Paulson and T Pogge (eds), *Rights, Culture and the Law: Themes from the Political and Legal Philosophy of Joseph Raz* (Oxford, Oxford University Press, 2003) 45, 55–58.

difficult to disentangle in a judicial ruling the two components, the passive and the creative. Thus, although it is undoubtedly important for a judge that a certain directive has been issued by the legislature, the existence of this directive will in some cases provide only a starting point for the judge's decision.[38] Often he will have to make fresh law where pre-existing-law is incomplete. In other cases he is empowered to change pre-existing law where he thinks it does not take certain specified reasons adequately into account. And even when he only applies the law, his applicative determination is authoritative. In these respects, legal systems with courts and a legislature manifest a plurality of authoritative sources.

B. The Legislature *and* the Courts

In the previous section we reached the conclusion that according to Raz the law often does not speak in one voice. Legal systems with courts and a legislature are the most obvious case. Both courts and the legislature claim for themselves a share of power over legal subjects. There seems to be no reason to regard any one of them as exclusively expressing law's claim to authority. Thus, the legislature-only reading overlooks the plurality of authoritative sources in legal systems with a legislature and courts. In this section I shall pursue this line of argument a bit further. What are the implications of having two legal authorities, the legislature and the judiciary? How does this plurality of legal sources affect law's claim to authority?

Consider the case of a statute banning interracial marriages passed in a legal system with an entrenched constitution and a practice of constitutional review.[39] Suppose further that the reviewing court strikes it down on the ground that it infringes privacy or some other similarly fundamental right enshrined in the constitution. Of course, it cannot be the correct understanding of the moral concept of privacy that makes it the case – even before the court's decision – that one is legally permitted to marry someone from another race. In fact, for Raz morality does not enter the question of whether the rule 'Interracial marriages are permitted' is a valid rule of the system. According to the sources

---

[38] Raz, *Authority of Law* (n 12) 96. Even in cases where judges apply statutory law, they are not necessarily reduced to mouthpieces of the legislator. Application of the law, it has often been noted, is not a mechanical process. It inevitably depends on the way the law is interpreted by the courts. In turn, principles of legal interpretation, as Raz himself notes, sometimes evolve from judicial conventions. See J Raz, 'Intention in Interpretation' in R George (ed), *The Autonomy of Law* (Oxford, Oxford University Press, 1996) 249, 271. Of course interpretative guidelines may be contained in statutes as well.

[39] *Loving v Virginia*, 388 US 1 (1967). To tighten the example, we also need to assume that the doctrine of constitutional review has evolved from a judicial convention that grants the constitution its authority and determines the way it ought to be interpreted by individual judges.

thesis, what makes it valid is that it has been issued by a de facto authority – in our case, the court.

Here then we have two allegedly valid legal rules, the one coming from the legislature and the other coming from the court, which pull in opposite directions. What form does law's claim to authority take in this situation? Does the fact that the two conflicting rules come from different sources make any difference? I am going to examine two routes Raz might take to answer these questions. Like the legislature-only reading they start from the premise that law claims unlimited authority in order to vindicate the sources thesis; in this sense they can be seen as fleshing out the Solution. But unlike the legislature-only reading, both try to accommodate the fact that in legal systems like that of our example law's claim to authority is made up of the contributions of both the legislature and the courts.[40]

The first route starts from the premise that each state institution claims authority to adjudicate on different reasons, in other words, that each has a different jurisdiction. Their respective claims to authority are supplementary. Taken together, courts and the legislature claim authority to adjudicate all the practical reasons that apply to legal subjects. Law's claim to unlimited authority is, so to speak, a combination of the two sub-claims. I shall call this the *division-of-labour reading*. Against it, it will be argued that it cannot save the Solution, because it makes the authoritative status of at least some of its norms depend on the test of jurisdiction. And this test, as I indicated earlier, is shot through with evaluative judgements concerning the dependent reasons.

The second route, by contrast, invites us to think of courts and the legislature as both claiming unlimited authority. Each of them claims to adjudicate on all the reasons that apply to legal subjects. I shall call this the dualistic reading. The dualistic reading does away with the test of jurisdiction and thus avoids the criticism levelled against the division-of-labour reading. Still, I shall argue, it comes at a significant cost. It does not have the resources to adequately explain the sense in which judicial duty is constrained by legislative decisions.

But before we turn to the examination of the two readings, it is important to clear out of the way a seemingly attractive but ultimately misconceived suggestion that trades on the doctrine of judicial discretion. According to this doctrine, recall, judges are often confronted with cases which pre-existing law has left unresolved. To settle these otherwise unregulated cases, judges have to exercise their discretion. In this limited law-making capacity, judges do not compete with any conflicting legislative will. Whatever the merits of the doctrine of judicial discretion, it is of no avail in the case under consideration. Constitutional review of legislation is also applicable in cases where the legislature has expressed

---

[40] There is nothing prima facie surprising about the existence of two or more authorities with overlapping jurisdictions. See J Raz, 'The Problem of Authority: Revisiting the Service Conception' (2006) 40 *Minnesota Law Review* 1003, 1020–21.

itself in a clear and unambiguous way. In fact, this is partly what makes it so controversial. In our example there is no doubt that the legislature claims the authority to dictate that interracial marriages should be banned. The judicial decision that interracial marriages are permitted flies in the face of the explicit legislative will. Hence, the neat distinction between the judicial task of applying pre-existing law and that of exercising discretion interstitially, in cases where pre-existing law has run out, cannot help explain away the conflict between the legislature and the court.

C. The Division-of-Labour Reading

The division-of-labour reading aims to recast the conflicts between the legislature and the courts that are typical of constitutional adjudication in jurisdictional terms. Suppose that the set of dependent reasons comprises reasons a, b, c, d and e. In addition, suppose that d and e stand for the reasons to promote the interests guaranteed by constitutional rights – call them *constitutional reasons*. On the division-of-labour reading, in legal systems with an entrenched constitution and a practice of constitutional review, the legislature claims authority to adjudicate on a, b, and c, whereas courts claim authority to adjudicate on d and e. As Raz has put it, judicial review gives courts 'when adjudicating on the compatibility of legislation with the constitutionally protected moral considerations, the power to modify the application of those moral considerations themselves'.[41] On the face of it, this reading explains why courts are bound by the legislative determination in the majority of cases; it's because with regard to most dependent reasons the legislature is an authority over authority-subjects, and hence its decisions are equipped with exclusionary force. It also explains why judicial rulings in cases implicating constitutional reasons typically override legislative decisions. If the legislature never claimed authority to adjudicate on constitutional reasons, then legal subjects are not pre-empted from acting on them, even after the legislature has issued its directive. If, further, courts claim authority with regard to constitutional reasons, then their ruling that the legislative directive is unconstitutional gives legal subjects reason to disregard that directive (assuming, as it is reasonable to do, that constitutional reasons are weightier than other dependent reasons).

There are two problems with this reading. First, it is unconvincing to portray courts as the *sole* authorities with regard to constitutional reasons. Even if it were possible tidily to single out the constitutional aspects of a political issue from its other aspects and entrust the former to one institution and the latter to another, such a division of labour would seriously misconstrue the institutional role of

---

[41] Raz, 'Incorporation by Law' (n 36) 13.

legislatures. We are intuitively disinclined to say that constitutional reasons lie beyond the jurisdiction of the legislature. We do not think that the legislature may simply take such reasons into account, but without claiming any authority concerning them. When Congress passed the Civil Rights Act of 1964, it clearly claimed to do more than that. Accordingly, it is probably more accurate to say that it is because we think it so important that legislatures have due regard to constitutional reasons that we have included the relevant constitutional guarantee.[42]

Furthermore, the division-of-labour reading is incompatible with the sources thesis. Since the authority that the two institutions claim is not unlimited, their directives must pass the test of jurisdiction before they can be identified as valid. Let me try to make this more conspicuous with an example. Imagine that the legislature has enacted a scheme of subsidies to boost the economy. The court would be acting ultra vires, if it replaced the bill with a different scheme, not in the name of constitutional reasons but because it is of the view that the goal of economic growth will be better served through an alternative scheme. But we cannot know this unless we determine that the reasons the court's decision adjudicates on are not constitutional reasons. Note that this problem also stings a modified version of the division-of-labour reading, whereby the legislature claims unlimited authority. This modification can fend off the first criticism but, insofar as it maintains that courts only claim authority concerning constitutional reasons, it violates the sources thesis.[43]

In short, the reconciliation this reading offers between the plurality of authoritative legal sources and law's claim to unlimited authority fails to vindicate the Solution. If it supposes that the legislature does not claim authority with regard to constitutional reasons, it offers a bad account of legislative power. At any rate, the division-of-labour reading introduces a jurisdictional component into the conditions of identification of (at least) judge-made rules. Thus, it flouts the sources thesis. The fact that the law as a whole presumably claims unlimited authority does not affect this conclusion.

D. The Dualistic Reading

A major shortcoming of the division-of-labour reading is that it concedes that the test of jurisdiction is inherent in law's claim to authority (at least as far as judge-made law is concerned). This, we have seen, is a consequence of the fact

---

[42] cp D Kyritsis, 'Principles, Policies and the Power of Courts' (2007) 20 *Canadian Journal of Law and Jurisprudence* 379, 385–87.

[43] In addition to that, the modified version has difficulties explaining why courts prevail over the legislature in constitutional cases, if the legislature is also an authority concerning constitutional reasons. I will have more to say about this in the next section.

that for the division-of-labour reading (at least) courts claim limited authority. The dualistic reading denies this; it states that both courts and legislatures claim unlimited authority. To repeat, this means that both claim the power to adjudicate on all the dependent reasons. On this view, law's overall claim to unlimited authority does not unify the voices of courts and legislatures. It is just made up of the claims to unlimited authority independently made by the two institutions. Arguably, then, the dualistic reading succeeds where the previous one had failed, that is, in defending the Solution. Since both courts and legislatures claim unlimited authority, the test of jurisdiction has no purpose; provenance from the right source suffices to identify a valid directive.

To test the dualistic reading, I shall examine whether it can provide an adequate explanation of the relationship between courts and the legislature. It is an integral part of that relationship that courts may not freely disregard legislative edicts and decide each case that comes before them *de novo*, just because they are of the view that a different directive from the one issued by the legislature better tracks the balance of dependent reasons. Quite the opposite, adjudication is commonly taken to depend in a special sense on what other legal institutions, including legislatures as well as other courts, have decided in the past, and, as we have seen, Raz agrees with this when he writes that courts 'are required to exercise [the power to determine the normative situation of specified individuals] *by applying existing norms*'[44] (emphasis added). Granted, as Raz and other legal theorists insist, past decisions do not necessarily provide courts with conclusive guidance. In legal systems with a practice of constitutional review, which are the focal point of our discussion, courts can sometimes override norms created by the legislature. Still, they may do so on a limited set of grounds (which I called earlier constitutional reasons). Accordingly, we think that a court that ignored past decisions or overstepped the boundaries of constitutional review would be making a serious mistake.[45]

How would the dualistic reading describe this kind of mistake? Or to put the same point differently: if courts claim authority to make a decision on any ground, why are they thought to be under a duty to decide on just a few – only on constitutional grounds – and to defer to the legislature with regard to the rest? Once again, we encounter jurisdictional considerations, namely considerations about the remit of authoritative institutions, this time in their relationship with other such institutions. The dualistic reading blocked them off from the conditions of identification of valid directives, but now they crop back up as determinants of judicial duty. To account for them, it is no use responding that past decisions contain valid legal norms. There seems to be no reason why rules

---

[44] Raz, *Authority of Law* (n 12) 109–10.
[45] More generally, we think that *jurisdiction is relevant to the moral evaluation of a decision*. For further elaboration of this point see below.

issued from one unlimited authority should make any difference to the decision of another unlimited authority, *just because they are valid*. Likewise, we cannot invoke the notion of a 'qualified' exclusionary force of legislative edicts, as applied to courts. For, we are not yet sure whether legislative edicts have any force vis-à-vis the courts, let alone an exclusionary force.

But perhaps courts really do not have a special institutional duty to follow the norms laid down by other authoritative institutions in their decisions, just because these norms are valid norms of the legal system. Perhaps, that is, legal validity does not even have this feature, that it is the property of a norm by virtue of which courts ought to apply it in deciding cases. Recall that for Raz judicial decisions are binding even if wrong. In turn, they are wrong if they misapply an existing norm but also, one would add, if they do not apply the relevant existing norm at all.

If the idea of validity cannot account for the limits of the judicial role vis-à-vis the legislature, then what's the alternative? Here is one suggestion: courts better perform their role as practical authorities over legal subjects if they show some measure of respect to norms created by the legislature, even when they have the power to constitutionally review them, than if they make law out of new cloth. It follows then that the mistake a court makes when it disregards pre-existing law, if it is a mistake at all, is one a court commits *qua* practical authority. The decision it makes in breach of its duty to apply a relevant existing norm to the case before it lacks merit, if it does, *qua* authoritative directive.

We are a long way from the familiar positivistic picture where pre-existing law is a given in adjudication and what courts ought to do is combine it with moral premises to arrive at a determinate answer in concrete legal questions. On the suggestion we are now considering, the duty of courts to follow the norms created by the legislature is, like the duty to create new rules beyond – or in combination with – the existing law, one that follows from their role as practical authorities. And as in the latter case 'judges do not just push away their law books and start to legislate without further guidance from the law',[46] so in the former case the judge will discharge his duty by combining certain facts (that the legislature has dictated *p*) and evaluative premises.

Let's examine this suggestion more closely. Recall that for Raz we treat someone as an authority if we better conform to the reasons that apply to us independently of the authority's intervention by following his directives than by trying on our own to achieve conformity. On this view, we compare two stages: one where we are left to our own devices to work out what is the right thing to do, and one where the authority makes judgements in our place, as we would make

---

[46] HLA Hart, *The Concept of Law*, 2nd edn with a new Postscript (Oxford, Oxford University Press, 1994) 274.

those judgements, only better. A directive then is a good exercise of authority when it correctly reflects the reasons that exist at the first stage, and it is a bad exercise of authority if it does not. If the court's reason to follow legislative edicts and to review them only on a limited set of grounds is one of the reasons that an authority does a better job at tracking with her directives, then it can easily be reconciled with Raz's theory. It belongs to the reasons that are covered by the directive's exclusionary force.[47] Furthermore, it pertains to the evaluation of a directive and as such does not bear on its existence.

At first blush, however, the court's reason in favour of deference does not have a counterpart among the dependent reasons. For, it only arises once a structure of authoritative guidance is put in place. Prior to this, it seems that legal subjects have no reason that authorities stay intra vires. And this is as it should be, since jurisdiction is a component of institutional morality. It appears to make little sense to say of jurisdiction that individuals fare better or worse in respecting it when acting on their own, absent the authority's intervention. Our intuitions track this aspect of jurisdiction. We think that respecting one's juris-diction is one thing and getting the balance of dependent reasons right is another and that the two may come apart. An authority can go dreadfully astray, even if it has stayed intra vires. And conversely, a decision may be very good in its content, while at the same time coming from someone who had no business making it. For example, a golf club committee may decide that all UK citizens should have a minimum income of £12,000. Now, it may well be that this is just the right thing to do, morally speaking, but that does not change the fact that the committee lacks competence to make this sort of decision for the UK. It comes as no surprise then that Raz himself singles out jurisdictional mistakes from other mistakes that may sting a directive and intends the pre-emption thesis to apply to the latter but not the former.[48]

If this is so, then the Razian test of what makes a directive a good exercise of authority does not capture the importance of jurisdiction and hence cannot explain the failure of an ultra vires directive.[49] This further entails that the exclusionary force of authoritative directives does not cover the court's reason for deference. Authority subjects may still act on it even in the presence of an

---

[47]   cp Raz, 'The Problem of Authority' (n 40) 1029–31.

[48]   Raz, *Morality of Freedom* (n 6) 62.

[49]   Jeremy Waldron has also noted the discrepancy between the reasons that apply to individuals and the reasons that authorities ought to take into account. See Waldron, 'Authority for Officials' (n 37) 59–63. Scott Hershovitz has made a similar claim against Raz's theory of authority by focus-ing on the value of democracy and pursuing its implications for the normal justification thesis. See S Hershovitz, 'Legitimacy, Democracy and Razian Authority' (2003) 9 *Legal Theory* 201. Note also that this discrepancy may provide the starting point for an explanation of the 'qualified exclusion-ary force' that Raz thinks legislative edicts may sometimes have on judges, as opposed to legal subjects. For a proposal that is largely sympathetic to the Razian framework, see A Marmor, 'Authority, Equality and Democracy' (2005) 18 *Ratio Juris* 315.

authoritative directive. They may still evaluate whether a judicial ruling has complied with it. Now, as has been argued in the account of jurisdiction offered at the outset of our discussion, in order to assess whether an authority has stayed intra vires, authority subjects will also have to have recourse to j-reasons. For instance, they must determine whether the court has overridden the legislative decision for constitutional reasons only. In addition, they will have to do this for every judicial ruling. Once again, then, jurisdiction militates against the stand-alone sources thesis. Before we can say of a judicial decision that it has created a valid directive, we need to assess whether, in issuing it, the court has respected the constraints that stem from its position in the legal system and its relationship to other institutions, notably the legislature.

But maybe this conclusion is premature. Maybe a proponent of the dualistic reading is able to recast the court's reason in favour of deference in terms of reasons that would apply to legal subjects even in the absence of an authoritative structure. In this vein he can argue that, once a legislative decision has been issued, it may affect the reasons that apply to legal subjects and hence also the task of the court. So, it may be that the legislative decision has established a system of coordinated action in cases where coordination is needed. In this case the judge has a reason to uphold this arrangement just because it has succeeded in securing coordination. Hence, it is likely that his decision will better track first-order reasons if he sticks to the solution chosen by the legislature than if he replaces it. But this justification inevitably works piecemeal. Coordination is not always needed. Hence, we cannot expect that coordination-based considerations always give the judge an extra reason to defer to the legislative determination. As a consequence, they cannot account for the court's reason to respect legislative edicts in general.

The proponent of the dualistic reading might attempt a different tack: he might propose that legal subjects have a blanket reason to want courts to heed legislative edicts. This reason has nothing to do with the merit of individual legal directives but with the merit of having a system of settled expectations. Thus, it might be argued that judicial activism is likely to disrupt the normal function of the legal system. Fewer and fewer people will be able to rely on the expectation that others will comply with pre-existing law, since there is no assurance that their rights and duties that flow from pre-existing law will be enforced by the courts. This will undercut the legal system's general ability effectively to regulate the behaviour of legal subjects. And *that* is something that each individual would evidently not want. However, in a decentralised judicial system, it would be quite unpersuasive to maintain that each and every instance of judicial activism will have such terrible consequences. At a minimum, we can say that it is easy to envisage a situation where this is unlikely to be the case. Take a private dispute over the enforcement of a contract brought before a lower court. In these circumstances, even though the threat of institutional breakdown is removed, our moral objection against judicial disrespect for pre-existing law does not disappear.[50]

Let's recap. What is the ground for the courts' duty of deference to legislative edicts? Accordingly, what kind of mistake would the court commit if it disregarded them? This duty, as we have seen, stems from considerations that determine how courts ought to exercise their authority given that they operate side by side with the legislature. Likewise, the mistake the court would commit if it disregarded legislative edicts would be that it did not adequately take such considerations into account. However, considerations of this type cannot plausibly be understood as reflecting reasons of a kind that authority subjects would have in the absence of an authoritative structure and are thus pre-empted from having recourse to according to the pre-emption thesis. Quite the contrary, authority subjects ought to take them into account when they are faced with a judicial ruling. This conclusion is not affected by the fact that courts as well as legislatures claim to adjudicate on all first-order reasons, as the dualistic reading urges. Thus, even on the dualistic reading, the fact that law claims unlimited authority does not block the relevance of jurisdictional considerations for the identification of valid law.

IV.   A JURISDICTIONALLY BOUND SOURCES THESIS

So far, I have been arguing that, contrary to what the Solution suggests, we cannot do without jurisdiction in our accounts of law despite the fact that the law claims unlimited authority. I shall now consider an objection whose main thrust is that I have overshot my conclusion. According to it, although jurisdiction deserves a place in our accounts of law, it can be reconciled with the sources thesis. I shall examine two versions of this objection, one suggested by Timothy Endicott and the other by John Gardner.

Endicott agrees that submission to authority does not pre-empt authority subjects from assessing the authority's jurisdiction. Quite the opposite, he thinks that they must do so, 'if they are to justify action in compliance with a directive'.[51] They must determine whether a given consideration is or is not excluded by the directive. He gives the example of a mother who instructs the child to stay at home. The house catches fire. Will the child be disobeying the mother's directive, if she runs to safety? The mother's directive, according to Endicott, cannot

---

[50] The case we are considering is to be distinguished from the example of someone deciding to break the speed limit when driving on a road with no traffic at all. Regardless of how we are inclined to describe his moral predicament, whether, that is, we think he has a moral obligation to obey the speed-limit rule in that case or not, the judge's position is very different. We think the latter has a special institutional duty to decide according to pre-existing law.

[51] T Endicott, 'Interpretation, Jurisdiction and the Authority of Law' (2007) 6 *APA Newsletter* 14, 17.

be interpreted as pre-empting the consideration that one ought to flee a house on fire, and hence it does not stand in the way of the child's acting on that unexcluded consideration. But in order to see this, the child must determine the jurisdiction of the mother's directive. Endicott also agrees that 'it may take a complex exercise in evaluative and normative reasoning to justify obedience to a claim of authority'.[52] Finally, he thinks that the situation is no different in law. He writes: 'Legal directives do not generally purport to exclude all considerations that are not legally recognized any more than your mother's directive to you to stay in the house excludes all considerations that she has not recognized'.[53]

Still, Endicott does not draw the radical conclusion in the theory of law that I do. This may well be because the focus of his proposal is not the conditions of legal validity and the truth of the sources thesis, but the compatibility of authority and autonomy. Nonetheless, he does advance a number of claims that someone who wants to reconcile jurisdiction and the sources thesis could be tempted to have resort to. I shall briefly describe each of these claims and argue that attempts at reconciliation based on them are bound to fail.

Endicott's first claim is that jurisdictional considerations will inform the interpretation of a directive. Interpreters, he says, should be guided by a sense of the 'purposes for which [someone] exercises authority over you'.[54] It follows from this that the meaning that they attribute to the directive cannot frustrate these purposes. So, interpreting the mother's directive as not excluding the consideration to flee a burning house makes better sense of the mother's authority. It is therefore to be preferred. As Endicott puts it, 'a limit on jurisdiction is a ground of interpretation of an unspecific directive'.[55]

In what sense does this claim help defenders of the stand-alone sources thesis? It does, because, by deferring jurisdictional considerations to the stage of interpretation, it allows them to say that jurisdictional considerations do not impinge on the validity of directives. But this manoeuvre will not get us very far. To begin with, it only makes sense to interpret valid directives. And a directive that is made without jurisdiction is not a valid directive at all. Perhaps legal subjects only *find out* when they begin to engage with a directive that has come from the right source. But legal validity belongs to the metaphysics of law, not its epistemology. A legal interpreter that judges that a directive has been made without jurisdiction discovers a fact that is true prior to his discovering it. Upon discovering this fact, he realises that he had been engaging with a directive that, as it turns out, was void all along.

The appeal of Endicott's claim lies in part in the fact that he focuses on unspecific directives. It is common to say of such directives that, because of

52 ibid.
53 ibid 18.
54 ibid.
55 ibid.

their vagueness, they ought to be interpreted. And, if possible, they ought to be given a meaning that does not raise jurisdictional concerns. But surely, someone might contend, before their meaning was specified at the stage of interpretation, they were already valid directives. It's just that they were unspecific. In other words, in the case of unspecific directives it seems more natural to distinguish their validity from their interpretation.

However, jurisdictional concerns may also be raised by a specific and clear directive. A directive may fail the test of jurisdiction not just at the margins but in its core. Take for example a directive by a golf club committee decreeing that all club members ought to go to Brighton on holiday or that they may not go to Blackpool. The directive has ultra vires written all over it. You do not need to interpret it or remove any ambiguity in its wording to be persuaded of this. So at least in the case of such failures the argument from lack of specificity is not available.

We can imagine the following objection to this line of thought: someone might say that this type of patent failure does not threaten the sources thesis. The sources thesis, recall, states that directives must be identifiable without recourse to moral considerations. However, according to the objection we are now considering, when a failure is so obvious, it does not require any recourse to the dependent reasons to identify it.[56] This objection is again guilty of over-relying on the deliberative process of authority subjects. For, the fact that it does not take them any time or effort to identify ultra vires directives does not negate the fact that a directive's validity depends on its not being ultra vires; and this, as we have seen, involves recourse to the dependent reasons.

Let me end the discussion of the first manoeuvre by saying a few words about unspecific directives. I want to suggest that the argument against the sources thesis offered here stings them as well. Directives are not strings of words in the statute book. They are norms. Only of norms can we say that they are valid. So, in order to determine the conditions of validity of a directive, we need to decide which norm it is we are talking about. The example of the mother ordering the child to stay at home shows that the norm 'stay at home, even if it catches fire' is not a valid norm of the system, because it is ultra vires, whereas the norm 'Stay at home barring exceptional circumstances' is. The lack of specificity attaches to the words but not to the norm. We may be inclined to say that we find out, when we interpret the words, but this way of putting the point, as I have been at pains to emphasise, is compatible with acknowledging that the validity of the directive depends on jurisdictional considerations.

---

[56] The objection also seems to echo Raz's understanding of jurisdiction in the passage from the *Morality of Freedom* quoted in section II. He thinks that jurisdiction would be an embarrassment to his theory, 'if in most cases it was particularly controversial or difficult to establish which are [jurisdictional mistakes] and which are not'. See Raz, *Morality of Freedom* (n 6) 62.

So far, I have argued that the sources thesis cannot be saved by deferring jurisdictional considerations to the stage of interpretation. But there is a different way of insulating the sources thesis from jurisdictional considerations that is closer to the spirit of the Solution. Law, says Endicott, 'need not claim that there are *or* that there are not any limits to its authority'.[57] Instead, it can and typically does leave the scope of its authority unspecified. Suppose Endicott is right in his description of law's claim to authority. A defender of the Solution can use this description to put forward the following suggestion: a theory of law is adequate if it accounts for the normal case and gives us the resources to explain what makes a situation exceptional. The idea that law's authority has an unspecified scope does both. Since the scope of law's authority is not specified, legal subjects can go about their daily dealings with the law without having to worry about jurisdiction, especially given the fact that law's authority is rather extensive anyway. Jurisdiction only becomes an issue in exceptional and critical situations, where a directive appears to test the limits of that unspecified claim. This, however, does not undermine the sources thesis. The sources thesis still stands as 'a claim about law that reflects the role that law generally has in a community, and the value that it potentially (and perhaps generally) has'.[58]

However, even if it were true that the jurisdictional limits of law's claim to authority are as a matter of course not spelled out, it does not follow that they do not exist. Neither does it follow that those limits only emerge in exceptional circumstances. At the epistemological level, exceptional circumstances merely serve to reveal to us the tacit assumptions of our understandings of law. In addition, as the previous analysis has shown, the jurisdiction of various state institutions is often defined in a more systematic way and standing limits are imposed on their power. In view of that it would be false to relegate the role of jurisdiction to the exception.

Whereas Endicott's strategy is to question the need for recourse to the test of jurisdiction, Gardner denies that the test of jurisdiction poses a threat to legal positivism, even when we have recourse to it to identify valid directives. To do this, he draws a distinction between the content of an authoritative directive and its merit. Gardner rejects the Solution. Validity, he writes,

> *can* depend on [the content of norms] so long as it does not depend on the *merits* of their content. That a certain authority has legal jurisdiction only to change the

---

[57] Endicott, 'Interpretation, Jurisdiction and the Authority of Law' (n 51) 17.

[58] T Endicott, 'Raz on Gaps: The surprising part' in L Meyer, S Paulson and T Pogge (eds), *Rights, Culture and the Law: Themes from the Legal and Political Philosophy of Joseph Raz* (Oxford, Oxford University Press, 2003) 99, 104. In this chapter Endicott considers cases where the validity of contracts is made dependent on moral considerations and argues that such cases do not undermine the sources thesis wholesale.

criminal law means that, by virtue of their content, its measures purporting to create new causes of action in tort do not create valid legal reasons.[59]

So, Gardner accepts that a legal authority may have limited jurisdiction and consequently that its directives are valid provided that they are intra vires. But he does not see this as a problem for legal positivism. According to Gardner, what is distinctive of legal positivism is the thesis that validity is independent of the moral merit of a directive. Jurisdictional considerations, however, pertain solely to its content.

Does Gardner's distinction cut any ice against the argument put forward in this chapter? To begin with, it should be remembered that I have taken as my target a particular theory of legal validity. According to this theory, legally valid directives are identifiable as such without recourse to any of the normative considerations that they are supposed to be based on. For Raz, we might say, legal validity is a completely value-free notion. I have based this interpretation of Raz's theory on two premises: first, the pre-emption thesis, namely the thesis that authorities make a practical difference to their subjects by pre-empting them from acting on the reasons that these authorities are meant to adjudicate on; and, second, the thesis that law does not accept any limits on its authority. The sources thesis, I have claimed, reflects this interpretation: it makes legal validity depend solely on the social fact that the directive has been issued by a de facto authority. Thus, it does not allow for the distinction between content and merit (and the inclusion of considerations pertaining to the former among the conditions of validity), at least insofar as content is taken to encompass issues of jurisdiction. In other words, I have argued that Raz cannot afford to make legal validity depend on jurisdiction.

But maybe Gardner's distinction between merit and content has independent philosophical appeal. We should therefore consider whether it can save legal positivism on its own. In order to do this, though, we must clarify the basis of the distinction. It may be that Gardner disagrees with my reading of Raz's conception of legal validity. Perhaps, he thinks that the pre-emption thesis should be read down to only block recourse to normative considerations other than jurisdictional ones. Or it may be that he has in mind a different theory of legal validity altogether, whereby content and merit should be treated differently. In both cases, it will be the different reading of Raz's conception or the different theory of legal validity that is doing the work and not the distinction of content and merit on its own. It would be premature to dismiss either of these manoeuvres. Still, I want to cast doubt over their availability in principle.

---

[59] J Gardner 'Legal Positivism: 5 1/2 Myths' (2001) 46 *American Journal of Jurisprudence* 199, 209. Gardner makes a claim relative to the validity of legal directives but his point can be applied to authoritative directives in general.

To be sure, I have already conceded that respect for jurisdiction is independent of the merit of the course of action dictated by the directive. I have thus accepted that the distinction can be drawn. But the fact that it is possible to draw it does not entail anything about whether a legal positivist can include jurisdictional considerations among the conditions of legal validity. In fact, the preceding analysis has given us reason to think otherwise, insofar as it has indicated that jurisdiction is relevant to the successful exercise of authority. Respect for jurisdiction, we have seen, is relevant when we come to evaluate a decision by an authority. That is because it seems to us a morally important thing for an authority not to stray beyond its proper sphere. And conversely, we are intuitively inclined to attach some kind of moral reproach to acts of an authority that are ultra vires, other things being equal. If that is the case, a legal positivist has as much reason to keep legal validity untainted by considerations of jurisdiction as by those of merit.

V. JURISDICTION REVISITED

In this chapter I set out to examine whether law's claim to unlimited authority can support a stand-alone sources thesis. I argued that, even if we accept that it is unlimited, law's claim to authority in is in fact inconsistent with the sources thesis: in legal systems with a practice of constitutional review of legislation by the courts this claim depends on respect of jurisdiction in a way that vitiates the sources thesis.

By way of conclusion I wish to locate the argument of this chapter in a broader jurisprudential canvass. One pretty straightforward way of cashing out the point of the exercise I have undertaken would be in the language of the theory of law. It would be to say that the claim I have advanced counts against legal positivism, insofar as the latter is committed to the view that for a standard to count as legal it must be identifiable just by appeal to social facts, without recourse to normative considerations. But the analysis so far has shown that this cannot be the case with jurisdictional considerations, which, as I have argued, are normative considerations, the very considerations that legal authorities such as courts and legislatures are supposed to adjudicate on. However, given that I am not at this point putting forward an anti-positivist account of the role of jurisdiction, I have rested content to point to a challenging case for legal positivism. It remains to be seen what, if any, role jurisdiction can play in an anti-positivist theory of law.

However, this conclusion might sound disappointing to those who find the debate about the truth of the sources thesis rather technical. So, here is a way of cashing out the point of the exercise that has hopefully somewhat wider appeal and furnishes some more tangible philosophical lessons that will be taken up in subsequent chapters. Raz accounts for the normative power involved in authoritative guidance in terms of the pre-emption of dependent reasons; the reasons that authority subjects have independently of their participating in a structure of authoritative guidance. The foregoing analysis suggests that this picture suppresses the importance of a whole host of moral concerns about the proper exercise of authority that have to do with who gets to decide what. Those concerns are not pre-empted even in an authoritative system as comprehensive as law. In fact, they seem to be a pervasive feature of legal practice, at least in legal systems with courts and a legislature. I am not saying that they are necessarily active in the minds of authority subjects, although undoubtedly it would be good if they were. This is not a point about vigilance. It is, ultimately, a point about what makes an exercise of authority successful. The test of jurisdiction points to a distinct aspect of an authority's success. This should come as no surprise. The existence of an authoritative system poses a distinct moral problem, namely to what extent and how an authority's power should be delimited and controlled. Jurisdiction forms part of the answer to this problem.

Philosophers discuss this problem in the context of the state as a whole.[60] They ask whether there are any limits beyond which it is impermissible for the state to encroach upon individuals. From this perspective we do not need to distinguish between state organs. But the problem is present – and very acute – within C-L legal systems as well.[61] Therefore, we should expect the C-L relationship to be structured and the jurisdiction of courts and the legislature to be carved out such that they are responsive to it. Of course, legal and moral philosophers – not to mention public lawyers and constitutional theorists – have for long been developing accounts of the C-L relationship along these lines. But they should do so free from the distorting influence of the sources thesis.

For one thing, they should not be constrained to explicate jurisdiction solely in terms of the range of dependent reasons that an authority adjudicates on. Those reasons, we have already noted, abstract from some of the moral concerns of life under authoritative institutions. C-L legal systems with their plurality of authoritative institutions provide a good illustration. There jurisdiction is not solely determined by the relationship between authority and legal subject but also partly by the relationship between the courts and the legislature. To perform well as authorities, courts and the legislature cannot single-mindedly look at the reasons that legal subjects have independently of their participation in the legal system. Rather, they must also properly interact with one another. Practices of constitutional review bring this observation into sharp relief. We do not want courts to review legislation for its compatibility with fundamental

---

[60] See eg Green, *The Authority of the State* (n 27) 78–83.

[61] As applied to C-L legal systems the moral problem of jurisdiction raises perennial themes of constitutionalism. See generally G Sartori, 'Constitutionalism: A Preliminary Discussion' (1962) 56 *American Political Science Review* 853.

rights just because they are better than legal subjects at deciding how to protect these rights, but also in order to check the legislature. The preceding analysis suggested that it is futile – and at any rate counter-productive – to connect this concern indirectly to the dependent reasons.

Secondly, since jurisdiction pertains to the solution of a moral problem, it makes sense to explicate it in value-laden terms. This seems to give anti-positivism an edge. Now, legal positivists have an interest in political morality as well. Nevertheless, they insist that political morality is not a condition of legal validity. The membership of a standard in law, they say, can be determined in a value-free manner. But by connecting legal validity and authority as Raz does, they run into the problems that this chapter has identified. It is here that the anti-positivist advantage is at its clearest. In principle, an anti-positivist should be happy to bring considerations of political morality relating to jurisdiction into the determination of the content of the law. It should be remembered, however, that an anti-positivist need not frame the role of such considerations in terms of conditions of legal validity. Nor need he accept the connection the sources thesis draws between membership of a standard in the law and the mode of its identification. Though it is entirely plausible to link legal epistemology and legal metaphysics in this way, the two can be kept separate.

Being immanent, the preceding critique of Raz's theory heeded neither suggestion. This will change in the ensuing chapters. Drawing on Ronald Dworkin's theory of law I shall articulate an anti-positivist account of the C-L relationship, which sees jurisdiction in the light of the more general moral problem that it is partly a response to. As it develops, this account will encounter the same phenomena and concerns that put Raz's theory to the test.

3

Dimensions of Interpretation

I. INTRODUCTION

COURTS, WE SAY, ought to decide cases according to the law. Even if it is true, as some philosophers claim, that this is not the whole of judicial duty, it is at least a very important part of it. A judge violates this aspect of his duty if his decision is not consistent with the law, even if it is superior along some other dimension.

It is widely accepted that deciding according to the law means enforcing the rights and duties (either genuine or putative) that we have by virtue of social facts about the institutional history of legal systems such as facts about the acts and sayings of the officials of those systems.[1] Let's call this widely accepted view the social-facts thesis. The social-facts thesis is most commonly associated with legal positivism.[2] But Ronald Dworkin, one of the main opponents of legal positivism in recent years, is no less concerned to accommodate the importance of institutional history in his theory. In *Law's Empire*, which contains the most sustained and comprehensive exposition of his theory of law, he offers the following description of the point of law:

> Law insists that force not be used or withheld, no matter how useful that would be to ends in view, no matter how beneficial or noble these ends, except as licensed or required by individual rights and responsibilities flowing from past political decisions about when collective force is justified.[3]

According to Dworkin, different jurisprudential theories flesh out this very general idea by specifying ways in which past political decisions characteristically give rise to rights and responsibilities. Famously, his preferred theory of law, interpretivism, also contends that past political decisions make a difference

---

[1] See eg M Greenberg, 'How Facts Make Law' (2004) 10 *Legal Theory* 157; N Stavropoulos 'Interpretive Theories of Law' in E Zalta (ed), *Stanford Encyclopedia of Philosophy (Winter 2003)* available at http://plato.stanford.edu/archives/win2003/entries/law-interpretivist.

[2] See eg J Raz, *The Authority of Law* (Oxford, Oxford University Press, 1979).

[3] R Dworkin, *Law's Empire* (Oxford, Hart Publishing, 1998) 93. Dworkin updated his theory in subsequent work, esp R Dworkin, *Justice in Robes* (Cambridge MA, Harvard University Press, 2006). He further developed his general account of interpretation in R Dworkin, *Justice for Hedgehogs* (Cambridge MA, Harvard University Press, 2011).

to our legal rights and duties. They do so because the distinctive virtue of law, namely integrity, commands that state coercion be used in accordance with the principles of political morality that – in Dworkin's terminology – best fit and justify the way the state has used its coercive force in the past. The account arguably respects the social-facts thesis, insofar as it makes the principles that determine the correct legal outcome in a specific case sensitive to facts of institutional history. Judges cannot enforce just any moral principle, because only some principles can plausibly be said to fit and justify this history. Thus, institutional history makes a difference to our legal rights and duties by constraining our interpretations of the law.

In this and the following chapters I shall employ the interpretivist framework to explicate the relationship between courts and the legislature. For this purpose, it is crucial to spell out how institutional history is meant to constrain legal interpretation. Clearly, legislative decisions form a large part of the institutional history that constitutes the database for the legal interpreter's task. In fact, they are likely to be the main determinant of legal duty in modern legal systems. Thus, an answer to the general question about the bearing of institutional history on legal interpretation may pave the way for the more particular theoretical inquiry that is the concern of this book.

There is a further reason for our interest in the dependence of legal interpretation on institutional history: it provides the focal point of one of the most persistent criticisms against Dworkin's account of law. According to this criticism, Dworkin is offering at best a theory of adjudication, which, however, presupposes a legal positivist theory of law. The chapter seeks to defend interpretivism from this criticism and thus prepares the ground for the positive proposal of the following chapter. To this effect, it reconstructs Dworkin's conception of legal interpretation, tracing its incremental development (partly in response to the aforementioned criticism) and thus integrating Dworkin's earlier view as expressed in *Law's Empire*, and his later one, most fully explored in *Justice in Robes*.

The crux of the proposed reconstruction is the idea that the content of legal duty must be sensitive to two distinct and independent dimensions of value that check one another. Thus understood, I shall argue, interpretivism can adequately explain the gravitational force of past political decisions and thus effectively respond to its critics. Given the overarching aim of this book, however, the analysis will focus on one specific facet of interpretation in the law, namely the bearing of legislative decisions on judicial interpretation.

II. THE TWO DIMENSIONS OF INTERPRETATION

Dworkin argues that law is an interpretive practice. By this he means that claims about the content of our legal rights and duties must be grounded on accounts that take the form of *constructive interpretations* of legal practice. In this respect, he claims, law resembles artistic genres, certain social rules and even justice.[4] In those other domains as well, claims and disputes are interpretive in nature: participants ascribe a point (or purpose or function) to the practice they are interpreting and assign a meaning to objects and concepts within the practice in the light of the appropriate point, such that those objects and concepts are shown to realise that point as best as possible.

Assuming that such things as interpretive practices exist, it is a further question to what extent and in what respects they differ from one another. Indeed, in the last book he published before his death, *Justice for Hedgehogs*, Dworkin claims that, unlike other interpretive practices such as historiography or morality, interpretation in law has a collaborative character. (In Dworkin's scheme, histories offer *explanatory* interpretations and moral theories *conceptual* interpretations.) 'Collaborative interpretation', he writes, 'assumes that the object of interpretation has an author or creator and that the author has begun a project that the interpreter tries to advance'.[5] In the case of law,

> a judge takes himself to aim at the same goal – justice – as the statesmen who made the law he interprets. Even when he sees his role as entirely subordinate to theirs, the subordination is, in his view, itself justified by the overall goal of justice he shares with them.[6]

In this sense, Dworkin suggests, legal interpretation is similar to most types of artistic interpretation. There, too, participants work together towards realising the same goal but they do so from different positions, the artist by contributing a work of art that seeks to advance the aesthetic and other purposes that are specific to an artistic genre and the art critic or art lover by interpreting the work as an example of its genre, that is, against those purposes.

The idea of a collaborative interpretive effort is key to the account of the relationship between courts and the legislature that I defend in this book. For this reason, in what follows, I will restrict my attention to law *and other practices like law* that manifest a strong element of interpretive collaboration. Accordingly, I will focus on interpretations of individual contributions within such practices, where the collaboration is clearest, rather than on interpretations of those practices as a whole.

What makes an interpretive claim about the meaning of, say, a statute or a poem true, if it is true? We must be able to offer a genuine criterion, one which interpretive claims may fail to satisfy. Take law for example. We firmly believe that law is not just what one thinks it is. We believe that there is a distance between our beliefs about our legal rights and duties and what legal rights and

---

[4] Dworkin, *Law's Empire* (n 3) 73–76.
[5] Dworkin, *Justice for Hedgehogs* (n 3) 135.
[6] ibid 136.

duties we *really* have. This distance is eliminated if there is no genuine standard that our beliefs must strive to track.

Dworkin juxtaposes his answer to this question to three alternatives. To begin with, since *Law's Empire* his main opponents have been the theories he calls semantic.[7] Semantic theories hold that the ground for the truth or falsity of a legal claim is the fact that it satisfies the criteria that practitioners explicitly or implicitly agree in treating as determining membership in law. The content of the law for semantic theorists, says Dworkin, is exhaustively determined by this area of communal agreement. That is not to say that on the semantic view the mere fact of disagreement precludes the existence of a right legal answer. For instance, practitioners may disagree about whether a specific fact has obtained, on which the correct legal resolution of the case hangs. But in cases of *theoretical disagreement*, where competent practitioners are inclined to apply different criteria in determining whether a standard governs the legal resolution of the case, there is no fact of the matter as to what the law requires. Hence, the judge who decides the case is free to develop the law in any way that he thinks fit. Apart from semantic theories, Dworkin also contrasts his approach to two further alternatives. The first says that jurisprudence generalises from certain recurring social patterns, and the second that law possesses a deep structure which determines its necessary features, just as animals have a DNA that is distinctive of each species.

Dworkin faults all these alternatives for supposing that the philosophical study of law can be *Archimedean*, in the sense that it can answer questions about the nature of law such as whether moral considerations necessarily figure among the truth conditions of propositions of law by merely describing legal practice. On these views, the theory of law is a second-order inquiry that is discontinuous with the discourse of legal practitioners and merely reports the salient features of that discourse. Contrary to such descriptive approaches, Dworkin's interpretive theory portrays philosophical claims about law as normative, operating at the same level as first-order claims made by practitioners. In cases of theoretical disagreement, the philosophers' claims side with one or the other view. They do not just report legal practice. Rather, they may on occasion discipline it.

Both practitioners' claims and philosophical claims about law are subject to the same interpretive standard: their correctness turns on the theory that *best fits and*

---

[7] Dworkin, *Law's Empire* (n 3) 1–44; Dworkin, *Justice in Robes* (n 3) 145–54. Although Dworkin counts John Austin and HLA Hart, two major figures of legal positivism, among semantic theorists, I shall as a matter of policy refrain from associating the 'semantic view' with the two aforementioned legal philosophers, let alone with legal positivism as a whole. There is an extensive literature on whether this attribution is fair, which I am not going to engage. Nicos Stavropoulos has sought to vindicate the attribution of the semantic view to Hart in N Stavropoulos, 'Hart's Semantics' in J Coleman (ed), *Hart's Postscript: Essays on the Postscript to the* Concept of Law (Oxford, Oxford University Press, 2001) 59.

justifies the relevant practice or a feature or aspect thereof, call it the 'object of interpretation'.[8] Correspondingly, fit and justification are the two dimensions along which constructive interpretations are appraised. What do these two dimensions stand for and how are they supposed to be combined in interpretation?

Consider, first, the dimension of justification. According to interpretivism, an interpretation justifies its object, in the sense that it shows that the object serves a value or, more generally, has a point.[9] Not just any justification will do, however. In Dworkin's words, it must be such that it fits the object of interpretation. Otherwise, it cannot be regarded as an interpretation of that object. For instance, it must respect the language of the statute or the choice of words of the poem. In this regard, the dimension of fit checks the assignment of a point to the object. Yet, fit is not so strict as to demand that the interpretation respect every aspect of the object. As Dworkin writes '[c]onvictions about fit will provide a *rough* threshold requirement that an interpretation must meet if it is to be eligible at all'[10] (emphasis added). As a general matter, constructive interpretations may disregard parts of their objects as non-essential or discount them as mistakes without failing the requirement of fit. Consider the following example. Imagine a community that practices a certain religion, which, let's assume, is interpretive in character. Imagine further that members of the community always have their coats on in church, because they happen to live in Greenland and their church is very badly heated. We tend to think that our interpretations of their religious duties need not be constrained by the fact that they wear their coats in church, on the ground that this fact does not reveal anything essential about their religious practice.

At once flexible and constraining, the requirement of fit poses a bit of a mystery. In what follows, I shall examine two attempts to further specify it, which I will call the threshold and the holistic conceptions. In the rest of this section, I shall argue that the former, though superficially attractive, renders the requirement of fit idle and thus virtually eliminates the element of interaction that is supposed to check the interpretive ascription of point. By contrast, the latter, properly understood, provides a superior articulation of the requirement of fit. Importantly, it is immune to a serious objection against interpretivism, which I will outline in the following section.

---

[8] There is very little one can say in the abstract to denote the content of the term 'object of interpretation', first, because what it comprises varies from one interpretive practice to the other, and, second, because, as we shall see below, even within a single interpretive practice different interpretations may define it differently. Suffice it for my present purposes that we have an intuitive, albeit vague, grasp of its meaning.

[9] Justification is used here in a broad sense. The point we ascribe to the object of interpretation need not be moral. This is true of many artistic practices. To say of them that they strive to achieve aesthetic purposes – whatever these are supposed to involve – will then be all the justification they need. See Stavropoulos, 'Interpretive Theories' (n 1) section 7.

[10] Dworkin, *Law's Empire* (n 3) 255.

On the threshold conception, the requirement of fit must be taken in purely quantitative terms. Whether the threshold has been met is a matter of how many features of the object of interpretation each interpretation was forced to discount as mistaken or unimportant. In cases where two or more interpretations pass the threshold, thus defined, justification takes over, and the competing interpretations are judged solely according to their attractiveness on that dimension. Presumably, then, the purpose of the requirement of fit is the gate-keeping one of eliminating the candidate interpretations that are too far removed from their object. Beyond that, fit has nothing to say in favour or against any of the remaining interpretations.

An apparent advantage of the threshold conception is that it offers a notion of fit that, being merely quantitative, is neutral between different sides in interpretive disputes and applies equally to all. But in fact the threshold conception reduces the requirement of fit to triviality because any conceivable interpretation can meet it. Imagine a situation where up until point t legal officials typically cited statutes in their decisions. Quantitatively speaking, their behaviour has optimal fit with an interpretation that maintains that what they have always been doing is following a rule that requires 'Cite statutes up to point t and then cite passages from your favourite book'.[11] If on the threshold conception the constraint of fit cannot even disqualify the deviant interpretation of our example, it surely cannot disqualify any interpretation at all. Therefore, it is not a genuine constraint. What's left to call the shots in interpretation is the dimension of justification. If a practice of citing statutes is more valuable as a matter of political morality than a practice of citing one's favourite book, then this is the meaning that the interpretation will ascribe to the judges' past behaviour. In other words, the element of interaction between purpose and object with its potential to check interpretations is lost. Interpreters are completely free to assign the object of interpretation any point they like. But the interaction is lost in another sense as well. The threshold conception fails to explain why it is important to show fidelity to the object of interpretation in the first place. It will not do to say that without fidelity we would not be interpreting that object. Why interpret at all?

The threshold conception is highly problematic. In fact, Dworkin dissociates himself from it, and unless we cannot find any more plausible reading of the dimension of fit, it would be uncharitable to saddle him with it. He warns that 'it is important not to misunderstand the distinction by supposing, as some commentators have, that the test of fit is only a mechanical test of consistency'.[12] I believe that such an alternative is available in the *holistic* conception of fit. To

---

[11] This type of example, originally formulated by Wittgenstein in L Wittgenstein, *Philosophical Investigations* (Oxford, Blackwell Publishers, 2000) eg §185ff, has famously been elaborated by Saul Kripke in S Kripke, *Wittgenstein on Rules and Private Language* (Oxford, Basil Blackwell, 1982).

[12] Dworkin, *Justice in Robes* (n 3) 15.

spell it out, I will take a lead from a point Dworkin makes in the context of literary interpretation, which we can apply to interpretation more generally. He argues that the contrast between justification and fit 'is *not* a contrast between those aspects of interpretation that are dependent on and those that are independent of the interpreter's aesthetic convictions'.[13] And he adds:

> Both major types of convictions any interpreter has – about which readings fit the text better or worse and about which of two readings makes the novel substantively better- are internal to his overall scheme of beliefs and attitudes; neither type is independent of that scheme in some way that the other is not.[14]

Applying this lesson to law, he writes that 'the two dimensions of fit and value represent different aspects of a single overall judgement of political morality'.[15] We can infer from the two quotations that for Dworkin the application of the requirement of fit is not merely a quantitative matter that is neutral towards competing interpretations; rather, that what it means more precisely and in what way the ascription of the point should be related to it are themselves questions to be settled by appeal to convictions that form part of and depend on the interpreter's overall account of the best justification of the practice.[16] The relationship between fit and justification is one of dependence in the sense that the interpreter's convictions about the level and shape of fit must cohere with his more general convictions about the proper point to be assigned to the practice. According to the holistic conception then, fit can be said to constrain justification in the sense that *an interpretation must fit those parts of its object that the point it assigns to it deems relevant and important.*

As a result of this sort of dependence, fit will vary from one practice to the other. For a story we tell our friends to be the same joke as the one we heard being told by someone else, it needn't be the case that we use the exact same words or even describe the same events and people. Suffice it that our rendition catches the drift or the spirit of the original joke.[17] Conversely, a rendition of a joke that pays too much attention to the words being used rather than the pun or the story is also a failure, even though superficially it 'fits' more of the original joke. It is entirely different with poems. For an interpretation of a poem to be successful, for example, it must attend to the words of the original poem. It would be preposterous to suggest that two poems both describing a sunset are to be treated as the same thing for the purpose of aesthetic appraisal. The different

---

[13] Dworkin, *Law's Empire* (n 3) 234.

[14] ibid 235.

[15] Dworkin, *Justice in Robes* (n 3) 15.

[16] Some commentators were careful to note the evaluative character of fit from early on. See J Finnis, 'On Reason and Authority in *Law's Empire*' (1987) 6 *Law and Philosophy* 357, 373 fn 23: 'the other criterion, "fit", is itself inherently evaluative, i.e, justificatory'; G Postema, '"Protestant" Interpretation and Social Practices' (1987) 6 *Law and Philosophy* 283, 293–95.

[17] R Dworkin *A Matter of Principle* (Cambridge MA, Harvard University Press, 1985) 150.

stringency of fit in the two cases depends on what we take the point of each practice to be.

To sum up, I have claimed that the interpretive test, the test that determines the truth or falsity of interpretive claims, takes the following form. Constructive interpretations must both fit and justify the object they are interpretations of. They must articulate a purpose the object of interpretation can be said to strive for or serve or exemplify, without discarding as mistaken or of little importance too much of that object.[18] In this sense, the dimension of fit is supposed to check the ascription of point. Only the point that best fits in the relevant sense the object of interpretation can be said to be its point. The interpretation that best fits and justifies its object is the standard that individual interpretations strive to meet.[19] Individual interpretations, of course, may fall short of it. In this sense we can talk of superior and inferior interpretations. They are superior or inferior vis-à-vis the best interpretation.[20] I have also claimed that, unlike the threshold conception of fit, the holistic conception makes the requirement of fit internal to each interpretation rather than neutral vis-à-vis competing interpretations.

III. PROBLEMS FOR INTERPRETIVISM

On the holistic conception, as we have seen, interpretive claims are 'interpretive all the way down'. In other words, they are not grounded in anything external to the interpretation. But this seems to many to render interpretivism vulnerable to a formidable challenge. In an early article critiquing Dworkin's account of interpretation before the publication of *Law's Empire*, Joseph Raz put this challenge in a particularly forceful way. He wrote:

> But what is this legal material? It is not a set of meaningless inscriptions on paper, etc. It is a body of interpreted history, of meaningful documents. Otherwise why fix on this legal history? If you regard the Constitution as an uninterpreted jumble of ink scratchings and regard legal theory as designed to give it meaning in accordance with the best moral theory there is, then there is no gap between ideal law and an interpretation of existing law. Under these conditions one can interpret the Constitution to

---

[18] Dworkin, *Law's Empire* (n 3) 47.

[19] Not the fact that most practitioners converge in accepting some claim as true, as the semantic theorist would have it. Since the best interpretation may correct individual interpretations, there is room in the interpretivist story for most or all of the practitioners to have got it wrong.

[20] This is not to say that people are always so reflective in real life. Of course, the way they argue their claims, try to persuade one another and defend their views from criticism aims – ideally – to track this standard. Yet, someone may have come to hold a certain view about his legal rights and duties, not because he has engaged in constructive interpretation of legal practice but because, say, he trusts his solicitor. Besides, people are all too often attracted to one or the other view for the wrong reasons. And we are well aware of the pervasive role of rhetoric and persuasion in achieving just that. There is no problem with these cases. For even then, people's views are true, if they are, because they are in line with the best interpretation of law.

mean anything at all. It can be read to mean the same as Shakespeare's Hamlet. (If, for example, it has double the number of words as the number of sentences in Hamlet, all you have to do is to read every two words as if they meant one sentence in Hamlet). Dworkin is of course aware of this. His method of coherence can only apply to the legal documents which are given their plain meaning.[21]

Here, Raz focuses on the criterion for identifying the materials towards which the requirement of fit is directed. He presents Dworkin with a dilemma, both horns of which undermine the philosophical appeal of the interpretive methodology: either the interpretive test does not impose a genuine constraint or law is not 'interpretive all the way down'. The interpretive test does not impose a genuine constraint if an interpreter can manipulate the object of interpretation to mean anything she wants. Were an interpretation only to fit the features of the poem or the statute that *it* designates as the relevant or important ones, it would seem that it cannot but be self-congratulatory. It allows interpreters free rein to gerrymander the object of interpretation so as to ascribe to it just any point or purpose, however eccentric or absurd. For instance, if they think that art is the supreme value, they can interpret the constitution 'to mean the same as Shakespeare's Hamlet'. Hence, so the suggestion goes, the poem or statute may just as well be 'meaningless inscriptions on paper'. Let's call this the no-constraint objection.

The no-constraint objection is not saying that interpretivism does not supply any standard by which to judge legal claims. Insofar as interpretations also seek to *justify* their object, they can be ranked according to which invokes the higher value. For instance, it may be that *Hamlet* is aesthetically superior to *The Tempest*. Perhaps, then, we have an aesthetic reason to prefer an interpretation that reads *Hamlet* into the constitution rather than *The Tempest*. But our reason will have nothing to do with the fit of the two interpretations. It is the latter kind of constraint that interpretivism fails to supply if it is vulnerable to Raz's objection. The passage quoted above alludes to a specific form of this failure that is of particular relevance to the theory of law. One of the fixed points in our understanding of law is the distinction between law and morality. Legal duty, we tend to think, is sensitive to facts of institutional history (such as the fact that a certain constitutional text has been enacted) and may therefore diverge from utopian morality, that is, from what we would be morally required to do absent those facts. But if institutional history does not genuinely constrain legal interpretation, then interpreters are free to read utopian morality into the law. Echoing a rather common sentiment among contemporary legal positivists, Brian Bix writes that the distinction between law and morality is 'a distinction Dworkin's theory fogs, when it does not erase it entirely'.[22]

---

[21] J Raz, 'Dworkin: A New Link in the Chain' (1986) 74 *California Law Review* 1103, 1119.

[22] B Bix, 'Legal Positivism' in MP Golding and WA Edmundson (eds), *The Blackwell Guide to the Philosophy of Law and Legal Theory* (Oxford, Blackwell Publishing, 2005) 29, 44.

The other horn of the dilemma questions the extent to which interpretivism is really an alternative to its rival, legal positivism. If it is true that by making the requirement of fit internal to interpretation interpretivism falls prey to the no-constraint objection, then arguably the only remaining option is to accept that the interpretive process must be directed at materials whose meaning and significance are already given and can thus act as an external constraint on candidate interpretations. But that would be to give the game away. It would mean that the status of something as law is settled prior to interpretation. Accordingly, many legal philosophers reinterpret Dworkin's theory as a theory of adjudication that seeks to determine how judges should decide cases. These philosophers have no problem accepting that, although the fact that a valid law governs the case before the court will very often be determinative, this will not necessarily be the case. They readily concede that a host of additional considerations bear on the question facing the judge, including considerations of political morality. It may even be that by virtue of those further considerations the judge must decide contrary to pre-existing law. However, according to this view, the task of a theory of law is different and more modest: it is solely to identify the criteria that determine a standard's membership in law rather than its impact on adjudication.[23]

IV. FIT AND THEORY

Does the interplay between the two dimensions of interpretation involve a sufficiently robust 'interaction between purpose and object'?[24] Or does interpretivism fall prey to Raz's challenge? In this section I shall elaborate an understanding of interpretivism that can resist the challenge. To do this, we need to delve deeper into the way the requirement of fit is meant to check interpretations and explain why the constraint of fit cannot be gerrymandered. As I shall I argue, this is because fit corresponds to a distinct evaluative component of the point we ascribe to collaborative interpretive practices like law and artistic genres.

Recall some of the examples mentioned above where the requirement of fit has obvious force. Why do we think it is inappropriate for an art critic to change the words of a poem, although she thinks the change will maximise its aesthetic impact? Why do judges generally give so much weight to the language of a statute, even in cases where they are convinced that doing so will produce a sub-optimal decision from the point of view of justice?

---

[23] J Gardner, 'Legal Positivism: 5 1/2 Myths' (2001) 46 *American Journal of Jurisprudence* 199.
[24] Dworkin, *Law's Empire* (n 3) 52.

The answer in both cases has to do with the value instantiated in the contribution of the poet or the legislator to the joint effort. Start with poetry. Whatever else it may be about, poetic experience is centred round the poem, which is a string of words *that have been chosen and combined by an author*. Of course we sometimes say of phrases uttered without any artistic intention that they are or – very instructively – sound poetic. But such cases seem to be parasitic upon the focal meaning of 'poetry' and 'poetic'. Poetic interpretation tracks this aspect of the poetic experience by showing fidelity to the words chosen by the poet. Let's call this dimension of poetic interpretation *authorship*. Authorship enters poetic interpretation as a value that good poems must instantiate.[25] Poetic interpretation must respect authorship because, insofar as a poem is shown to instantiate that value, it is a *pro tanto* good poem. Of course, it is not only authorship that makes a good poem. Good poems also affect and engage the artistic sensibilities of the reader. We might say that they then instantiate the value of aesthetic impact. But the two values are independent. Though, clearly, authorship is guided by the goal of creating something that has aesthetic impact (and is thus shaped to a greater or lesser extent by extant artistic understandings and expectations in the author's intellectual environment), it does not collapse into it. As we noted above, there is beauty in phrases uttered without a poetic intention, and, conversely, authorship does not necessarily make any claim to aesthetic excellence, and does not necessarily attain it, even when it does make such a claim.

I said above that authorship denotes a value that good poems instantiate. It may be objected to this that authorship merely refers to the contingent fact that the poet chose certain words and not others. Although it is true that poetic interpretation is successful when it is faithful to those words, that's because the choice of words has fixed the poem as the object of interpretation, not because the interpretation thereby respects any value. There is an obvious relationship between this objection and the Razian criticism rehearsed in the previous section which insists that laws are fixed by an act of communication independently of any evaluative judgements, interpretive or otherwise.

Appealing as it may seem, this suggestion should be resisted. The practice of writing and reading poems is more than just about communicating a message that the author intended to convey. Consider again the practice of telling jokes. When someone recites funny stories to a group of people, they do so in order to achieve a specific aim, make them laugh. This aim will typically require fine-tuning the recital to the circumstances of the audience and the time of the recital. This means that different recitals of the same joke may on occasion vary in the choice of words or the description of people, settings and strings of events.

---

[25] On the importance of this value, though with important qualifications, see TS Eliot, 'Tradition and Individual Talent' in TS Eliot, *Selected Essays* (New York, Harcourt, 1950) 4.

It follows then that, contrary to poetry, authorship does not impose as rigid a constraint in the practice of telling jokes. The difference cannot be explained if we focus solely on the two types of utterance – there are written jokes as there are oral poems. Additionally, we must invoke practice-specific evaluative considerations. For instance, we can appeal to the fact that the practice of poetry praises the values of originality and individual genius, whereas these values do not hold as much sway in the practice of telling jokes. If that's true, it is no surprise that poetic interpretations must be respectful of the exact wording of the poem as far as possible. Because of the value we ascribe to authorship in poetry, we cannot replace at will or disregard any words of the poem we are interpreting, in order to maximise its aesthetic impact on a certain audience.[26]

How does this account of authorship in the practice of poetry help vindicate the holistic conception of fit? If the success or failure of interpretation were judged along only one evaluative dimension, then perhaps it would make sense to argue that the holistic conception of fit is vulnerable to the no-constraint objection; it would do nothing to dismiss interpretations that make the constitution 'mean the same as Shakespeare's Hamlet'. But if we take, as I have urged in the case of poetry, the point of the interpretive practice to be sensitive to two distinct, though interrelated, values, we have reason to resist this claim. In this picture, the dimension of fit reflects a value commitment to originality as distinct from aesthetic impact. In fact, originality seems very well-suited to account for fit, as it provides interpreters with a reason to heed the contribution of a fellow-participant in the practice of poetry. Critics care for the exact words of the poem because an interpretation that brings out the aesthetic impact that they make vindicates the genius of the poet.

This reading of fit undercuts the no-constraint objection because it builds an effective internal check into the interpretive process. Good interpretations must be responsive to both originality and aesthetic impact. They must determine the precise import of each through judgements of the sort: Which reading of a given poem vindicates the individual genius of its creator? Which enhances its aesthetic impact? To repeat, these are not quantitative questions. Insofar as originality and aesthetic impact stand for values, these are evaluative questions, and unless one endorses a thorough-going scepticism about value judgements (and Dworkin's critics typically do not), one can reasonably expect that they will

---

[26] A rejoinder to this line of argument may draw on a distinction between the object of interpretation and its meaning. As Raz puts it '[i]nterpretations explain and do not change their objects. They explain their objects by making plain their meanings... What they affect is the meaning, not the object which has it' (J Raz, *Between Authority and Interpretation* (Oxford, Oxford University Press, 2009) 303). It is not necessary for present purposes to question whether there is a sense of the 'object of poetic interpretation' that is exclusively determined by the poet's utterance. What is more pertinent is to establish that interpretive ascriptions of meaning to a poem are not checked by the object, thus understood, but by aspects of it picked out as relevant by values of poetic excellence such as authorship.

for the most part admit of determinate answers.[27] Furthermore, insofar as the two values are independent of each other, an interpretation cannot trade originality for aesthetic impact without cost. By exerting its own evaluative pull towards fidelity for the poem, originality checks the pursuit of aesthetic impact. As a result, competing interpretations will be poor unless they accommodate both values to some degree. Their competition is what gives edge to the interpretive methodology. It detracts from interpretations that ignore one dimension in favour of the other and accordingly gives persuasive force to more balanced accounts.

That is not to say that it will be easy to figure out the correct answers to interpretive questions. One's convictions about, say, the weight of authorship in poetry inescapably draw on a whole set of further beliefs about communication, the importance of individual talent, facts about individual and collective psychology, the place of poetry in the larger culture and so on that must hang together in a successful interpretation. Different people are bound to hold widely divergent views on these issues. As a result of varying higher-order convictions, for instance, one interpreter will consider it appropriate to have reference to biographical details about the poet and will think that an interpretation that does not fit those details is *pro tanto* poorer. Another, more sympathetic to the view that poems have a life of their own, will object that the life of the author and indeed her artistic intentions are irrelevant for the purpose of poetic interpretation; what is more important is that the poem becomes a site for the engagement of the artistic sensibilities of successive generations. Accordingly, our assessment of the relative merits of conflicting interpretations will at times be extremely complex and open to controversy. But this does not necessarily make it any less determinate.

In the previous paragraphs I argued that the holistic conception of fit fends off the no-constraint objection. But it also does a better job than the threshold conception at motivating the interpretive process as a whole. If it is a value that orients interpretations towards their object, then interpreters have a genuine reason to engage with the original poems; values are the sort of thing that can do that. Following up from this, the holistic conception vindicates the collaborative nature of the practice of poetry. It does not just so happen that poetic interpretation focuses on the original poem. Interpreters must 'collaborate' with poets, in the sense that they heed their contribution, insofar as this contribution embodies a value that their practice is meant to promote. We might go as far as to say that both the poet and the interpreter collaborate in a joint project – a project of attaining a specific kind of aesthetic excellence. This project is bound together and structured by values which make the contributions of each participant worth engaging with.

---

[27] I discuss the determinacy of interpretive judgements in more detail below.

V. INTERPRETATION AND THE PROJECT OF GOVERNING

I shall now elaborate the connection between the more general discussion of interpretivism of the previous section and the specific jurisprudential concerns that discussion was meant to help us address. Interpretivism in law invites the same challenge that confronted interpretivism in general: namely that it falls prey to radical indeterminacy. If interpretation determines both the way past political decisions matter to and constrain the ascription of meaning to them as well as which parts thereof should be discarded as mistakes, the following question arises: How can our interpretations not be self-congratulatory? Can past political decisions really check legal interpretation? On the interpretivist story, it seems, the test that legal claims have to pass is such that they will always come out true; it is not a genuine constraint.

Recall how the no-constraint objection directed against interpretivism in law is related to the topic of this book. Consider again the relationship between courts and the legislature. Judges, we tend to think, have an institutional responsibility to decide in accordance with past political decisions. In particular, we think they have a special duty to defer to the decisions of the legislature. But the idea of deference would be no more than illusion if interpretivism in law were vulnerable to the no-constraint objection. If the interpretive test that judicial decisions must meet were not genuine, judges would be left free to twist and turn past political decisions to make them fit their personal political and moral convictions. In essence, past political decisions would make no difference to the way judges decide cases. Hence, figuring out in what way past political decisions are meant by Dworkin to constrain legal interpretation becomes a cardinal task. On the one hand it helps us rebut the no-constraint objection and on the other it may, as I believe it will, cast light on how interpretivists can conceive of the relationship between courts and the legislature.

The argument of the previous section offered a response to the no-constraint objection in literary interpretation. According to this response, the point of literary interpretation involves two distinct evaluative dimensions. Their contest, it was suggested, provides a genuine standard by reference to which we can judge interpretive success and failure. Can we say something similar about law? Does legal interpretation exhibit an analogous interplay of two distinct values? Dworkin offers an answer. For him, 'procedural fairness . . . is the nerve of the dimension of fit',[28] while, conversely, 'substantive justice . . . is the nerve of political justification'.[29] Accordingly, he thinks that legal interpretation is 'sounder on the whole' when it is 'fairer and more just in the right relation', that

---

[28] Dworkin, *Justice in Robes* (n 3) 171.
[29] ibid.

70   *Dimensions of Interpretation*

is, when it combines procedural fairness and substantive justice in the right proportion.[30]

We need to spell out these claims. To simplify things, I shall focus on the case of a judge interpreting a statute. In due course, we will introduce some complications to this simple picture, but for the moment the simple picture will do because it clearly brings out what law and artistic genres share, namely that they are both types of collaborative interpretation. What difference does it make to interpretation that the judge is participating in a joint institutional project, the project of governing? In this project, other bodies, notably the legislature, also have the power to affect through their decisions the content of our legal rights and duties. An important aim of judicial interpretation is determining the bearing of those decisions on the court's duty. Just as in the case of literary interpretation, the answer to that question is a function of two dimensions, which I will refer to as *content* and *institutional design*.[31]

Content will direct the judge's attention to the course of action that the decision dictates. Is it the right or wise or desirable one? If the decision imposes a tax, does it distribute burdens justly? If it restricts the legal subjects' freedom, does it do so justifiably? If it threatens sanctions for some type of behaviour, is the behaviour seriously antisocial? Does it respect our basic rights? Clearly, the proper interpretation of legislative contributions to the project of governing must make reference to such standards; they define the public good that the legislature is there to serve. A successful interpretation of a statute shows it to strive for the promotion of the public good and thus to track those standards. Conversely, a statute is bad *qua* statute if it fares very poorly when judged against them.

The standards or considerations of content are a matter of ideal political theory, in the sense that their specification is independent of any statute they help interpret. However, it is not accurate to say that they are independent of political institutions *tout court*; they do not define the rights and duties that we would have in the absence of any such institutions. There are a variety of legal systems, at national, supranational and perhaps sub-national level, and it is likely that we have special rights and duties as members of a specific legal system eg the national state. It may be, for instance, that we have more demanding duties of egalitarian justice towards our fellow-citizens in a national community than towards fellow-participants in supranational political associations such as the EU.[32] If this is the case, it should come as no surprise that the dimension of content will identify a different set of standards as pertinent, depending on the

---

[30] Dworkin, *Law's Empire* (n 3) 263.

[31] The two concepts are meant to echo a familiar though ambiguous distinction from the law of judicial review of administrative action between substance and jurisdiction.

[32] See T Nagel, 'The Problem of Global Justice' (2005) 33 *Philosophy and Public Affairs* 113.

moral character and purpose of each system. In this sense, the dimension of content obviously tracks different political institutions. However, political institutions like the state are typically also equipped with bodies that make decisions in their name and thereby affect the rights and duties of the members of those institutions. Call these bodies agents of governance. We can then say that content comprises the rights and duties that members of this or that political institution should have as a matter of ideal theory, prior to any intervention by agents that govern in that institution's name.[33]

The legal systems that we are familiar with are not just sets of rules about what legal subjects ought to do. In addition, as already noted, they assign certain bodies the power to make decisions that affect the rights and duties of legal subjects. Earlier we referred to such bodies as agents of governance. The dimension of institutional design refers to the kinds of consideration that justify the assignment of such power and thus supply an answer to the question: Who are you to tell me what to do? Of course, in the case of law these considerations are not furnished by the values of originality and creativity. When we empower a political institution to make a decision about what we ought to do, we do not care whether that institution is going to make a novel and distinctive contribution to the law. But we do care, for instance, that it has the right pedigree and that it has followed the right procedures. If this is the case, then, other things being equal, we have reason to heed it when that institution tells us what to do.

Dworkin uses the term 'structuring principles'[34] to refer to the kinds of consideration that 'justify the settled arrangements of power and authority. . .in the nation'[35] and 'limit those powers in various formal and informal ways'.[36] In *Law's Empire*, he had written that a political society that is governed in accordance with such principles exhibits the virtue of 'procedural fairness', which he had juxtaposed to the virtue of 'justice'.[37] The operation of these principles in a certain political society creates a 'complexity within morality itself'. It gives rise to moral rights and duties that we would not have but for our membership in that political society. This is because the bodies that are bestowed power and authority by the structuring principles can affect the moral rights and duties of members of that political society through their acts and decisions.

---

[33] cp the distinction Dworkin drew in his earlier work between institutional and background rights. Whereas background rights 'provide a justification for political decisions by society in the abstract', institutional rights justify 'a decision by some particular and specified political institution'. See R Dworkin, *Taking Rights Seriously* (London, Duckworth, 1978) 93. Hence, 'no one may claim an institutional right by direct appeal to general morality' (ibid 101).

[34] Dworkin, *Hedgehogs* (n 3) 409.

[35] Dworkin, *Justice in Robes* (n 3) 17.

[36] ibid 16.

[37] Dworkin, *Law's Empire* (n 3) 177–78.

Institutional design also encompasses the notion of jurisdiction that we encountered in chapter two. There, jurisdiction was taken to mean the range of issues that an agent of governance is recognised as having the power to regulate or the kinds of acts that it may dictate in the exercise of its power.[38] Thus understood, jurisdiction may be thought to bear on the content of a decision, rather than the way that decision was produced. This would be a mistake. As we noted in chapter two, jurisdiction reflects a concern that a certain decision is made by the proper agent of governance.[39] Think about the kinds of consideration that respond to this concern, such as expertise or coordination ability. They all make reference to the institutional capacity of that agent reliably to do the right thing rather than what the right thing would be on a specific occasion. This is why it is perfectly conceivable that an ultra vires decision has dictated the right thing and an intra vires decision has committed a blunder. Nonetheless, to fully appreciate the role of jurisdiction in institutional design, we must go beyond the understanding of jurisdiction that the Razian framework allows. Jurisdiction is not judged only on the basis of a comparison between the reason-tracking capacity of an agent of governance and legal subjects. It includes the limits on that agent's authority that stem from its relationship with other agents of governance, with whom it cooperates.

But if what considerations of institutional design do is justify an agent's having the power to affect the rights and duties of legal subjects, the question arises why they should be at all relevant to the duties of other agents of governance such as courts. Surely, if they make any difference, it must be from the perspective of legal subjects who are the addressees of those agents' decisions. The answer is that the same considerations also structure the joint project of governing, in which courts and the legislature are fellow-participants. The court's role in that project is not a given, as many legal positivists seem to think. Rather, it is a function of the reasons of institutional design that make that project worth

---

[38] See ch 2.

[39] We can envisage hard cases. Consider, for example, the norm that the state may not compel individuals to do something that falls within one of their fundamental rights eg read a book. This, we think, is a choice that is properly left to the individual to make. Is such a norm a consideration of content or institutional design? It seems plausible to say that by placing private choices out of bounds for the government, this norm delimits its jurisdiction. Seen in this light, it appears to be a matter of institutional design. If you are a hard-nosed state perfectionist, you may be more drawn to this view. You may think that there is nothing in principle wrong with the state making it its business that people read the right books and that it is a contextual matter whether this or that agent of government can be trusted to make the correct choice. By contrast, proponents of liberal neutrality will perhaps be more inclined to treat this and other similar norms as in principle belonging to the dimension of content. They will argue that, for a political community to be morally in order, it is irrelevant whether people read the right books; rather, the political community goes badly when it coercively interferes with this choice, even if it prescribes good books. In addition, they will point to the fact that such norms typically set limits on all state action rather than on the role of this or that agent of governance. This suggests that they have nothing to do with the institutional structure that decides in the name of the political community, the domain of institutional design.

participating in. Suppose that part of the reason why a legislature has the power to affect the law is its democratic credentials. As a general matter, we do democracy a good service if, among other things, we have our political community effectively governed in accordance with democratic principles. The project of governing is crucially also geared towards the same aim. In fact, given their critical role in the running of a political community, participants in this project like judges are expected to pursue this aim in a special way. They are expected to implement and possibly also further the decisions that have been made by the democratically elected legislature. Their reason will not just be that they happen to take part in a joint project. It is rather the more complex reason that, insofar as the joint project is relevantly governed by the principle of democracy, it is *pro tanto* a morally worthwhile project, to which they have a *moral duty* to contribute.

As a participant in the joint project of governing, we have seen, the judge must bring considerations of institutional design to bear on the interpretation of a legislative decision. These considerations will in large part determine how much weight he ought to assign that decision and what, more precisely, fidelity to it requires. Fundamentally, they will determine whether he should take any interest in that decision at all. Unless the judge finds some good reason for the assignment of a certain power to the legislature – or any other agent of governance for that matter –, he fails no official duty in disregarding the decisions coming from it, just as he would not if he disregarded a decision made by a private citizen dictating what the rest of us ought to do. In short, by virtue of considerations of institutional design the judge is enjoined to make his interpretation 'fit' the relevant political history.

At the same time, though, the judge cannot blindly follow the political decisions that considerations of institutional design designate as pertinent. He must also take into account considerations of content. His convictions about what the legislature ought to be doing must inform his judgement about the extent to which he will give effect to its decisions. That's because a legislative decision is shown in its best light, interpretively speaking, when it fares well along the dimension of content, too. A very unjust decision cannot plausibly be seen as a contribution to the joint project of governing. Considerations of content, then, play the role of justification in an interpretive exercise, and judges must balance them alongside considerations of institutional design. To use a familiar example from many legal systems, the judge will assign a narrow meaning to a statute that imposes criminal liability or a tax burden because the principles of political morality that govern these areas of the law put a high premium on predictability. But he will be less restrained when he is interpreting, say, a piece of commercial law. The requirement of strict construction of tax laws and criminal laws has nothing to do with the credentials of the body that has passed them; it is the same body that passes ordinary commercial laws as well. That requirement is grounded in the variable weight of certain considerations of content across different domains of social life.[40]

Many legal philosophers agree that there is a philosophically interesting connection between legislative decisions and considerations of content. However, they resist the further thought that the decisions' contribution to our legal rights and duties must depend on such considerations. They claim for instance that it may well be a necessary truth about law that legislative decisions claim or aspire or even attempt (the list of possible modalities is endless) to prescribe the right thing as far as content is concerned, but of course it does not follow from this that they always or typically do prescribe it. To urge judges to take into account considerations of content when interpreting the contribution of legislative decisions to our legal rights and duties is to make the very same mistake that interpretivism has been accused of all along, namely that it licenses the manipulation of legal materials to yield whichever result the interpreter prefers. That is not to say that considerations of content will not play a role in determining whether we should obey the law, as this has been shaped by a legislative decision. But this task comes after the identification of some standard as the law.

This objection is misguided, but it is critical for our purposes to explain where it goes wrong. Why is it not enough for a judge interpreting a legislative decision that it *claims* to be a genuine contribution to the joint project of governing? Why must he construe it in the light of the relevant considerations of content and even assess it against them? To answer these questions, we have to appreciate why the judge interprets the legislative decision in the first place. His goal is not the theoretical one of identifying the meaning of this or that decision. Rather, it is the very practical one of determining what he ought to do as part of his official role. This also requires assessing what difference a contribution by one of the judge's fellow-participants has made to his official duty. Unless that contribution is supported by the right reasons, it is not a genuine contribution to the project of governing which the judge has a moral duty to respect and, possibly, help implement and further. The interpretive exercise which combines considerations of content and institutional design will decide just that. From this

---

[40] It could be asked whether the example of strict construction tells against the neat correlation I seek to draw between fit and institutional design and instead suggests that fit is not solely a matter of institutional design. Doesn't the example show that the way interpretations must 'fit' political decisions is also partly determined by considerations of content? In response, it must be noted that there is an understanding of what happens in cases of strict construction that preserves the distance between the two types of consideration. We can say that institutional design makes eligible a certain interpretation, say, that a certain tax rebate be extended to a class of citizens, which can be said to be covered by a word used in the relevant legislative decision, but content disqualifies this interpretation because it runs afoul of the kind of predictability we expect in tax matters. Still, there is an element of truth in this criticism which will be explored further in the following chapter: doctrines of statutory interpretation are best viewed as a compound of considerations of institutional design and content, and it is not always easy to disentangle analytically the effect of either in the mix.

perspective, the thought that judicial duty is sensitive to considerations of content should be as unproblematic as that it is sensitive to considerations of institutional design. Their combination will determine what on any given occasion the judge has to do in order to do his share in the joint project of governing, as this has also partly been shaped by the legislature's contributions. The real question should be what the right mix is.

This marks an important difference between the law and other practices of collaborative interpretation such as literary critique.[41] It is common to treat individual works as the target of literary interpretation. Here the analogy with law breaks. The focal point of the judge's interpretive judgements will not necessarily be 'discrete political decisions',[42] but, rather, their official duty in the joint project. Decisions bear on it, but only when there is good reason for that. Besides, important though they may be, they are not the only factors that bear on official duty. Decisions must typically be combined with other factors, and often the judge will determine what he ought to do in the absence of such decisions. That is because considerations of institutional design and content do not require the existence of such decisions to be operative in judicial reasoning.

In the following chapter, we shall flesh out in more detail how judges ought to combine the two types of consideration, in order to determine their duties in the joint project of governing. Here, I want to make some general observations about the interaction between content and institutional design. To begin with, I want to highlight how this interaction offers a solution to our original problem. I want to claim that, recast in terms of the distinction between content and institutional design, the two dimensions of interpretation are shown to be sufficiently distinct from each other, notwithstanding the fact that they are both components of an overall judgement of political morality. That is because they point to two different things that we demand from government. We want government to make morally sound decisions that affect our interests and the common good. But being governed well also means being governed by the right people and according to the right procedures. Further, these two concerns can genuinely check one another. For one thing, they issue requirements that may sometimes come apart. Considerations of institutional design may direct a judge to give effect to a legislative decision that is morally sub-optimal as far as its content is concerned. By assuming the role of a judge in the legal order he has, to use John Rawls' terminology, 'abdicated his title' freely to act solely on the basis of what by his own lights is just and equitable.[43]

[41] From this perspective the analogy of the chain novel that Dworkin has elsewhere employed seems more apt. Of course, the analogy must be qualified to accommodate the fact that, unlike two chain novelists, the judge does not occupy the same role in the project of governing as the legislature.

[42] Dworkin, *Law's Empire* (n 3) 190.

[43] J Rawls, 'Two Concepts of Rules' in J Rawls, *Collected Papers* (S Freeman ed, Cambridge MA, Harvard University Press, 1999) 20, 31.

Although few would dispute that institutional design and content refer to distinct normative concerns, some may be sceptical about their potential to check one another, on the ground that they are incommensurable.[44] To evaluate the force of the challenge, we need to distinguish between two types of incommensurability, strong and weak. Let's start with strong incommensurability. Two values are strongly incommensurable, when it is never possible to compare a loss in one value with a gain in the other. Should institutional design and content be found to be incommensurable in this sense, the challenge would be devastating for the interpretivist project. However, there is ample reason to suppose that this is not the case. One reason has been put forward by Ruth Chang. Chang has developed a general strategy for dealing with strong incommensurability: she takes two values that we are inclined to regard as strongly incommensurable and she compares a *notable* example of one and a *nominal* example of the other, where a notable example is one that embodies a value to a great degree and a nominal example is one that barely embodies it. In such a comparison we have no hesitation to prefer the notable to the nominal. Thus, there is at least one pair of tokens of the two values with regard to which comparison is possible. Hence, strong incommensurability is false.[45] Take for example artistic excellence. This value can be attained through various combinations of more specific aesthetic virtues. Both Beethoven and Picasso were excellent artists, but in very different ways. It would not surprise us if it turned out that we cannot compare those two individuals along the dimension of artistic excellence. But let's now imagine an artist who combined the virtues that Beethoven exhibited, only to a far lesser degree. This artist provides a nominal token of artistic excellence. About him, we are more confident to say that he was inferior to Picasso.[46] We can say the same thing about the judicial task. Some of the options facing the judge in a specific case may be impossible to compare because they display very diverse institutional and substantive virtues. For example, one option may be doing a very good job at protecting an important right but at the cost of fair notice, whereas another gives effect to a considered democratic judgement in a controversial human rights case in which judges lack expertise. But pointing to such examples does not suffice to establish that all comparisons of institutional design and content will encounter a similar dead-end.

As the preceding discussion suggests, it may be that the interaction between content and institutional design will not always yield one right answer. Perhaps,

---

[44] One such critic is TRS Allan. See TRS Allan, 'Human Rights and Judicial Review: A Critique of "Due Deference"' (2006) 65 *Cambridge Law Journal* 671, 688. I have raised doubts about Allan's criticism in D Kyritsis, 'What is Good about Legal Conventionalism' (2008) 14 *Legal Theory* 135, 163–66. Here I offer a summary of the arguments I advance in that article.

[45] See R Chang, 'Introduction' in R Chang (ed), *Incommensurability, Incomparability and Practical Reason* (Cambridge MA, Harvard University Press, 1997) 1.

[46] R Dworkin, 'Objectivity and Truth: You'd Better Believe it' (1996) 25 *Philosophy and Public Affairs* 87.

with regard to some interpretive questions it will be neither true nor false that one answer is better than another nor that they are equally good. As a result we have no reason to regard any one of them as the *right* legal answer, although we may have other types of reasons to prefer one to the others. (For instance, one interpretation may be more useful to a political struggle that we are mounting.) Many philosophers think that this kind of indeterminacy is endemic. John Finnis has suggested that it is characteristic of hard cases. He writes: 'A hard case is hard (not merely novel) when not only is there more than one answer which violates no applicable rule, but the answers thus available are ranked in different orders along each of the available criteria of evaluation'.[47] Timothy Endicott claims that indeterminacy is caused by the inherent vagueness of evaluative considerations.[48] Joseph Raz adds the complexity of certain values as a source of indeterminacy.[49] Both of these factors afflict legal interpretation as well: on the account offered here, interpretive judgements are complex, involving the assignment of relative weights to evaluative considerations which are distinct and independent of each other. There is a good chance, then, that they will turn out to be indeterminate around the edges. Still, this will be an indeterminacy of the weak sort. As such it does not threaten interpretivism. The interpretive test is still genuine even if it does not yield fully determinate answers to some interpretive questions. For one thing, it is genuine insofar as it dismisses certain options, with regard to which it is determinate that they are sub-optimal.

Thus far, I have assumed that it is appropriate to balance institutional design and content. The argument from incommensurability that we have just examined questions the determinacy of this kind of balancing exercise but not its appropriateness in principle. It is the latter issue that we must now probe. Does it make sense to balance evaluative considerations such as democracy and justice? Jeremy Waldron answers this question with an emphatic no. He argues that to do so would be to commit 'something of a "category mistake"'.[50] Although he agrees that these two considerations are independent of one another, he points out that

> one is functionally related to the other. It is the task of political fairness to address the situation that arises when people in a society disagree about justice, and thus cannot act univocally *as a society* on the basis of an appeal to justice alone.[51]

[47] J Finnis, 'Reason and Authority' (n 17) 372–73.
[48] T Endicott, *Vagueness in Law* (Oxford, Oxford University Press, 2000), and, more recently T Endicott, 'Raz on Gaps: The Surprising Part' in L Meyer, S Paulson and T Pogge (eds), *Rights, Culture and the Law: Themes from the Legal and Political Philosophy of Joseph Raz* (Oxford, Oxford University Press, 2003) 99.
[49] J Raz, *The Morality of Freedom* (Oxford, Clarendon Press, 1986) 332–35.
[50] J Waldron, 'The Circumstances of Integrity' (1997) 3 *Legal Theory* 1, 10.
[51] ibid.

According to Waldron, given the problem of disagreement in politics, what we collectively ought to do cannot turn on the considerations that we disagree about. This is why we have fair political procedures like democratic rule. Adherence to such procedures gives legitimacy to state action in a political community fraught by reasonable and ineradicable disagreement. It goes without saying that our moral objections to a policy are likely to persist despite the fact that it has been decided upon by fair procedures. The fact that the policy has garnered the support of the majority does not change the *ex ante* balance of the policy's pros and cons. As Waldron puts it, it

> offers a different kind of reason, operating on a different level. It is a reason *for society and for those who act in society's name* to settle on [the policy] as a social decision given that a social decision is needed and that people disagree about the first-order reasons in the matter.[52]

Waldron argues that it would be at odds with the functional relation between the second-order reasons regarding fair political procedures and first-order reasons like justice to balance them as if they were on the same level. This would betray a lack of sensitivity to the solution that second-order reasons hold out for political communities fraught by disagreement. In fact, it would betray something even more disturbing, namely disregard for the moral claims of citizens in such communities. We disrespect them, when we impose on them a vision of justice which they do not share, solely on the basis that we think it is correct. We show them the respect they are due, Waldron contends, when fair procedures displace consideration of first-order reasons of justice. In this way, the winning side arguably offers the losing side a justification that is independent of the point of contention, namely that they have lost in a fair political contest.[53]

In this chapter, I have talked about democracy and other considerations of political fairness in the context of the joint project of governing, as considerations that inform institutional design, and more specifically the judicial role vis-à-vis the legislature. Hence, I have framed their function in a slightly different way from Waldron. However, as has already been noted in the first chapter, Waldron is quite explicit that these considerations also govern official duty.[54] In the passage quoted earlier he says that fairness applies to individual citizens as well as 'those who act in society's name'. The latter as much as the former must discharge their responsibilities in full awareness of the existence of ineradicable disagreement over justice within the political community they are charged to

---

[52] ibid 11.

[53] Waldron makes a comprehensive case for this view of political legitimacy in J Waldron, *Law and Disagreement* (Oxford, Oxford University Press, 1999).

[54] See J Waldron, 'Authority for Officials' in L Meyer, S Paulson and T Pogge (eds), *Rights, Culture and the Law: Themes from the Legal and Political Philosophy of Joseph Raz* (Oxford, Oxford University Press, 2003) 45 and ch 1, s IV above.

govern.[55] This means, among other things, that when a political decision has been reached in accordance with the proper procedures an official acquires a duty to respect it, other things being equal. In Waldron's scheme, to do otherwise would be to presume that one's own view about what ought to be done is superior to that of the rest of the political community. This, to return to my previous example, is the case of the judge faced with a decision made by a democratic legislature.

How will fairness and other considerations of institutional design interact with justice in the context of the joint project of governing? Will they altogether displace it from the deliberation of officials? Waldron is certainly right that the problem of what an official ought to do is transformed in a joint project shaped by values such as democracy. The transformation takes various forms. A scheme of government where fairly reached decisions by one institution completely pre-empt the independent judgement about justice of other officials is but one possibility. Alternatively, a scheme of government may allocate to a number of different officials a partial responsibility to act on such a judgement.[56] Many C-L legal systems make this choice, and those that we are familiar with almost invariably do. In them the decisions of one institution put limits on any individual official's power to rely on his independent judgement but do not obliterate it. Rather, the individual official must make judgements about justice that are framed by the efforts of his fellow-participants. To use Waldron's terminology again, he 'approaches issues of justice from an oblique angle'.[57] If he disregards the settlement embodied in these efforts, he elevates himself above his fellow-citizens. If he does not act on his view of justice, he abdicates his official responsibility. Hence the need for trade-offs between justice and fairness, or institutional design more generally. These trade-offs represent the limits on any one official's power posed by the shared character of the project of governing. This is precisely the picture that I have been outlining in this chapter. Far from pre-empting the balancing of considerations of content and institutional design, this picture necessitates it.

In addition, the picture of the joint project of governing that is emerging from the foregoing analysis strongly suggests that institutional settlement in the C-L legal systems that we are familiar with has a distinctly precarious quality. Political settlement is of course transient. It is natural for political communities to revisit their previous decisions. But the joint project of governing introduces a further dynamic element. Since it is possible that a legal system comprises a

---

[55] Waldron, 'Circumstances of Integrity' (n 50) 16–18.

[56] In fact, a political community can entrust this power to just one official. Waldron calls this elective dictatorship. (ibid 17) Importantly, he acknowledges that 'it is not always inappropriate for an official acting in a public capacity to act on the basis of his or her own tendentious views about justice' (ibid).

[57] ibid 12.

variety of institutions making judgements of justice in the name of the community as a whole, the fact that one institution does not re-open a certain issue need not entail that another institution must refrain from doing so. To be sure, this will depend on whether the second institution has the corresponding power. In turn, this is determined by the combination of considerations of institutional design and content. In light of this, it would be misleading to view political settlement as a one-off thing, in the sense that a resolution in one corner of the joint project of governing – even in the corner occupied by the democratic legislature – must settle the matter across the board. No doubt, a system of one-off settlements coming from the democratic legislature has the advantage of simplicity. I do not want to preclude the possibility that in some legal systems or over a certain range of issues the simplicity of such a one-off settlement is desirable. Still, the fact that political communities very often give a measure of discretion to legal officials to act on their views about justice is evidence that we are comfortable with more decentralised arrangements, provided that the project of governing meets certain specifications.[58] We shall return to those specifications in the next chapter.

VI. THE RETURN OF LEGAL POSITIVISM

Having completed the positive case for interpretivism, I turn to a number of positivist comebacks. Their thrust is that, even in its revised form defended here, interpretivism is not really an alternative to legal positivism. In fact, they counter, interpretivism cannot but presuppose legal positivism at some level. They insist that at best it is a theory of adjudication.

A. Jurisdiction and the Project of Governing Over Time

The first comeback to be examined brings back into focus the issue of jurisdiction. In what follows, I shall focus on Andrei Marmor's version of this comeback.[59] Marmor criticises Dworkin's seminal argument against Hart in *Taking Rights Seriously*.[60] His criticism (I claim) could be replicated to apply to the proposal offered here. Showing why it would fail not only strengthens the proposal but also locates the C-L relationship in a broader constitutional landscape.

---

[58] I have drawn out some implications from this feature of our legal practice regarding the legitimacy of constitutional review and Waldron's argument against it in D Kyritsis, 'Representation and Waldron's Objection to Judicial Review' (2006) 26 *Oxford Journal of Legal Studies* 733.

[59] See A Marmor, *Social Conventions: From Language to Law* (Princeton NJ, Princeton University Press, 2009) 155–75.

[60] Dworkin, *Taking Rights Seriously* (n 33) chs 2 and 3.

As is well known, Dworkin argues that Hart's explanation of law as based on a social rule binding on officials made up of a pattern of convergent behaviour and an attitude of acceptance cannot account for the existence of widespread and reasonable disagreement in law. Disagreement negates the existence of a social rule. And yet, when judges disagree in hard cases, they argue for their own view irrespective of the fact that it is not shared. In addition, they claim that their view better captures the law on this issue. They do not make a proposal about how the law should be developed.

In countering Dworkin's challenge, Andrei Marmor suggests that, whatever may be said about the standards that judges apply, Dworkin's challenge does not reach far enough, in that it leaves untouched the rules defining judicial role. Surely (the argument goes) we cannot run the challenge, unless we assume the existence of such rules, which determine what makes someone a judge and what is in general terms his or her role in the legal system. Never mind how they decide hard cases. We first need to determine what makes it the case that they get to be the ones who decide hard cases. On this question, arguably, Dworkin's challenge remains silent. As Marmor puts it:

> Before judges can come to disagree about any legal issue, they must first be able to see themselves as institutional players, playing, as it were, a fairly structured role in an elaborate practice. Judges can only see themselves as such on the basis of the rules and conventions that establish their role and authority as judges, namely, the rules of recognition. In short, pointing to the fact that judges often have certain disagreements about the content of the rules of recognition simply cannot prove that there are no such rules. On the contrary, we can only make sense of such disagreements on the basis of the assumption that there are rules of recognition that constitute, inter alia, the courts system and the legal authority of judges.[61]

Can a similar objection be raised against the proposal offered here? Here's how the point may be put. All that the revised interpretive methodology can do is explain how values bear on judicial interpretation. But it comes too late to cut any ice against legal positivism. We care for judicial interpretations because the people articulating them have an important place in the joint project of governing. We would not have any reason to direct our attention to them, were it not for the rules constituting the office of the judge. We know that their interpretations matter because they occupy that office.

It is one of the strengths of the proposal offered here that it represents a convincing response to Marmor's critique. It acknowledges that theories of law must account for the existence of standards that distinguish the institutional role of judges from that of other officials. But it insists that these standards can be fully explained in terms of the considerations of political and institutional

---

[61] See Marmor, *Social Conventions* (n 59). Marmor contends that the rules that constitute the office of the judge are rooted in what he calls constitutive conventions.

morality that underpin the joint project of officials. Such considerations determine the judge's position in the joint project of governing, his jurisdiction relative to that of the legislature. In turn, his jurisdiction has a bearing on the way he interprets legislative decisions. Will he construe them narrowly or broadly? Will he construe them in line with constitutional imperatives that he is entrusted in the final instance to enforce? The correct answer to these and similar questions crucially depends on our understanding of his position vis-à-vis the legislature. Jurisdiction is a suitable concept to structure our thinking about this issue. In other words, on the revised version of interpretivism I am advancing, it is not true that there is an independent set of standards that define someone as a judge and a separate set of standards that govern how that judge ought to decide cases. Rather, the same standards play out in both cases.[62] Jurisdiction is a determinant of interpretation, and, conversely, we need to interpret in order to define jurisdiction.

It may be said (as Marmor does say) that the considerations of institutional and political morality of the kind I am invoking underdetermine the content of the institutional roles assigned to judges, legislators and other officials within any given legal system. But if that is so, then they cannot provide the full normative explanation of the standards defining those roles. They leave it open that some positivist-sounding idea like a convention has to be added in, at the very least for the purpose of specifying which of the morally eligible schemes of division of labour is the one that is legally binding around here. In fact, the objection continues, it is extremely likely that, whether determinate or indeterminate, many of these issues will be settled by the constitution. This seems to be the case in most modern legal systems. Their constitutions typically include rules about allocation of political power among officials, thus arguably blocking recourse to considerations of institutional design.

In response to this counter-argument, one cannot warn enough against overestimating the ability of constitutional provisions and conventions to settle difficult questions of institutional design. Controversies inevitably arise, and although different sides couch their views in terms of the correct application of the relevant provisions and conventions, the fact of the matter is that they typically invoke considerations of institutional design to make their case. Admittedly constitutions and conventions do sometimes appear to settle such questions. Should the interpretivist concede that, when they do, they pre-empt any moral reasoning? Should he rest content to explain how ambiguities and disputes are resolved around the edges of these settlements? This concession

---

[62] In ch 2 we distinguished two stages in the test of jurisdiction. We first delineate in the abstract the powers assigned to an agent of governance, and then we ascertain whether a specific decision, issued by, say, the legislature is a genuine exercise of those powers. On the view advocated here, the distinction is not all that sharp; it is more apt to view the two stages as points along a continuum of abstraction.

would seriously undercut the reach and ambition of the proposal and must be rejected.

How can the interpretivist case be bolstered then? There is, I think, another, more effective answer to the counter-argument that has special relevance to the account offered here. My depiction of the joint project of governing has so far focused on the synchronic relationship between the courts and the legislature. But that project is one that spans over time. So, the partners whose contributions bear on the determination of the institutional duty of current officials are not just their contemporaries but also past participants, including those who sought with their decisions to shape the division of labour for the future. Think of constitutional assemblies. Decisions like those made by constitutional assemblies may help more closely to determine the content of institutional roles where, absent those decisions, abstract considerations of political morality would have left the issue underdetermined. Judges of today have (if they do) the same kind of reason to heed those decisions that they have to heed any other contribution to the joint activity of law. Those decisions form part of the institutional tapestry that judges must interpret in order to determine what it is within their power to do in order to do their share in the joint project of governing. To elaborate, the reason is not simply the social fact that, say, there is a constitutional convention that assigns a certain task to judges or the social fact that a decision of constitutional significance happened in the past that has the same effect. Rather, what makes the social fact pertinent is a *moral fact*: the legitimacy and political standing of the constitutional assembly or the continuing adherence of key political actors to the constitutional convention are crucial considerations of institutional design that go a long way towards morally justifying the decision or convention binding courts and the legislature into the future. Without these considerations, the constitutional assembly or the convention would have no more force than the say-so of a private individual.

There is nothing incoherent or mysterious in the thought that judges of today participate in the same joint project with the founding fathers. At the very least, this thought should be no more incoherent or mysterious than the thought that judges and legislators engage in such a project. Judges are called to implement the decisions of long-dead legislators. They do so because the relationship that connects them is institutional, not personal. The same applies to the founding fathers. It is the project of governing, as structured by the relevant considerations of institutional design that directs courts to heed their acts and decisions, not any sort of actual proximity.

I said above that the temporal distance between different officials does not by itself negate their participation in the same project. Still, the passage of time since the enactment of the constitution can be of moral relevance to what judges may or may not do in their official capacity today. Quite plausibly, the need for a working division of labour that governs the practice of officials from time to time may sometimes undercut the moral weight of decisions made at a distant point in the past, even if that point is the founding moment.[63] This is another important consideration of institutional design which tempers the authority of the founding fathers and thus loosens the grip of previous generations on present-day politics. It thus explains why ideas like the 'living constitution'[64] have currency in constitutional law. Of course, it is a further question of institutional design who gets to update the constitutional framework, once it is accepted that it is legitimate to update it.

It may be objected that this line of argument deals with Marmor's challenge but in a way that falls prey to the no-constraint objection. That is because interpreting the power-conferring provisions of a constitution does not involve any interplay between content and institutional design. Such provisions regulate matters of institutional design. Therefore, considerations of content may, at best, form part of the background or may delineate outer limits to their interpretation. This critique misses the mark but is onto something. What matters for interpretivism to address the no-constraint objection is not that we find the same interplay across all legal interpretation – it is no accident that I have specifically focused on just one of its areas. What matters is that we identify (at least) two sets of sufficiently distinct and independent considerations, one of which gives moral weight to institutional history and thereby constrains the extent to which we can appeal to the other. We have no difficulty doing that in the present instance. That's because the kinds of considerations of institutional design that bestow authority on the constitutional assembly are not the same as the considerations that the constitutional assembly had to take into account in designing the general framework of government. The latter are, say, the democratic pedigree of the legislature, the rule of law, separation of powers, efficiency and the like, whereas the former are the legitimacy that the constitutional assembly enjoyed, the fact that it was effective in securing the support of the nation around the political settlement it devised and so on. We can see that the two kinds of consideration check one another by considering that we are inclined to treat the constitution as binding, even if we think that the framework of government it lays down could have been better along the dimension of democracy, the rule of law etc.

B. Varieties of Reasons and the Law

Marmor questions whether my reformulation of interpretivism extends to rules defining institutional roles, while remaining agnostic about whether it correctly

---

[63] J Raz, 'On the Authority and Interpretation of Constitutions' in L Alexander (ed), *Constitutionalism: Philosophical Foundations* (Cambridge, Cambridge University Press, 2001) 152.

[64] WH Rehnquist, 'The Idea of a Living Constitution' (1976) 54 *Texas Law Review* 693.

captures the nature of judicial interpretation. There is another positivist come-back that will not even concede that. The theorists that propose this comeback do not deny that considerations of content and institutional design may bear on judicial duty. However, they maintain that this is compatible with the view that another very important determinant of this duty is the set of norms created by the legislature. Legislative decisions make a difference to the role of courts, insofar as they constitute exercises of a certain normative power, the power of an authority to create norms. It is through such norms that the legislature con-tributes to the joint project of governing. It is quite likely that in some legal sys-tems courts are bound or permitted to combine them with further norms, moral or other. What is more, these further norms may include norms of political morality concerning the political credentials of the legislature and the courts' own institutional position in the project of governing, especially vis-à-vis the legislature. The account proposed here merely seeks to explain how all these different norms bear on the judge's duty in those legal systems where they do bear on it. But the explanation of the creation of norms by the legislature is independent of it.

To make the contrast sharper, I shall employ a distinction recently proposed by David Enoch between robust reason-giving and triggering reasons.[65] What is characteristic of robust reason-giving is that one person intends to give another a reason to ϕ and communicates this intention to her, intending that the other person recognises this intention and that the reason will depend in an appropri-ate way on that recognition.[66] Enoch claims that robust reason-giving differs from (in the sense that it is a philosophically interesting sub-set of) reason-giving by *triggering* pre-existing reasons. One triggers pre-existing reasons by manipu-lating the non-normative circumstances such that these reasons now apply. An example of mere *triggering reason-giving* is the case where you and I are heading towards each other and you move to one side of the pavement. I have a pre-existing reason not to crash into people which your act has triggered. Thus, I now ought to take the other side of the pavement. Of course, Enoch contends, promises create reasons because they trigger a pre-existing reason to do as promised. But this does not collapse the two types of reason-giving. It is still important to single out robust reason-giving because of the distinctive connec-tion that it envisages between the intention of the person who promises, requests, commands etc to give a reason and the resulting reason: the reason comes about 'merely by the very forming of the intention to give a reason'.[67] It is also possible to intend to give one reasons in the triggering mode. It may well have been your

[65] D Enoch, 'Reason-Giving and the Law' in L Green and B Leiter (eds), *Oxford Studies in Philosophy of Law* vol 1 (Oxford, Oxford University Press, 2011) 1.
[66] ibid 10–14.
[67] D Enoch, 'Authority and Reason-Giving' (2014) 89 *Philosophy and Phenomenological Research* 296, 302.

intention all along to make me move to one side of the pavement, and the course of action you chose – to pick a side first – was particularly effective in achieving this. However, the thought is that in the triggering case what gives the reason is not the intention itself but rather the circumstances which you intentionally manipulated with your act so as to trigger the reason.

Enoch maintains that having practical authority consists in having the power robustly to give reasons. Assume, as some legal philosophers contend, that law – or, more relevantly for present purposes, the legislature speaking on law's behalf –[68] claims authority. Then, on Enoch's view, we have to explicate the legislative contribution to judicial duty in terms of robust reasons. Obviously, this is not the only way in which the legislature gives judges reasons when it does. But this is how it gives judges reasons when it rises up to its claim, that is, when it succeeds in exercising legitimate authority. Let's call this the voluntarist view. Other voluntarists insist that it is not intentions but the communicative acts such as utterances by which those intentions are conveyed that are crucial for the giving of robust reasons. I do not take sides in this debate, so I will be speaking interchangeably of the intentions and the say-so of legislatures as giving rise to robust reasons.[69] If true, voluntarism can serve to vindicate the legal positivist strategy of carving up the space between theories of law and theories of adjudication. It does so, primarily because it makes the legislative contribution to judicial duty rest solely on the intentions (once properly communicated) or utterances of the legislature. Thus, it isolates this contribution as an object of philosophical study from any further normative impact that it might have, perhaps in combination with other reasons that bear on the judicial role.[70]

A fully-fledged evaluation of Enoch's proposal and of the voluntarist view, more generally, lies beyond the scope of this book. Rather than do that, I shall offer the following two-pronged response in Dworkin's defence: I shall first suggest that, although interpretivism may be compatible with the voluntarist view, it does not entail it. I shall then go on to claim that, even if it were true that the voluntarist view furnished the best account of the normative powers of

---

[68]   Enoch broaches this line of argument in Enoch, 'Reason-Giving and the Law' (n 65) 36. I have examined and qualified it in ch 2 by reference to Joseph Raz's theory of legal authority.

[69]   Enoch also talks about authorities giving reasons rather than creating norms. In what follows, I am going to ignore this division within voluntarism, as it does not affect my argument.

[70]   There is a further sense in which Enoch's theory can be said to lend support to legal positivism. He writes that we can separately study the structure of attempts to give robust reasons, whether or not these attempts succeed in creating those reasons as intended. He further distinguishes normative from non-normative conditions for the success of these attempts. An attempt meets the non-normative conditions when the communication of the intention is successful in affecting the practical reasoning of the receiver in the intended way. An attempt further meets the normative conditions when the receiver has a pre-existing reason to do as he is told because he has been told, which has been triggered by the reason-giver telling him to do something or other. There is an interesting symmetry between this distinction and Raz's distinction between a legitimate and a de facto authority. See J Raz, *Ethics in the Public Domain* (Oxford, Clarendon Press, 1994) 215ff.

legislators, this would not necessarily make it the best account of the nature of law.

Let me begin by outlining a plausible view about the kind of power legislators wield, which is markedly different from the voluntarist view but equally compatible with the interpretivist story offered here. Its gist is, to use Enoch's terminology, that legislative decisions merely trigger reasons; they do not robustly give reasons. As my goal here is solely to establish that interpretivism does not entail the voluntarist view, I shall not argue for the superiority of the alternative view. All I shall do is explain why it is a genuine alternative to the voluntarist view.

On the alternative view legislators do not affect the content of our moral rights and duties by their mere say-so, but rather because their decision triggers non-robust reasons. Consider a situation where doing the morally right thing requires that we converge on one among several mutually exclusive but equally effective courses of action. Imagine further that this convergence is unlikely to occur spontaneously, or that it is too costly to wait for it to emerge spontaneously. It may be that having the legislature opt for one of those courses of action solves our coordination problem, because it gives that course of action the requisite salience. In this case, what gives us reason to follow it is not the legislative say-so, but the fact that it has become salient. In fact, the salient solution need not coincide with the one the legislature had intended to make us follow. What matters for the alternative view is that the legislature's decision has played a crucial causal role in creating a salient solution. In addition, this was no accident. The legislature produced this effect precisely because it was assigned the power to do so.

This is but one illustration of a more general strategy, according to which the distinctively *legal* impact of legislative decisions should be cashed out in terms of reason-triggering, without appeal to the idea that the mere intention or say-so of the legislature generates robust reasons.[71] Nicos Stavropoulos summarises this strategy thus:

> [F]or the interpretivist, the role of institutional action as a determinant of legal obligation is explained by some distinctive political virtue that is realized or some purpose that is served by institutional action's having that role. Thus, the legal relevance of institutional practice is derivative from the moral relevance of some of its aspects.[72]

---

[71] See generally N Stavropoulos, 'Obligations, Interpretivism and the Legal Point of View' in A Marmor, *The Routledge Companion to Philosophy of Law* (New York NY, Routledge, 2012) 76. Stavropoulos contrasts the alternative strategy to Joseph Raz's account of promissory and legal obligation. For a view of promissory obligations that is congenial to Raz's, see D Owens, *Shaping the Normative Landscape* (Oxford, Oxford University Press, 2012) chs 5–6.

[72] ibid 89.

Here the explanation of the obtaining of legal obligations is indirect.[73] Because of its moral relevance institutional practice has the effect of changing the moral circumstances of legal subjects, and thereby also their legal rights and duties. Now, some aspects of the moral relevance of legislative decisions are systematically linked with the institutional credentials of the legislature. This is the case in the example that I gave a couple of paragraphs ago. There, the legislature effectively coordinates because of the position of prominence it occupies in the legal system. That the relevant legal norm in this scenario does not come about directly or robustly, through mere legislative say-so, is evinced by the fact that its content need not coincide with the content of the legislature's intention or utterance.

Compared to Enoch's view, the alternative strategy acquires even more traction as an explanation of the C-L relationship. It is worth remembering that the legislature is just one partner in a complex system of institutional collaboration. Among other things, this means that legislative decisions have to go through a series of institutional hoops before they can be enforced. In every institutional round, new reasons of institutional design are brought to bear which may qualify the impact of those decisions. In such a setting it is bizarre to think that the intentions of legislators when they enact a statute are the same as the intentions of a lone practical authority. More specifically, it seems unwarranted to insist that in the face of this complexity legislators will continue to have the kind of intention necessary for robust reason-giving, that is, an intention that the addressees of their decision should ϕ and that they should take that intention as their reason for ϕ-ing.

To resist this line of argument, Enoch could argue that in the robust reason-giving case, it is not necessary 'that the reason-giver intend the reason-receiver actually to ϕ'.[74] The reason-giver may not know what other reasons apply to the reason-receiver and thus whether the robust reason he is giving him will eventually be outweighed. In such situations, the reason-giver 'has an intention to make a difference to the reasons applying to you (and also to their balance) without necessarily intending that the weight of reasons will ultimately support you [acting on the robust reason]'.[75] However, I doubt this move can reinforce the plausibility of the voluntarist view in the case of legal systems with courts and a legislature. It is not that the legislature is unaware of the other reasons that apply to the reason-receivers, say the courts, which may compete with the reason to do as the legislature intended. In fact, the legislature knows full well some of those further reasons – or at least is typically expected to know them. These

---

[73] ibid 82. On the idea of directness, see M Greenberg, 'The Standard Picture and its Discontents' in L Green and B Leiter (eds), *Oxford Studies in Philosophy of Law* vol 1 (Oxford, Oxford University Press, 2011) 39.

[74] Enoch, 'Authority and Reason-Giving' (n 67) 14.

[75] ibid.

reasons apply to the reason-receiver in a systematic way, because of the reason-receiver's position in the project of governing. At the same time, this is a project the reason-receiver shares with the legislature. The legislature knows that its decision is a contribution to that project. Knowledge of this fact is bound to change the intentions of the legislature when it makes a decision. It seems more apt to say that in light of such knowledge the legislature intends no more than to contribute to the project of governing in a way which will crucially depend on the considerations of institutional design that structure it. By decoupling the distinctively legal impact of the legislative contribution to the content of the law from the legislature's intention or say-so, the alternative view can accommodate this insight.

But let's assume, for the sake of argument, that, when compared against the view just rehearsed, the voluntarist view of the normative impact of legislative decisions has the better argument. This still would not suffice to give legal positivism the edge over interpretivism. All the voluntarist would have achieved is to explicate one of the determinants of legal duty. It takes further argument to show that this determinant must enjoy a privileged position in our accounts of law. In other words, even if the legislature creates robust reasons, this does not mean that it is those reasons that are distinctly legal. As I shall argue now, it is still available to the interpretivist to part ways with the voluntarist at this point.

There is no doubt that legislative decisions are a central element of the C-L relationship. Small wonder that in fleshing out interpretivism I have been focusing on the impact that legislative decisions have on judicial duty. However, it is not true that by doing so I have committed to a view about the order of philosophical explanation that is congenial to voluntarism, whereby legal obligation is normally created by the making of an authoritative decision. That is because the focus on legislative decisions was chosen for purposes of illustration. The proposal works also without reference to them. For one thing, considerations of institutional design determine judicial duty even in the absence of legislative decisions. Take the following example. Although it may be a good idea, morally speaking, that every citizen have a right to a minimum income, this is for many a paradigmatic case of a right that the courts have no business enforcing.[76] And this is so on the basis of the position that courts occupy within the joint activity, especially vis-à-vis the political branches, rather than on legislative say-so.

Isn't this just the flipside of a positivistic understanding of the relationship between courts and the legislature? It would be the law that every person has a right to a minimum income if the legislature passed a law to this effect, but, until it does, it is the law that there is no such right. Again, this may be compatible with the proposal but it is not entailed by it. We can easily imagine a variant of

[76] Larry Sager offers a thoughtful and sustained argument for such a limit to judicial power; see L Sager, *Justice in Plainclothes* (New Haven CT, Yale University Press, 2004) chs 6–8. I discuss his argument in more detail in the next chapter.

the proposal that says that, although courts cannot of their own initiative enforce a right to a minimum income, they may still have the power to do other things in the name of equality – that is, on the strength of a pressing considera- tion of content – independently of legislative action. They may, for instance, have the power to quash a legislative decision that violates equality, or extend a benefit that the legislature has given a certain class of citizens to other classes.

Needless to say, legal positivists have proposed various ways to accommodate the aforementioned examples of judicial decision-making in the absence and even in the teeth of legislative decisions. We critically examined some of these ways in chapter two. For example, they say that judges themselves have a limited power to create norms by say-so through the exercise of discretion or by virtue of a constitutional convention. They go on to claim that the kinds of norm mentioned above ('Benefit x ought to be extended to class y of the population') become part of the law, only once the judicial power has been exercised. But they insist that such cases are properly treated as pertaining to adjudication; they are evidence that adjudication comprises a variety of tasks alongside the task of applying norms created by the legislature.

This is an important view, and anti-positivists must reckon with it. Nevertheless, it must be stressed that the mere fact that there is an alternative explanation of the phenomena that my proposal also seeks to explain does not affect the dialectic of this chapter. My aim here has not been polemical. It is rather to sketch an alternative understanding of law, one which challenges the distinction between law and adjudication as conceived by legal positivists. On this understanding, the dependence of judicial duty on legislative decisions must be placed in the context of the joint project of governing in which courts and the legislature participate. The project is structured by considerations of institutional design that distribute power between the two bodies and regulate their cooperation. They prescribe that judges heed legislative decisions, but they prescribe a host of other things as well which also determine judicial duty. Accordingly, judges are there not fundamentally to give effect to legislative deci- sions but to govern well within the project that they share with the legislature. To do so, they must combine a variety of considerations, the existence of a legislative decision being only one among them. From this we can reasonably conclude that legal duty is what comes out of the mix, not one component. The fact that legislative decisions give rise to robust reasons does not seem to make any difference. In the next chapter, I shall furnish some reasons of political morality for taking the C-L relationship as the focal point of theories of law. Granted, these reasons will not necessarily hold much appeal to those legal philosophers who believe that the subject matter of theories of law is conceptu- ally fixed and not a matter of substantive moral argument. However, they will serve to establish that from within the interpretivist framework the move towards the joint project of governing is not ad hoc.

In the last couple of paragraphs I have argued that there is much more to law than legislative decisions and that this makes a difference in the theory of law. So even if you think that the legislature's say-so creates norms *pace* the voluntarist view, you need not also identify law with exercises of this normative power by the legislature – or any state institution for that matter. This defence of interpretivism echoes Dworkin's charge that much legal positivism, including Raz's theory examined in chapter two, studies what Dworkin calls the *taxonomic* concept of law. The taxonomic concept of law furnishes criteria that make a standard legal. Dworkin is sceptical about the point of the taxonomic enterprise in law, which, for him, is premised on a 'scholastic fiction'.[77] In fact, he blames this fiction for a persistent misunderstanding of his early critique of legal positivism. He claims that many legal theorists, blinkered by the taxonomic frame of mind, took Dworkin to be arguing for the inclusion of a class of standards – principles – among legal standards alongside source-based rules. Of course, should the voluntarist turn out to have the best argument, there would be nothing fictional about the norms created through legislative (or, more generally, official) say-so. But, even so, the taxonomic enterprise would still be open to the scholasticism charge. Whether the charge sticks depends on which view of the nature of law we take. If we agree with Dworkin that the task of jurisprudence is to determine the truth conditions of propositions of law, then the identification of norms created by legislative norms is an idle wheel or, at best, a side-show. What really matters is how these norms bear on the truth of propositions of law. On the interpretivist account outlined above and further elaborated in the following chapter, this will necessarily involve recourse to moral considerations of content and institutional design that give shape to the joint project of governing that courts and the legislature are part of.

VII. CONCLUSION

In this chapter I have sought to reformulate and vindicate Dworkin's contention that judicial interpretation is subject to a constraint of fit. I have claimed that fit is required by the principles of political morality that determine the judicial role within the joint project of governing. In order to perform his role adequately, the judge must always look over his shoulder to see whether the legislature has decided something that is relevant to the case before him. If he finds in the legislative record a pertinent decision, he must further ascertain whether he has a special kind of moral reason to give it effect. This reason is furnished by the considerations of institutional design that define the relative position of different participants in the project of governing and specify how they should work

---

[77] Dworkin, *Justice in Robes* (n 3) 4.

together, combined with considerations about what rights and duties we would have in a perfectly just society.

I want to finish by delimiting the scope of my claim in this chapter. It was not my intention to offer a general theory of interpretation or a general explanation of the concepts of fit and justification in interpretivism. To begin with, the account of the interplay between fit and justification does not extend beyond collaborative interpretation. For instance, it is not designed to explain why and how far our interpretations of the concept of justice must be faithful to the beliefs and intuitions about justice of the concept-users. Neither does it offer any guidance to, say, historians, who engage in what Dworkin calls explanatory interpretation. Historiography, too, must fit the past, but not because historians collaborate with the people whose lives they study. This should not come as a surprise. If fit is best understood as a component of a complex interpretive judgement, as the holistic conception urges, it is bound to vary from one type of practice to the other, since it will be sensitive to the values and considerations that shape different types.

But even if we restrict our attention to collaborative interpretive practices, the understanding of fit proposed here does not explain what constrains our ascriptions of a point or purpose to the whole practice rather than to individual contributions within it. Thus, in the example of poetry I have assumed that literary practices value originality, which directs us to assign weight to the work of art, as it has been handed down to us by its creator. However, I have not offered any reason for the claim that originality is part of the point of those practices. Nor, importantly, have I explained how we should go about testing such claims. Insofar as those claims are, according to Dworkin, interpretive, they must also be subject to a requirement of fit. Surely, though, originality cannot ground this requirement on pain of circularity. It falls outside the scope of this book to defend the interpretive methodology from all the challenges that it faces, including the one just mentioned. (Given that Dworkin thinks all value hangs together in a whole, whose components are interdependent and mutually reinforcing, it is to be expected that challenges will come from very different fronts.) I have focused on the challenge which is most pertinent to the main concern of the book, namely the explanation of the bearing of legislative decisions on judicial duty. Besides, this is the challenge most closely associated with the no-constraint objection. Since literary genres only serve as an illustration of the general point I want to make, my discussion of them relied on nothing more than a number of reasonable and commonly held assumptions about their point. I produced more argument when I elaborated the interaction between fit and justification in the case of law in terms of content and institutional design. Even there, though, certain assumptions did a lot of the work.

4

Legality, Integrity and Institutional Design

I. INTRODUCTION

ACCORDING TO INTERPRETIVE theories of law, the content of the law is determined by the principles of political morality that best fit and justify institutional history; we have a legal right or duty if it is morally justified in the relevant sense that we do. The interpretive test also applies to the determination of the official duty of judges in legal systems with courts and a legislature. In the last chapter it was argued that this test constrains judges, when they decide cases, from acting on the best understanding of abstract principles of justice. Judges are not deciding in an institutional vacuum. Among the principles of political morality that will bear on the determination of judicial duty there are those, principles of institutional design as I called them, that direct judges to give weight to the acts and decisions of the legislature, even when doing so will mean deciding the case before them in a way that is sub-optimal, as judged against the best understanding of justice. This is not to say that the job of courts is merely passive, subservient to that of the legislature. At the most general level, the aim of courts is to create and sustain a just and well-ordered society. But it is an aim that they share with the legislature. As participants in a joint project, they have good moral reason to heed the legislature's contributions. They must balance that reason alongside considerations of content – considerations regarding what rights and duties we would have in a perfectly just and well-ordered society.

In this chapter I want to say more about this joint project and the respective roles of the two institutions. We cannot expect to go into too much detail. Predictably, the specifics of the joint project vary from one jurisdiction to the other. At the very least I want to defend the idea that courts and legislatures are involved in a joint project to begin with. Though this idea was frequently invoked in the previous chapter, it was largely taken as a given. This is due to the fact that the purpose of the previous chapter was to present and argue for a certain understanding of the interpretive methodology, such that it becomes a genuine alternative to legal positivism. I have sought to do this by introducing the thought that legal interpretation consists of the interplay between moral considerations of content and moral considerations of institutional design; this is a central element of the reformulation of interpretivism proposed here. Accordingly, the relationship of courts and the legislature was, for the main part, used as an illustration of how the interplay operates.

Here, the relationship between courts and the legislature is placed front and centre. My aim is to show that this project instantiates a distinctive virtue, which is characteristic of law. I shall begin, negatively, by critically examining an enduring characteristic of Ronald Dworkin's jurisprudential outlook, namely his focus on courts. I shall ask: Is there a valid reason for privileging the judicial perspective in our theories of law? This will lead to an investigation of the value that Dworkin ascribes to law. In *Law's Empire* Dworkin contends that, when legal systems perform as they should, they manifest integrity. He claims that integrity is the best articulation of a more abstract value we associate with law, that is, legality. In *Justice for Hedgehogs* he further claims that integrity is primarily a virtue of judicial decision-making. I shall suggest that, if we acknowledge the importance of the considerations of institutional design highlighted in the previous chapter, we must question the connection between legality and integrity. By doing so, we will end up dethroning courts from their position of prominence in the interpretivist edifice. Once we abandon the court-centric view of the law, we will also be in a better position to appreciate the role of institutional design in the study of law and to locate courts within the broader institutional enterprise in which they participate.

In large part, the argument of this chapter will proceed in juxtaposition to Dworkin's views. It should be remembered, however, that at this stage we have left legal positivism behind. Hence, the claims I shall be making are claims about what an *interpretive* theory of law should look like. Accordingly, my critique of Dworkin will be internal to interpretivism, and, but for a short digression toward the end of the chapter, I shall not engage with the interpretivist's opponents. We might say that, whereas the previous chapter answered (in the affirmative) the preliminary question whether it is moral values that determine the respect judges owe legislative decisions, this chapter addresses the more specific question what those moral values are. This is a normative exercise. It requires being responsive to concerns in political morality which a political society ordered by law faces and its being ordered by law may serve to deal with. Nonetheless, it does not start from a clean slate. It builds on the lessons of the previous chapter. More specifically, it employs the idea that legislatures and courts participate in a joint project shaped by considerations of institutional design concerning how political authority should be distributed among institutional actors. The scope of the claims made here is accordingly restricted to legal systems with courts and a legislature. Our question is: What is good about such legal systems? The answer given will go some way towards fleshing out the idea that considerations of content and institutional design interact to ground our legal rights and duties. This idea was presented in a skeletal form in the previous chapter. Here, we will survey some of the more characteristic ways in which it is manifested in legal systems with courts and a legislature, making these legal systems worth having.

II. THE VIEW FROM THE COURTS

As is well known, Dworkin started off elaborating his interpretive theory of law from the perspective of an ideal judge, Hercules, who is equipped with unlimited intellectual powers and unlimited time and whose Herculean task consists in identifying the set of principles that best explain and justify the entire political history of the legal system to which he belongs.[1] Originally, Dworkin's focus on the judicial perspective seems to have primarily served a heuristic purpose.[2] Thus, in *Law's Empire* he wrote:

> We will study formal legal argument from the judge's viewpoint, not because only judges are important or because we understand everything about them by noticing what they say, but because judicial argument about claims of law is a useful paradigm for exploring the central, propositional aspect of legal practice. Citizens and politicians and law teachers also worry and argue about what the law is, and I might have taken their arguments rather than the judge's. But the structure of judicial argument is typically more explicit, and judicial reasoning has an influence over other forms of legal discourse that is not fully reciprocal.[3]

In his last book, *Justice for Hedgehogs*, Dworkin offers a different rationale for his focus on 'legal argument from the judge's viewpoint'. It is no longer merely the choice of a 'useful paradigm'. Instead, it is now nested in the broader interpretive approach to value that runs through Dworkin's later work. On this approach, value is an integrated whole, and the law is but one province of its domain. To understand law is to identify the value that underlies or is 'fundamental to' legal practice as well as the connections of that value with other values. It is also to make our accounts of legal practice sensitive to this constellation of values, in the sense that the claims we make within the practice must be answerable to the best interpretation of these values. In fact, Dworkin argues, law does hold a distinct role in this constellation. 'Law', he writes, 'is a distinct part of political morality'.[4] That is because law fulfils the need for a special kind of moral

---

[1] R Dworkin, *Taking Rights Seriously* (London, Duckworth, 1978).

[2] Even then, though, it has been informed by moral considerations alongside epistemic ones. See eg Dworkin, *Taking Rights Seriously* (n 1) 85–86. There, Dworkin argues that a judge who creates new law in hard cases, as legal positivism enjoins him, is retroactively changing the rights and duties of the litigants, and especially the losing party. His decision thus suffers from a serious moral defect, from which, by contrast, a decision decided on interpretivist grounds is immune.

[3] R Dworkin, *Law's Empire* (Oxford, Hart Publishing, 1998) 14.

[4] R Dworkin, *Justice for Hedgehogs* (Cambridge MA, Harvard University Press, 2011) 413.

justification, which arises in a political community that possesses the power to coerce its members. But a political community has a variety of institutions that act in its name over time, and not all their activity requires for Dworkin that special justification. Thus, Dworkin distinguishes the moral standards that apply to acts of the legislature and of the courts. Courts are 'institutions that direct the executive power of sheriff or police',[5] to enforce certain individual rights. In exercising this power, courts do not require 'further legislative intervention'.[6] In addition, the processes that enforce such a right are 'directly available' to aggrieved individuals, in the sense that they can be set in motion upon their demand.[7] No doubt, we also have certain expectations from the legislature concerning the protection and promotion of important rights. But the rights whose protection and promotion we properly demand from legislatures, our legislative rights in Dworkin's terminology, 'even when acknowledged, are of no immediate force';[8] an individual will need to await legislative action before he can enforce them.[9] Arguably, this makes a crucial jurisprudential difference. In order for a right to be equipped with on-demand enforceability, it must pass a heightened moral test that mere legislative rights need not.[10] Rights that pass this moral test and are thus properly called 'legal' belong to the extension of the doctrinal concept of law.[11] Dworkin takes the doctrinal concept of law to be the subject matter of the theory of the nature of law, whose central task, accordingly, is the articulation of the moral test that determines membership in the extension of that concept.

---

[5] ibid 406.

[6] ibid.

[7] ibid.

[8] ibid.

[9] Both legal and legislative rights are institutional rights, in the sense defined by Dworkin in *Taking Rights Seriously*. Institutional rights justify 'a decision by some particular and specified political institution'. See Dworkin, *Taking Rights Seriously* (n 1) 93. A claim of institutional right must be grounded in the 'special constitutive and regulative rules' of the relevant institution. The legislature is one such institution. Courts are another.

[10] The epistemic rationale for the focus on courts is not completely lost in this picture. eg when contrasting the philosophy of international law to that of domestic law, Dworkin writes that since in national legal systems institutional structures 'broadly distinguish between courts, which have the responsibility and power to enforce rights and obligations on demand, and other sorts of political institutions, like legislatures that do not', 'we can *helpfully frame* our political question in institutional terms'. See R Dworkin, 'A New Philosophy of International Law' (2013) 41 *Philosophy and Public Affairs* 2, 13 [emphasis added].

[11] Dworkin only talks of rights, but of course his point must also apply *mutatis mutandis* to legal duties, even when individuals do not have a corresponding right to demand that these duties be enforced in adjudicative institutions. Criminal law typically includes such duties. It would not be accurate to say that the adjudicative processes that enforce these duties are 'directly available' to individuals, but it makes sense to maintain that they can be triggered, if those duties are breached, without legislative intervention. For the sake of simplicity, I shall ignore this complication and follow Dworkin in focusing on rights.

It is evident that this view significantly narrows the scope of the theory of law. It gives pride of place to courts and their role in a political community, as opposed to other institutional actors such as the legislature. It thus lends a certain shape to the jurisprudential study of the project of governing. The legal theorist's primary task is to ascertain the effect that, say, legislative decisions have on the content of the rights and duties that are judicially enforceable on demand; the same decisions are bound to have other types of effect but they are not the subject matter of the theory of law.[12] In what follows, I wish to argue, *contra* Dworkin, for a wide scope view of the joint project of governing. I shall challenge the primacy Dworkin accords to courts, and I shall suggest that the alternative yields significant philosophical gains that the court-centric view conceals.

III. INTEGRITY AND LEGALITY

How are we to adjudicate the disagreement between Dworkin's view and the one I am advocating? Let's first consider the following simple answer. Perhaps we can define the disagreement away. If legal rights are just defined in terms of their amenability to judicial enforcement on demand, then rights that fall outside this definition will not be deemed legal rights. Maybe they are legislative, or maybe they are not institutional rights at all. This is compatible with saying that they are considered as part of the law in other respects – such as that they are routinely referred to as law as a matter of sociological fact. Indeed, it may be crucial for our understanding of the political practices of our community that we pay attention to and analyse them.[13] But their examination is not the task of

---

[12] Even more controversially, Dworkin has expanded his court-centric view of law to international law. See Dworkin, 'International Law' (n 10). There he argues that the doctrinal concept of international law comprises all the rights and duties that would be enforceable upon individual demand by 'an international court with jurisdiction over all the nations in the world'. (ibid 14) He asks us to imagine that 'cases can be brought before that court reasonably easily and that effective sanctions are available to enforce the court's rulings'. (ibid) Conceding that this is 'fantasy upon fantasy' (ibid), he nevertheless insists that this speculative exercise is philosophically valuable because it allows us to identify international law duties which states currently ignore or reject and can afford to do so because these duties cannot be enforced upon them. Although the motivation is important, it is questionable whether it is well served by postulating such a court. As I shall suggest below, law goes beyond the on-demand enforceability that is the courts' responsibility. A theory that focuses on them is therefore liable to distort our accounts of law's point. For obvious reasons the risk is accentuated in the case of international law, but I cannot elaborate this point here.

[13] Thus, Larry Sager insists that, even if we accept Dworkin's conception of law in terms of judicial enforcement, what is left out is 'still crucially relevant to the best understanding of the constitution as a whole, to the justification and measure of the rights that are recognized by courts, and to discussion of other, possibly far-ranging issues of constitutional interpretation and adjudication'. See L Sager, 'Material Rights, Underenforcement, and the Adjudication Thesis' (2010) 90 *Boston University Law Review* 579, 585.

a theory of law. Accordingly, courts can simply be defined as the institutions, whichever they are, whose job it is to identify those moral rights that may properly be enforced on demand.

However, this answer will not get us very far. The definitional approach does not provide an argument why on-demand enforceable rights, the doctrinal concept of law as understood by Dworkin, are the proper subject matter of jurisprudence. This approach would appear as unmotivated as the distinction between the theory of law and the theory of adjudication that was criticised in previous chapters. Fortunately, there is a better way to judge the merits of Dworkin's understanding of the province of jurisprudence. As he insists: 'Vocabulary should follow political argument, not the other way around'.[14] We therefore have to ask whether the primacy assigned to the idea of judicial enforcement on demand is defensible as a matter of political philosophy. We must ask, that is, whether respect for our legal rights, as understood by Dworkin, exhibits a special type of moral virtue. Additionally, we must decide whether that virtue may be said to be distinctive of legal practice.[15]

Consider the following account of political legitimacy: in order to be legitimate, a state need not be fully just; it suffices that it acts in accordance with an appropriate conception of equality among citizens. This conception prescribes that the state extend to a group of citizens a right or a benefit that it has granted another similarly situated group on the basis of a plausible scheme of moral principle. When state action meets this condition of legitimacy, it manifests the moral virtue of integrity. This, as is well known, is the answer to the problem of political legitimacy that Dworkin offers in *Law's Empire*.

What does this account say about the issue at hand? The idea of integrity has evident affinities with Dworkin's understanding of judicial interpretation. A judicial decision conforms to the requirements of integrity, when it treats the litigants in accordance with a scheme of principle that can be said to govern previous instances of state action. So integrity can be seen as a moral basis for the interpretive requirement that judges identify the principles that fit and justify past political history, since it is these principles that should guide their decision in the case before them. In addition, the concern for integrity arguably explains why we care for legality. For Dworkin, legality or the rule of law is the value that the law aspires to. He takes it to be commonly accepted that the law meets this aspiration when '[the state's coercive power is] exercised only in accordance with standards established in the right way before that exercise'.[16] It

---

[14] Dworkin, *Hedgehogs* (n 4) 407.

[15] Dworkin notes that a virtue is distinctively legal when 'understanding the value better will help us better to understand what claims of law mean and what makes them true of false'. R Dworkin, *Justice in Robes* (Cambridge MA, Harvard University Press, 2006) 169.

[16] ibid. See also Dworkin, *Law's Empire* (n 3) 93: 'Law insists that force not be used or withheld, no matter how useful that would be to ends in view, no matter how beneficial or noble these ends, except as licensed or required by rights and responsibilities flowing from past political decisions

follows from this understanding of legality that a state that respects legality also thereby manifests integrity. Furthermore, this is not just a happy accident. On the contrary, integrity is what you characteristically get when judges do what they are required to do by law. On this account, their legal duty is precisely to uphold the integrity of the political community. Once again, the hedgehog's method is at work. We interpret our values not one by one but in relation to one another, showing how they support each other. Here Dworkin's aim is to connect our account of law and our account of political obligation. He seeks to show that, if the law goes well, inasmuch as it serves the value that is characteristically linked to it, the political community goes well too, because by adhering to standards of legality it makes itself worthy of its citizens' allegiance. He does that by arguing that we have a legal right or duty if and only if it would be legitimate for a state to enforce that right or duty. That's because the standard imposed by legitimacy and legality is the same, namely integrity.

Do these connections between integrity, interpretation and legality furnish an adequate basis for Dworkin's court-centric view of jurisprudence? There is an obvious difficulty: Dworkin maintains that integrity is also relevant to the responsibility of the legislature. He states that the concern for integrity 'takes hold immediately politics begins and is sustained through legislation and adjudication to enforcement'.[17] Accordingly, alongside integrity in adjudication he identifies a distinct principle of integrity in legislation which 'restricts what our legislators and other lawmakers may properly do in expanding or changing our public standards'.[18] In fact, Dworkin cites as a paradigmatic violation of integrity one that is perpetrated by legislators: checkerboard statutes. Checkerboard statutes are afflicted by 'internal compromises' which aim to split the difference between two opposing sides on a matter of principle. They do so by treating two groups of people in accordance with two different principles, each espoused by one of the opposing political sides, although no principle that either side espouses can account for this differential treatment and in fact the principle of each side condemns the treatment reserved for the other group. Checkerboard statutes could be said to be expedient because they give each side some of what they want. Still, Dworkin thinks they manifest a grave political defect: they lack integrity.

The example of checkerboard statutes suggests that the idea of integrity by itself does not differentiate the moral test we apply to courts and legislatures. If legal theorists must orient their accounts towards integrity, they should look at

---

about when collective force is justified . . . This characterization of the concept of law sets out . . . what is sometimes called "the rule" of law'.

[17] ibid 213.
[18] ibid 217.

the latter as much as the former. Perhaps, then, it is the way that integrity impacts on the judicial role that makes judicial enforceability the litmus test for legality. On Dworkin's view, courts are there primarily to sum up the moral impact of institutional history up to the point of the decision. Once they make a decision, it too becomes part of the institutional history, which future judges must accommodate by recalibrating the scheme of principles that vindicates their practice. But at the time of the decision a judge committed to integrity will always look backwards. He will not look around at what other institutional actors are doing at the same time as the decision. Neither is it part of his official duty to look into the future to predict what effect the decision he makes will have in terms of maintaining a just and well-ordered society.

Now compare the legislative role. Does it also have a backward-looking element? Clearly, it is possible for integrity in legislation to operate diachronically. We can achieve the internal compromise that is typical of checkerboard statutes by splitting it into two separate statutes, enacted one after the other, rather than by incorporating it into one and the same statute. One statute will treat one group of people, say automobile manufacturers, in accordance with the principle championed by one political faction, and the next statute will treat electrical appliances manufacturers in accordance with a competing principle championed by the first faction's political opponents. If the single-blow compromise is problematic from the point of view of political morality, then the step-by-step compromise must be problematic too. 'Integrity is flouted', Dworkin writes, 'whenever a community enacts and enforces different laws each of which is coherent in itself but which cannot be defended together as expressing a coherent ranking of different principles of justice or fairness or procedural due process'.[19] In order to avoid such compromises, legislators minded to uphold their political community's integrity will have to look to their past record. They, as much as judges, will have to interpret the institutional history of their community and act within the constraints imposed by the principles that show that history in its best light. Furthermore, they must resist political offers, expedient though they may be, to negotiate spheres of influence that leave the legal system a patchwork of conflicting principles.[20]

---

[19] ibid 184.

[20] Likewise, integrity sets limits upon the extent to which the legislator of today may correct what he perceives to be mistakes of the past. I am not talking here about decisions that amount to egregious injustices; Dworkin's account has a built-in moral constraint that denies such decisions gravitational force in the name of integrity. See ibid. On the character of this constraint, see also D Smith, 'The Many Faces of Political Integrity' in S Hershovitz (ed), *Exploring Law's Empire: The Jurisprudence of Ronald Dworkin* (Oxford, Oxford University Press, 2006) 119. Even so, there will be decisions which are perceived by one political faction as sub-optimal, albeit not egregiously so. Integrity dictates that, once that faction ascends to power, it should give effect to those decisions, but justice dictates that their lingering influence should be cut short.

And yet, that's what legislators do all the time.[21] Sure enough, cynical legislators will engage in all sorts of internal compromises if they can get away with it. But, much more innocuously, legislators create patchworks that diachronic integrity would condemn whenever their party wins a majority in the legislative body on a platform which is at odds with the policies of the previous majority. It is here that the verdict of integrity seems to diverge, depending on whether it applies to judges or legislators. Thus, it potentially opens up the space for a tighter connection between legality and integrity in adjudication. On the one hand, it would be counter-intuitive to think that the new majority would violate *legality*, were it to refuse to reconcile its policies with the principles espoused by the previous majority. If we are convinced by Dworkin, we may come to regret such a failure on the part of the new majority, but it is not particularly clear what institutional sanction attends it. In particular, we are reluctant to say that the new majority has made a *legal* mistake. On the other hand, matters are different for courts. If a judicial decision fails the test of integrity because it does not flow from political history in the right way, it will rightly be quashed on appeal. Its mistake is more readily treated as a *legal* one. So even though integrity governs both the legislative and the judicial role, it appears to pose a very weak requirement in the first case and a stringent one in the second.

What explains the moral difference between integrity in adjudication and legislation? Recall that, for Dworkin, the characteristic of legal rights is that they can be enforced on-demand. As already mentioned, these rights do not exhaust what political rights we can claim under what we take to be the best conception of political justice. It is not incoherent to maintain that I have a political right to a minimum income and, in the same breath, that I do not have an enforceable right to a minimum income. In fact, the mere existence of a political right to a minimum income does not even entail a right that appropriate legislation be enacted.[22] What stands in the way is the need for the political community to somehow commit to the right to a minimum income. Given the fact of reasonable pluralism in politics, one cannot presume that one's political community will follow one's preferred conception of political justice; as Bernard Williams puts it, one cannot 'suppose that all the urgency and dignity of justice

---

[21] Dworkin is of course aware of this: 'We know that our own legal structure constantly violates integrity in this less dramatic way . . . We cannot bring all the various statutory and common law rules our judges enforce under a single coherent scheme of principle.' (Dworkin, *Law's Empire*, (n 3) 184) Not everyone thinks that this is a problem or that, even if it is, integrity in Dworkin's sense is the answer. Jeremy Waldron lists a number of possibilities, which are prima facie appealing or at least not outright reprehensible. Importantly, he suggests that principled political disagreement among members of a political community need not be seen as something that legal interpretation must attempt to transcend or paper over. See J Waldron, 'The Circumstances of Integrity' (1997) 3 *Legal Theory* 1, 4.
[22] B Williams, *In the Beginning was the Deed* (G Hawthorn ed, Princeton NJ, Princeton University Press, 2005) 124–25.

applies to one's own political interpretation of justice'.[23] Mind you, a political community need not expressly recognise a certain political right, for it to become enforceable. As we have noted time and again, for an interpretivist it is the *principles* underlying the decisions rather than the decisions by themselves that determine the content of our legal rights and duties. The point is that only once the political community has committed in the right way, whatever that is, can one presume that one's preferred understanding of one's political rights is vested with 'the urgency and dignity of justice'. Arguably, what marks this shift is on-demand judicial enforceability. When I claim that a right of mine is judicially enforceable on demand, I thereby assert that I do not need to look over my shoulder to see whether the rest of my fellow-citizens are prepared to go along – they have already committed to granting me this right. I can demand its enforcement precisely because it is already equipped with the urgency and dignity of justice. By contrast, when I put forward a claim of right in the course of democratic deliberation, I implicitly accept that the matter is not yet settled; there is still some convincing – or winning – to be done. It is of course no accident that the struggle over the content of our political rights ordinarily takes place in the legislature. This is the forum where our political differences and disagreements play out and a solution that takes them into account is forged – sometimes in a winner-takes-all fashion. This is not what courts are for. Since they are entrusted with enforcing rights on demand, their decisions must as a general matter track the commitments of a political community rather than make new ones. It is therefore appropriate that they be governed by the backward-looking principle of integrity. For them, legality holds sway.

I want to offer two critiques of this picture of the division of labour between courts and the legislature. First, even if accurate, it would still be insufficient for our purposes. Granted, it would give us an answer to the question why judicially enforceable rights are subject to a different and stricter moral test that makes reference to past political decisions. But we need an account of integrity, according to which it applies to legislation as well as courts, though not with the same stringency. What we have got so far explains only why it applies to the latter but not the former. There seems to be a mismatch here. On the one hand, if integrity pertains to the 'urgency and dignity of justice' which warrants on-demand judicial enforcement, it is not clear why legislators should bother for it at all. On the other hand, if integrity is the answer to the problem of legitimacy, then it must capture legislative action; after all, legitimacy should be the concern of all public officials. We can put the same point slightly differently: if integrity is primarily a judicial virtue, we stretch it beyond recognition in order to extend it to the legislature. If, by contrast, integrity is already sufficiently comprehensive to encompass the legislative role, then it does not give legal theorists a reason to

---

[23] ibid 125.

focus on the rights that are judicially enforceable in their study of the nature of law.

In fact – and here I turn to my second critique –, there is something formalistic about the proposal we are examining, insofar as it makes the judicial role the narrow focus of integrity. Should it turn out that the legislative role allows compromises that offend integrity, many of those will then be reflected in judicial interpretation as well. There is only so much that judges can do to bring the disparate policies of successive legislative majorities under a single scheme of principles.[24] For instance, they can intervene when the legislative change has violated the requirement of fair notice, in order to mitigate the negative effects caused by the frustration of citizens' legitimate expectations. But it would be impermissible for them to disregard a fresh political decision just because it is not aligned with a previously established course of action. How else can it be, if we grant that integrity in legislation does not render that decision in some sense legally mistaken? What is more, it is not entirely clear what judges ought to do in the case of the cynical legislator, either. For one thing, the cynical legislator's decisions stay in the books, notwithstanding that they are tainted by cynicism, unless they contravene constitutional provisions that furnish criteria for the legal bindingness of those decisions. Predictably, quite a few cynical compromises will pass under this radar. In both these cases the dependence of judicial duty on legislative decisions returns to haunt us. If integrity requires judges to impose coherence on whatever legislative decision has landed on their laps, then it arrives on the scene too late.[25] By this I mean that there seems to be little value in upholding the equality of citizens in the limited way that integrity, thus understood, recommends, and whatever value there is should be easily outweighed by considerations of justice. If so, it can hardly qualify as a basis for political legitimacy.

I am not saying that judges have a legal duty to give effect to whatever decision comes from the legislature. In the interpretivist framework that duty, if it exists, must be grounded in moral considerations counting in favour of them doing so. It may well be that those considerations will require that we discount the cynical legislator's decisions. What I have tried to show is that those considerations are not powered by an overarching concern for the integrity of the legal system. They have more to do with the value of democratic government and justice and with the way those values can be combined in real political life. If these values can do the trick, there is no independent role for integrity. I will revisit this point in the following section.

---

[24] Jeremy Waldron has explored these limits of integrity in J Waldron, 'Did Dworkin Ever Answer the Crits?' in Hershovitz (ed), *Exploring Law's Empire* (n 20) 155.

[25] I have mounted a structurally similar criticism against Dworkin's distinction between principle and policy in D Kyritsis, 'Principles, Policies and the Power of Courts' (2007) 20 *Canadian Journal of Law and Jurisprudence* 379.

I have so far sought to cast doubt on Dworkin's claim that integrity is a good candidate for explaining the predicament facing judges in their official capacity in systems where they govern together with the legislature. However, even assuming that adjudication did answer a pressing moral problem that can adequately be distinguished from the one falling on legislators, it remains to be seen whether answering that problem is the distinctive virtue of law. We have reason to be sceptical about that, too. We should hope that our accounts of the virtue of law do not drive as sharp a wedge between courts and their fellow-participants in the project of governing. It is with this aim in mind that I now turn to the positive part of my argument.

IV. LEGALITY AND SEPARATION OF POWERS

I suggested in the previous section that integrity, if it exists at all, is an elusive political virtue. Nonetheless it captures some key elements of the idea of governance by law. Thus, it is natural to associate state coercion with the enforcement power of courts and hence legality with the constraints and standards that govern the exercise of that power. But this conception of legality is overly narrow. I want to propose instead a more comprehensive conception of legality which encompasses the legislative role. To this effect, I too will follow the hedgehog's approach. I shall interpret legality in the light of a further normative ideal that has not been given much attention by jurisprudents in recent years. This is the ideal of separation of powers. Further, I shall contend that this is the value characteristically embodied by the joint project of governing in which courts and the legislature participate, when that project goes well. Having thus spelled out the nature of the relationship between courts and the legislature, I shall then go on to weave integrity back into the picture. Predictably, it will be relegated to a secondary role. I shall argue that whether judges care for integrity or not, as Dworkin insists, they care for a lot else besides.

A. Systemic Legitimacy

Dworkin's court-centric understanding of legality and, accordingly, of the subject matter of jurisprudence has been challenged by constitutional theorists like Lawrence Sager. They claim that the 'adjudicated constitution' is just one part of the constitution; another part, they argue, remains judicially 'under-enforced' because it is primarily directed at legislators. But according to these theorists, this does not mean that the judicially non-enforceable portion of the constitution is not part of the law.[26] In fact, given that it furnishes a warrant for the

---

[26] cp Sager, 'Material Rights' (n 13). For Sager's more general account of constitutional interpretation, see L Sager, *Justice in Plainclothes* (New Haven CT, Yale University Press, 2006).

political action of officials other than judges, 'it seems both awkward and mis-leading'[27] not to treat it as such.

It seems to me that underpinning the 'under-enforcement' view outlined above lurks an alternative understanding of legality, which I shall seek to tease out. Start by taking off the table a distracting thought. The under-enforcement view does not take issue with Dworkin over the *scope* of judicial power (though such a disagreement will possibly crop up further downstream). For one thing, Dworkin's court-centrism is not meant to issue into a defence of judicial activ-ism. Dworkin takes great care to stress that the political rights that are properly enforced by the courts may diverge from what utopian political morality dic-tates. That is because, as we have already seen, judicially enforced political rights are for him sensitive to 'structuring principles'.[28] These are moral princi-ples that make the history of a political community 'morally pertinent'[29] and include 'principles about the best allocation of political power in a coercive state'.[30] Thus, Dworkin countenances the possibility that such principles will direct judges to abstain from enforcing a political right by virtue of the fact that the scheme of separation of powers in a certain state assigns that right's protec-tion to another state institution, as theorists such as Sager maintain. Likewise, although the under-enforcement view furnishes the basis for a theory of judicial self-restraint, its difference from the Dworkinian view goes deeper than that. More specifically, it is, I think, animated by the belief that legality has what we might call a systemic as well as an adjudicative dimension. Along the adjudica-tive dimension legality is perhaps promoted by courts that enforce the rights of individuals flowing from past political decisions. Along the systemic dimension, by contrast, it is served by the existence of mechanisms, judicial and non-judicial alike, whose function is to check abuses of political power.[31]

---

[27]   Sager, 'Material Rights' (n 13) 589.

[28]   Dworkin, *Hedgehogs* (n 4) 409. See also Dworkin, *Law's Empire* (n 3) 401: '[T]he content of the law [is] sensitive to different kinds of constraints, special to judges, that are not necessarily con-straints for other officials or institutions. When judges interpret legal practice as a whole, they find reasons of different sorts, specifically applying to judges, why they should *not* declare as present law the principles and standards that would provide the most coherent account of the substantive deci-sions of that practice'.

[29]   Dworkin, *Hedgehogs* (n 4) 409.

[30]   ibid 413. These structuring principles are among the 'constitutive and regulative rules' of the institution of the court, in the sense defined in Dworkin, *Taking Rights Seriously* (n 1) 93.

[31]   The connection between law and coercion suggests a further line of inquiry: Rather than start from legality, we explore the moral justification of the coercive power of the state; law then becomes the set of standards that govern the use of that power, and legality is seen as the value that a state exhibits when it uses that power well. Recently, the jurisprudential significance of focusing on coercion has been forcefully asserted in N Stavropoulos, 'The Relevance of Coercion: Some Preliminaries' (2009) 22 *Ratio Juris* 339. Of course, even on this line of inquiry, it may be that the state coerces in a number of ways, only one of which is the on-demand enforcement of certain rights by adjudicative institutions, but establishing this claim goes beyond the scope of this book.

Classic political theorists like Montesquieu and the US founding fathers stressed the importance of such mechanisms and maintained that they exemplify or realise the idea of separation of powers. They regarded separation of powers as denoting more than just the fact that political authority is allocated among multiple state bodies; rather, they saw it as a virtue that political orders must aspire to. That is, they thought that political power is exercised well when it is shared between a variety of institutional actors who work together and at the same time check one another; thus if properly designed, this institutional arrangement is more likely in the long run to create and sustain a just and well-ordered society. This is clear from the following famous extract from *The Spirit of the Laws*:

> [Political liberty] is there only when there is no abuse of power; but constant experience shows us, that every man invested with power is apt to abuse it, and to carry his authority as far as it will go. Is it not strange, though true, to say, that virtue itself has need of limits? . . . To prevent this abuse, it is necessary from the very nature of things, power should be a check to power.[32]

I shall mention a couple of examples to focus the discussion. In many legal systems members of the cabinet are understood to have a responsibility to appear before the legislative body and give account of their actions. In others, the Head of the Executive is recognised as having the power to dissolve the legislative body and call an election under certain conditions. Such duties and powers are commonly thought to have their footing in the constitution, and they are said to exist despite the fact that typically they are not judicially enforceable.[33] At this stage we should refrain from assuming that this sort of ideas and beliefs, however widespread, report existing legal powers and duties rather than merely suggestions for reform.[34] Still, anticipating the ensuing analysis it is important to indicate what makes people hold them. We think that by giving an independently powerful political actor a say in the dissolution of parliament and instituting mechanisms of ministerial responsibility we put in place safeguards against self-serving, reckless and tyrannical government. Clearly, a political majority that can freely determine when to call an election has a powerful

---

[32] Charles de Secondat, Baron de Montesquieu, *The Spirit of the Laws* (1873 rev edn, first published 1748) Bk XI, ch IV, 172–73. That is not to say that the value of legality, as Dworkin understands, is absent from Montesquieu's account. The passage just quoted continues as follows: 'A government may be so constituted, as no man shall be compelled to do things to which the law does not oblige him, nor forced to abstain from things which the law permits'. Note, though, that Montesquieu talks about the constitution of government. This formulation does not seem to favour courts.

[33] Sager gives the related example of Congress enacting a regulatory framework that governs funding decisions of officials. He maintains that we are inclined to say that the officials have a legal duty to comply with the framework, even if their compliance is monitored by Congress only. See Sager, 'Material Rights' (n 13) 589.

[34] I am grateful to Nicos Stavropoulos for pressing this point.

weapon for extracting the submission of individual MPs and of the opposition. Equally, a minister will think twice before abusing her power if she knows that she is likely to be called to account for her actions in a public forum before public officials with their own political mandate (and perhaps a strong incentive to embarrass ministers).

The systemic dimension of legality – its connection with separation of powers – is suppressed by Dworkin, even when he refers to Montesquieu. Rather, Dworkin takes from Montesquieu the rough idea that in the tripartite distinction of government powers, the power of the judiciary is the enforcement of individual rights on demand. Thus, in the course of drawing the distinction between legal and legislative rights he remarks that 'legal rights can sensibly be distinguished from other political rights only if [a community] has at least an embryonic version of the separation of powers Montesquieu described'.[35] But, of course, Montesquieu's distinction of the three governmental powers has been widely criticised as overly simplistic, even for his time.[36] In particular, the role he reserves for the judicial function grossly overlooks the creativity involved in legal interpretation. Moreover, it is impossible to reconcile the judicial function, as Montesquieu understands it, with the Herculean task Dworkin assigns judges in his work or with practices of judicial review of legislation for its compatibility with constitutional norms. Against this background, Dworkin's reference to Montesquieu is puzzling. It assumes broad agreement on Montesquieu's understanding of the role of courts where there is none, and despite the fact that an agreement would not serve his purposes, even if it existed. More importantly, Dworkin's casual reference to Montesquieu passes on an opportunity to appreciate the full import of separation of powers. Though framed in essentialist language, Montesquieu's scheme of government powers is, as Laurence Claus has persuasively argued, best understood as primarily driven by the structural concern identified above; in other words, it was meant to be a theoretical response to the political imperative to prevent the abuse of power through its distribution among multiple actors. The same applies to his definition of the judicial function. We can make best sense of it by viewing it – at least in part – as a component of a scheme of separation of powers. If we favour a different definition, we have to defend it – also – by appeal to the same idea.

How can we give separation of powers its proper place? There is, it seems to me, a natural home in political morality for the kinds of concerns associated with this idea. But in order to identify that home, we must make a fresh start. Rather than adopt the perspective of the rights that individuals can assert in court, we must look at the legal system from the perspective of its various institutions cooperating to keep the political community in good working order. Why

---

[35] Dworkin, *Hedgehogs* (n 4) 404.
[36] See the detailed analysis in L Claus, 'Montesquieu's Mistakes and the True Meaning of Separation' (2005) 25 *Oxford Journal of Legal Studies* 419.

do that? Some will probably complain that this is a distraction. They will argue that the nub of the moral problem that law is an answer to is that in political life we can sometimes enlist the coercive force of the state to satisfy some demand of ours. Now, there is no denying that the ability to do so is formidable and stands in need of justification. What can we say to justify it? Dworkin contends we should approach this problem from the judge's perspective, retail so to speak. But it seems that a principal guarantee for our rights and for the proper exercise of coercion in a political society is the existence of a structure of government whose operation over time ensures the effective realisation of justice.[37]

To unpack the importance of this form of guarantee we need to return to the theory of political legitimacy. Let's start with a commonsensical observation. Political philosophy is not only concerned with our rights and duties in a perfectly just political society. Neither is it only concerned with the rights and duties we have given that there are certain institutions in place whose job is to govern us. It is also concerned with the way those institutions are arranged so that they are geared towards justice. This latter concern is well illustrated in the four-stage sequence that John Rawls envisages in Part Two of *A Theory of Justice*.[38] After identifying the two principles of justice, Rawls turns to the problem of selecting 'the most effective constitution, the constitution that satisfies the principles of justice and is best calculated to lead to just and effective legislation'.[39] Rawls discusses this problem in the context of determining the 'grounds and limits of political duty and obligation'.[40] This is as it should be. Institutional forms are absolutely crucial for political legitimacy. Consider, first, that, an essential function of politics is to fix what ought to be done in a way that overcomes the problem of intractable reasonable disagreement. Institutions are there to achieve that. So we need to design them, in order to make them fit for purpose. Consider also that even under the most favourable circumstances a political regime can only be nearly just, and so it cannot properly function unless citizens are prepared to comply with policies that are unjust or at least sub-

---

[37] Not all political philosophers agree that the justification of state coercion is the aim of theories of political legitimacy. Many take the view that such theories primarily seek to explain and justify political authority, which they take to be the power of the state to put us under obligations by telling us what we ought to do. It goes beyond the scope of this book to adjudicate between these different views. Since my immediate goal is to criticise Dworkin's account of legality, I focus on the theory of political legitimacy that is most congenial to it. In addition, I do not discuss the legitimacy of a political regime as something separate from its being justified to use coercive force in a given territory. For many theorists, this distinction is crucial, because different considerations govern legitimacy and justification. See among others AJ Simmons, 'Justification and Legitimacy' (1999) 109 *Ethics* 739. I take it that the considerations canvassed in the text are a significant part of an account of legitimacy, leaving it an open question what other considerations must be present as well. I am indebted to Massimo Renzo for urging me to come clean on this issue.

[38] J Rawls, *A Theory of Justice* (Cambridge MA, Belknap Press, 1971) 195–201.

[39] ibid 197.

[40] ibid 196. cp ibid 353–55.

optimal, as far as justice is concerned. This allowance extends the moral warrant of political society to affect our lives. It also necessitates that we make
judgements about what outcomes certain forms of government are likely to
produce. As Rawls puts it, we must determine the conditions under which 'in
the long run the burden of injustice [is] more or less evenly distributed over
different groups in society'.[41]

Structural considerations play a crucial role in answering these aspects of the
problem of political legitimacy. They are meant to give an assurance that the
agents of governance of a political society will on the whole tend to act justly
and efficiently. Without such assurance, we cannot reasonably expect others to
do their part. At the very least, we increase the appeal and likelihood of defec-
tion. Political obligation, as is often noted, is not a one-off thing. It must be
grounded in a standing disposition to obey. A government that is structured in
the right way strengthens this disposition. Even when it enacts a policy with
which I disagree or inflicts an injustice on me (albeit one, for which it has a moral
warrant for obedience), my faith in it is not undermined. It is not unreasonable
for me to believe that things will be different next time round and thus willingly
assume the cost of compliance on this occasion.

I propose we use the concept of separation of powers to collect together such
structural considerations. As already mentioned, this usage of the concept
should be familiar from the classical political theory of Montesquieu, John
Locke and the founding fathers. The way I will be using it, separation of powers
comprises two types of consideration, those that pertain to the proper division
of government power and those that pertain to checks and balances.[42] The division of labour dimension of separation of powers evaluates institutional
arrangements by the extent to which they assign a certain government power to
the institution that is well suited to exercise it. The checks and balances dimension reflects the importance of putting in place institutional mechanisms that
monitor the exercise of government power and can effectively prevent its abuse.
From the perspective of separation of powers, then, the joint project between
courts and the legislature goes well if, among other things, it is organised on the
basis of a reasonable division of labour and incorporates an adequate system of
checks and balances.[43]

---

[41]   ibid 355.
[42]   See generally MJC Vile, *Constitutionalism and the Separation of Powers*, 2nd edn (Indianapolis,
Liberty Fund, 1998).
[43]   Separation of powers is further fleshed out by appeal to a range of more concrete considerations of political and institutional morality, such as democracy, institutional independence, expertise, efficiency and the like. These considerations help specify whether it is morally appropriate to
assign this or that state institution a certain government function. In this way, they add more flesh
to the constitutional division of labour.

B. Legality without Integrity

All this may be well and good, but what does it have to do with legality? Answering this question will provide the bridge between our account of the problem of political legitimacy and the theory of law. Recall that legality recommends that our rights and duties be sensitive to institutional history. Separation of powers explains why this is so without relying on a dubious ideal of political integrity. It furnishes considerations about institutional competence etc that constitute (part of) the ground for judicial decisions; these considerations typically dictate that courts give effect to the past political decisions of other state institutions such as the legislature or, more generally, heed those political decisions in determining what is within their power to do in the joint project of governing. Take division of labour considerations. The flip side of the prescription that a certain power be exercised by a state institution is that other institutions respect that assignment and, perhaps, also assist in the exercise of the relevant power, depending on their own institutional credentials. The C-L relationship provides an apt illustration. For a host of institutional reasons, courts are well placed to give effect to legislative decisions. This, we might say, is one of the powers they ought to have under the scheme of separation of powers governing their relationship with the legislature. A judicial determination in accordance with that scheme is, all else equal, legitimate by virtue of the fact that it is the product of a system of governance organised in a way that addresses the systemic dimension of legitimacy.

In the previous chapter, I noted that the courts' duty to further legislative decisions is also sensitive to considerations pertaining to the content of the rights and duties produced by those decisions. There I gave a general argument for this claim. In a nutshell it goes like this: the joint project of governing, in which courts and the legislature participate, is supposed to be geared towards the realisation of justice. In principle, individual participants have a reason to assist in the implementation of a decision by a fellow-participant, provided that decision reasonably advances that cause, even if it is sub-optimal from the point of view of justice. The fact that legal duty is determined by the right combination of considerations of content and considerations of institutional design reflects both that the project of governing aims at justice and that it is joint. Hence, there is no need to search for the kind of coherence in the law that integrity holds to be essential. What makes it legitimate to have a certain legal duty is that it flows from the correct principles of political justice, as realised in a specific institutional structure.[44] In turn, deviation from the requirements of

---

[44] As Gerald Postema has put it: 'Integrity . . . simply is justice properly situated in politics, keeping the essential tension between the ideal and consensual dimensions of justice clearly in sight. The moral force of integrity lies, at least in part, in the need to approximate justice in the political

political justice is only allowed if it is compensated by institutional considerations. The idea that the state must additionally act on the same principles across the board, in a single voice, is neither here nor there.

Of course, what I have said so far is compatible with integrity in the much weaker sense that acting on the correct principles of political justice is also acting consistently.[45] As Scott Hershovitz has recently argued, courts have a general moral reason to exhibit integrity in their judgements, namely that

> whatever doubt we have about particular moral views, we are confident that the demands of morality are coherent. We are also confident that morality does not demand that we act capriciously or whimsically in matters of importance. Thus, if we are striving to act morally, we will act with integrity.[46]

Hershovitz is here offering a variation on the theme that treating like cases alike is '*one* essential element of the concept of justice'.[47] It is clear that on his understanding, as in mine, integrity is not a distinct political value, but an element of the realisation of justice within an institutional structure.

Note also that this modest type of integrity is obviously important for any official, not just the judge. In this way, we avoid having to choose whether integrity only applies to judges and not legislators, or to both, where either option is fraught with difficulties. Instead, we can say that legislators and judges care about the same thing, namely justice, but that the extent to which they may pursue it is constrained by separation of powers. In addition, since they occupy different positions in the scheme of separation of powers, they are constrained to varying degrees. Typically, legislators are given more leeway to develop and change public policy because – at least in the legal systems with which we are most familiar – they possess democratic credentials which are taken to justify this assignment of power. On the other hand, the lack of such credentials explains why judges have for the most part a subservient role to that of the legislature.[48] Naturally, legislators, too, must observe certain outer boundaries. Nevertheless, we are not forced to think of these boundaries as precluding the kind of change of policy that is so familiar in democratic politics.

---

circumstances in which we find ourselves'. See G Postema, 'Integrity: Justice in Workclothes' (1997) 82 *Iowa Law Review* 821, 843. In this intriguing article Postema goes on to defend an account of integrity that is much closer to Dworkin's than the one advanced here, basing it on his highly original conception of fidelity, but I cannot explore it in any further detail here.

[45] See S Hershovitz, 'Integrity and *Stare Decisis*' in Hershovitz (ed), *Exploring Law's Empire* (n 20) 103.

[46] ibid 114 (citation omitted).

[47] See HLA Hart, *The Concept of Law*, 2nd edn with a new postscript (Oxford, Clarendon Press, 1994) 185–86; See also D Réaume, 'Is Integrity a Value? Dworkin's Theory of Legal Obligation' (1989) 39 *University of Toronto Law Journal* 380.

[48] For a comparison of the constitutional position of the two bodies with particular reference to the legitimacy of constitutional review, see D Kyritsis, 'Constitutional Review in Representative Democracy' (2012) 32 *Oxford Journal of Legal Studies* 297.

Still, there is arguably one respect in which the integrity-based account of political legitimacy seems to fare better than the alternative defended here. On one reading, integrity is supposed to be able to secure legitimacy in the face of reasonable and persistent political disagreement. The idea is that, even though we disagree about justice, we acquire an obligation to submit to the authority of a political community when it treats us according to the same conception of equal treatment that it had implemented in the past. Such a community preserves the sense that 'no one [is] left out, that we are all in politics together for better or worse, that no one may be sacrificed, like wounded left on the battlefield, to the crusade for justice overall'.[49] The account of the project of governing I am arguing for could be said to authorise legal officials to pursue the type of monolithic crusade for justice overall, and thus to be *pro tanto* defective from the point of view of legitimacy.

To evaluate this challenge, we must be clear what the alleged problem is. I do not have the space to venture into a full-blown exploration of the significance of disagreement in the context of the theory of political legitimacy.[50] For present purposes, it suffices to focus on the relative merit of the justice-based account of legitimacy vis-à-vis Dworkin's integrity-based one. We can begin by noting that the latter does not state that the use of the coercive force of the state is legitimate only when *it is generally agreed* that integrity licenses it. It is thus not supposed to cure controversy as a matter of fact. It is to be expected that many citizens will disagree that a given instance of state coercion passes the test of integrity, even if the official believes in good faith that it does. *They* will certainly believe they are left behind. Maybe then, it is not what citizens *believe* integrity requires but what it actually requires that determines whether an instance of state coercion is legitimate. Accordingly, the fact that some citizens mistakenly hold the opposite view does not impinge on its legitimacy. But on this version of the claim, the integrity-based account loses its alleged advantage over the justice-based account. If an appeal to the correct – though controversial – view of integrity leaves no one behind, then surely so does an appeal to the correct – though controversial – view of what justice requires within an institutional structure.

Up to this point, I have made room for the alternative account starting from the theory of political legitimacy. But does it have any resonance with legal practice? Or does it paint a picture that is too far removed from the phenomenology of the C-L legal systems that we are familiar with? Of course, it is impossible to survey the wide variety of constitutional arrangements in actual C-L legal systems. What I shall try to do instead is look at some recurring puzzles that confront C-L legal systems through the lens of the account I have put forward.

---

[49] Dworkin, *Law's Empire* (n 3) 213.

[50] For two diametrically opposed views, see J Raz, 'Disagreement in Politics' (1998) 43 *American Journal of Jurisprudence* 25 and J Waldron, *Law and Disagreement* (Oxford, Oxford University Press, 1999).

To begin with, it seems well suited to explain practices of constitutional review. Such practices grant judges the authority to refuse to apply or invalidate statutes when these are found to pass a certain threshold of injustice. Many legal theorists, including some positivists, claim that this threshold reflects a moral condition of legal validity. For them, while the legislature is a norm-creating institution, its decisions have normative effect provided that they also meet moral standards. It is this type of complex criterion of legal validity that practices of constitutional review track. But the explanation looks slightly different on the revised interpretivist account. Here, the focus is on the terms of the joint project of governing, more specifically the terms under which courts assist the legislature. Nothing in the account precludes that, in discharging their duties under the joint project of governing, courts may sometimes make direct reference to principles of justice. In fact, the account gives us a good reason for the courts having this power: in exercising it, they will be performing an important checks and balances function and can thus improve overall compliance with justice. Note, though, that this does not negate the link between separation of powers and legality. Legality only requires that our rights and duties depend on institutional history, if it is justified that they should so depend. Separation of powers justifies this dependence, but at the same time places limits to it.

Natural lawyers who claim that moral standards necessarily figure among the criteria of the legal validity of norms created by the legislature are hard-pressed to explain why practices of constitutional review are themselves contingent. The account offered here avoids these difficulties. Although, like other natural law theories, it is committed to the view that justice is necessarily a determinant of legal duty, it maintains that their bearing on legal duty is mediated by considerations of institutional design.[51] This gives the account sufficient slack to account for the contingency of practices of constitutional review. The reasons of institutional design counting in favour of constitutional review are not overriding. They have to be balanced against other reasons of institutional design, such as efficiency and democracy and the need to avert abuse of power by the courts themselves. The interplay of these reasons will determine the extent of the courts' supervisory role. This exercise is unlikely to yield a one-size-fits-all scheme of judicial supervision. A lot will depend on contingent characteristics of specific legal systems.

It is not only constitutional review which is better explicated in light of separation of powers, but also the day-to-day dependence of the judicial role on legislative decisions. In particular, the separation of powers analysis allows us to recognise doctrinal differences across legal systems, when it comes to issues such as methods of statutory interpretation, the role and weight of legislators' intention, and the relationship between statute and judge-made law. Such doctrinal

---

[51] This has important consequences for legal epistemology, which I explore in section VI below.

differences reflect different arrangements of the C-L relationship, underlain by different combinations of principles of institutional design and content. On the contrary, the supposition that there exists a common concept of rule-application that unites all the instances of judicial reliance on legislative acts and decisions leads either to vacuity or parochialism. It leads to vacuity, if it blocks out questions, say, about the relevance of intention in interpretation as not pertaining to rule-application. It leads to parochialism, if it attempts to present one contingent type of judicial reliance on legislative acts and decisions as paradigmatic and then to squeeze all other types into this one mould.

C. The Scope of Jurisprudence Revisited

I said earlier that one aim of this chapter is to challenge the court-centric view of jurisprudence. With the help of the preceding analysis we can see why. If legality is interpreted in the light of the ideal of separation of powers, then it must capture our systemic response to the problem of political legitimacy. For example, on this view the legal interpreter would do well to pay attention to the judicially under-enforced portion of the constitution, insofar as that portion defines the powers of key participants – other than the judiciary – in the joint project of governing. Their contribution, even if it is not judicially enforceable, performs a crucial legitimating function. Given the connection between political legitimacy and legality, the scope of the study of law is accordingly broadened. It comprises the normative standards, adherence to which provides a systemic response to the problem of legitimacy, whether or not the enforcement of those standards is assigned to the judiciary and their judicial protection is available on demand to the individual citizen.

To this line of argument the following objection may be raised: if separation of powers is so integral to political legitimacy, why not make requirements of separation of powers judicially enforceable? Why not say that, until they are bestowed with judicial enforceability, they are no more than recommendations for reform? This objection would sting examples like the ones I mentioned above where state actors are understood to have powers and duties, whose enforcement lies beyond the remit of the courts. It will not suffice to point to the fact that some of these rights and duties have a textual basis, say, in the constitution. The texts of constitutions contain all sorts of statements, including programmatic, exhortative and symbolic ones, and we need theory to discern their true normative content.

Now, as it is precisely the connection between the existence of a legal right or duty and judicial enforceability that is in dispute here, we must be careful not to beg the question in either direction. That is, we must be able to explain why separation of powers would or would not single out judicial enforceability as the crucial benchmark for legal duty. It cannot be because effectiveness requires judicial enforceability. It doesn't. Other types of pressure, such as electoral disapproval, bad press and the availability of counter-measures, will often ensure that the minister will not fail to appear before the legislative body to answer questions and the head of the executive will exercise her power to dissolve parliament responsibly. Conversely, it is not necessarily the case that judicial enforcement is always preferable or even particularly effective. We should not forget that, despite their independence, courts are not external to the political regime. They have particular features, strengths and weaknesses, and in light of those they interact with the other state institutions in certain ways and not others. This does not mean that it is never warranted for them to take on the other branches of government. But it does mean that whether they should will vary. Although in some areas separation of powers will dictate that an issue be decided by a court of law – criminal charges are a good example –, in others it will encourage institutional cooperation, competition and checks and balances without need for judicial intervention.[52] The very task of enforcing certain rights on individual demand must be seen from the same perspective. It is now regarded as an option for institutional design whose appropriateness is also assessed against separation of power standards, importantly the imperative that 'power should be a check to power'. Like any other option, it comes with advantages and disadvantages, and we cannot be certain that the advantages will always outweigh the disadvantages.

In light of this more complicated picture of legal institutions, it appears unwarranted to treat as legal only those standards, which judicial decisions strive to track, and to relegate all the other standards that I have examined to the sphere of mere political aspiration. First of all, these further standards are crucial from the point of view of political morality, since they go a long way towards defining what a political regime must look like to have a good claim to moral legitimacy; in fact, judicial power itself makes better sense in light of these overarching standards. Secondly and related, these standards offer a reasonable articulation of the meaning of legality, inasmuch as they explain why it is important for legal duty to depend on institutional history. Thirdly, their force is undiminished by the fact that they cannot be judicially enforced on demand.

Needless to say, the proposal offered here is likely to take legal philosophers – and perhaps interpretivists more than others – out of their comfort zone. For Dworkin's privileging of the judicial perspective echoes a common sentiment among legal scholars, and I do not mean only those trained in common law systems.[53] If we want to know what the content of the law is, it is natural to turn

---

[52] A classic study of the latter kind of institutional interaction is J Choper, *Judicial Review and the National Political Process* (Chicago, The University of Chicago Press, 1980).

[53] Carl Schmitt criticises this tendency in the context of the Weimar Republic in C Schmitt, *Der Hüter der Verfassung* (Munich and Leipzig, Dunkler/Humblot, 1926). He attributes it to a formalist

to those officials whose job it is to interpret it. Besides, given that these officials carry out their task by offering a rationale for their interpretation in an articulate and sustained way, we can, so the thinking goes, glean from their judgements the considerations that determine whether something is part of the law. As Dworkin puts it, in courts the interpretive attitude that is the touchstone of legal practice is 'dressed for inspection'.[54] The version of interpretivism I have put forward opens up a different perspective from which to look at legal practice, the perspective of the constitutional designer as it were. From that perspective courts make an important, albeit local, contribution to the law. Because it is important, our scheme of separation of powers must be able to explain it. Because it is local, the view it presents of the law's dress is partial; separation of powers inevitably transcends it. Below we shall rehearse some reasons why its locality sometimes makes focusing on the judicial perspective misleading, too.

D. Back to Integrity

It was argued above that the separation of powers analysis displaces integrity from the role Dworkin had reserved for it.[55] In order to assess the legitimacy of the extant distribution of burdens and benefits in a political society, we only need to consult justice, not integrity. It's just that, because of the systemic dimension of political legitimacy, the requirements of justice must be combined with institutional considerations. However, the fact that integrity is not the value that underpins legality does not mean that it – or something like it – should be completely discarded. But if it does have a role to play, that role is likely to arise further downstream. Especially in legal systems with strong doctrines of stare decisis, a value akin to integrity may turn out to be crucial in determining judicial duty. I have in mind things like the importance of consistency for fair notice. Now, fair notice is not the same as integrity. The former is sensitive to the expectations of the group of people who take their cue from the sayings and doings of the court, whereas the latter is not. Still the two principles seem to lead to similar results in most cases. At any rate, even if integrity, thus understood, has a special bearing on the legitimacy of judicial decision-making, it must be combined with the institutional requirements that also attach to the judicial role

conception of the rule of law principle (*Rechtstaat*), which underpins the view that the protection of the constitution is the ultimate preserve of the judiciary. He notes acerbically: 'Sobald man das Recht in Justiz verwandelt und dann Justiz nochmals formalisiert, indem man alles Justiz nennt, was eine richterliche Behörde tut, ist das Problem des Rechtstaates schnell gelöst'. (ibid 22) Schmitt's own preference for a plebiscitary President as the guardian of the constitution is rightly vulnerable to criticism as well, but his theoretical point against the default of thinking that the judiciary is the be-all and end-all of constitutionalism stands.

[54] Dworkin, *Law's Empire* (n 3) 413.
[55] See also Smith, 'The Many Faces of Political Integrity' (n 20) 151.

as well as other considerations of content. This is evidence that its role is not basic but secondary.

Alternatively, take Hershovitz's proposal that integrity, understood as principled consistency, is a necessary element of the pursuit of justice. As was already mentioned, both judges and legislators will be driven by the requirements of integrity in this modest incarnation. But again, the measure to which they will display this kind of integrity is checked by the institutional considerations that structure the pursuit of justice (though these, too, must be acted on in a consistent and non-capricious way). For example, the consistent application of a scheme of tort liability that underlies past case law may require that automobile manufacturers also be liable according to the same standard as other mass product industries. But now suppose that a legislative decision explicitly excludes their liability. This is a case where consistency in the application of the liability standard competes with institutional design. On the account offered here, it is their competition that yields the correct legal answer for the court, not consistency taken on its own. Here, too, integrity in this limited sense is shown to have a subsidiary position in the order of justification.

V. GOVERNING TOGETHER?

In the previous section I argued that, in order to understand how law answers the problem of political legitimacy, we must also look at the relationship between state institutions such as the courts and the legislature. I offered separation of powers as the regulative idea for our exploration. I also contended that, seen through this lens, legality itself changes, and with it the philosophical study of law. But so far I have rested content to present this proposal and compare it to Dworkin's original account. It is now time to defend it from a number of objections from further afield.

One objection zeroes in on the idea that the two bodies are involved in a joint project of governing. It could be argued that, although it is entirely plausible to think that officials take each other's acts into account, it does not follow that they participate in a joint activity. Instead, we can think of the acts and decisions of others merely as constraints on the pursuit of whatever agenda a given official wishes to pursue. According to the objection, judges and legislators cannot be indifferent to one another's actions and decisions. If they want to have their agenda furthered, they must act in ways that anticipate those actions and decisions. In fact, judges and legislators may have a moral reason to take each other's actions into account. Suppose that a legislator wants to remedy a grave social injustice but that his proposal is seen with distrust by the conservative judiciary. Clearly, he has a moral reason to adjust his strategy, in order to curb or bypass judicial resistance and achieve his morally worthwhile goal. But his moral reason has nothing to do with a putative commitment to a project that he shares with the judiciary. Michael Bratman captures this by distinguishing mutual responsiveness from mutual commitment and support. He thinks that all three elements ought to be present before we can say of a collective activity that it is a truly joint activity. Responsiveness by itself is not enough. The legislator may be *responsive* to the acts of other officials, but without being *committed* to a common goal or prepared to *support* other officials to perform their part in achieving it.

Not only is an alternative description readily available, but there also seems to be good reason not to go along with the suggestion that the two bodies are involved in a joint activity. Consider, first, that their relationship is often antagonistic. Especially in cases of constitutional moment, courts and legislatures clash. One need only think of the constitutional and political impasse that was caused by the striking down of social legislation during the early years of the New Deal. Neither does it seem to be true that the acts of the two bodies are united by a common purpose. Legislators are more likely to be motivated by a political platform or by a desire to promote the interests of their constituents. Sometimes judges themselves will be driven by partisan agendas, which may or may not coincide with those of the legislators.

Let me address the negative side of the objection first. It would be a mistake to make much of the existence of dissonance in the relationship between courts and the legislature. Our mistake would be two-fold. To begin with, we would be ignoring that joint activities do not require that the aims of participants are identical through and through. It is sufficient that they are shared up to an appropriate point. Beyond that point, they may diverge or even conflict. Two people walking side by side are still taking a walk together, even if one is there because he enjoys the other's company and the other because he wants to ask a favour. The legislator may use his political power to crush the judiciary, if it opposes his plans. But as long as he continues to pursue his plans in a way that takes proper heed of the judiciary, he can be said to participate, at some level, in a joint activity with it.

Secondly, competition, disagreement and conflict are not necessarily incompatible with participation in a joint activity. In fact, such elements are sometimes seen as partly constitutive of the joint activity and conducive to the achievement of its aim. A good illustration of this is provided by James Madison's classic exposition of the point of separation of powers in the US Constitution. Madison thought that 'ambition must be made to counteract ambition'.[56] He anticipated that agents of government would be driven by a desire for self-aggrandisement, but he believed that, if they were pitted against each other, their interests would

---

[56] J Madison, 'The Federalist No. 51' in JE Cooke (ed), *The Federalist* (Middletown CT, Wesleyan University Press, 1961) 331. Of course, Madison was talking about the relationship between Congress and the President but his point can be generalised.

cancel themselves out or keep one another in check. The result would be less state interference with the lives of citizens, which for Madison was the recipe for better government. Turning to courts and the legislature, we do not think, of course, that the former have the political capital to antagonise the latter in pursuit of a partisan agenda. Nor do we necessarily share Madison's faith in smaller government. Be that as it may, as we have seen, a legal system regulated by separation of powers goes well when it also incorporates checks and balances mechanisms. Practices of constitutional review of legislation and other forms of judicial review which pit the two bodies against each other can be seen as such mechanisms.[57] Although there may be cases where the conflict between them gets out of hand, there is nothing disconcerting about it in principle.

More positively, it makes good sense to view the acts of judges and legislators as contributions to a joint plan rather than side-constraints of individual plans in spite of all the conflict and dissonance. Just as a successful joint camping trip is not the same as the separate successful camping trips of two people who just happen to share the same camping plot, so there is a special type of success that is associated with participation in a joint project which is distinct from one official making an individual impact subject to constraints imposed by the acts of other officials. The joint activity of governing tracks that type of success, and conversely the success sheds light on the character of the joint activity. First of all, it is important to note that it is not up to either institution individually to govern. The two institutions are assigned distinct roles which are understood to complement each other. This is most obvious in legal systems with a written constitution which sets out the broad contours of the institutional positions of each and of their relationship. In such an arrangement the two bodies work well precisely when they work together as envisaged by the constitution. The example is an obvious one because it is easier to regard the two institutions as partners in a joint project when that project has been conceived and put into effect by a political actor of superior authority like a constitutional convention. But even in the absence of a written constitution, where the terms of their relationship were never intended by a single political actor (either a person or group of persons) but rather evolved over time such as in the UK, the idea of a joint project is apt to describe their interaction. First, it is more or less stable and systematic. Secondly, it involves elements of mutual commitment and support. Most characteristically, courts display such commitment and support when they defer to the legislature and implement its decisions. But equally they display it when they disregard or even strike down a statute passed by the legislature – assuming, of course, that they have the power to do so. For, they have a duty to defer only to those legislative contributions to the joint project that are worthy of deference. Their role under the project is not always to stay out of the legislature's way, in

---

[57] See Kyritsis, 'Constitutional Review' (n 48).

the same manner that the role of a chessplayer is not to avoid frustrating her opponent. Thus, a legislator that sees his plan for social reform curtailed by the judiciary in the name of, say, due process rights, may well have reason to feel defeated or angry. But if the courts have acted within their constitutional role, there is something that she can set against this feeling, namely the recognition that they have jointly achieved the goal of governing together.

VI. SHAPIRO AND THE ECONOMY OF TRUST

Maybe the problem lies elsewhere. Maybe it is not the mere fact of disagreement and competition that makes the joint project impossible but the kind of disagreement and competition engendered or allowed for by the interpretivist framework. Some philosophers believe that the joint project of governing would break down, if it were subjected to this sort of strain. The fact that in many circumstances it works smoothly provides evidence that it is not governed by interpretivist principles. In his recent book, *Legality*, Scott Shapiro particularly emphasises this concern.[58] He finds that Dworkin's theory of law is overly demanding on institutional actors because it 'requires for its implementation a great deal of philosophical competence, moral rectitude and political homogeneity'.[59] It requires philosophical competence because '[t]o determine proper interpretive methodology, as well as to apply it in any particular case, the legal reasoner must engage in extremely abstract philosophical reflection and confront questions that have baffled humanity for millenia'.[60] Although some judges may have received a philosophical education, many haven't, and in any case Dworkin would presumably have us think that our judges must overcome a perennial philosophical bafflement in order to do their job. Secondly, Dworkin's theory requires a high degree of moral rectitude because it calls on institutional actors to be guided by moral values, as without recourse to them they cannot identify their official duties, at least in hard cases. For the same reason it requires homogeneity, otherwise interpretivist officials would be routinely imposing on each other and on citizens moral values not shared across the board.

For Shapiro the aforementioned requirements are impossible to square with the operation of most legal systems. Joint activities, Shapiro thinks, pursue more or less complex plans, and plans, to function properly, must be based on an

---

[58] S Shapiro, *Legality* (Cambridge MA, Harvard University Press, 2011) 259–330. There Shapiro amplifies a number of arguments that he had made in previous work against natural law theory in general. See S Shapiro, 'Law, Plans and Practical Reason' (2002) 8 *Legal Theory* 387. I have criticised these arguments in D Kyritsis, 'What is Good about Legal Conventionalism' (2008) 14 *Legal Theory* 135, 145–59. The ensuing paragraphs develop my earlier critique.
[59] Shapiro, *Legality* (n 58) 329.
[60] ibid 284.

economy of trust. This is especially so in cases where the content of the plan is partly left to be spelled out by its participants as they go along. This is how Shapiro defines the economy of trust in planning:

> Insofar as the aim of a plan is to capitalize on trust and compensate for distrust, the proper way to interpret the plan must not frustrate this function. It must not, in other words, permit interpreters to exercise competences and other character traits that the plan denies they have and for whose absence it seeks to compensate; nor may it refuse them the use of capacities that the plan assumes they possess and on whose possession it wishes to capitalize.[61]

The same applies to law, but with a vengeance. Law, according to Shapiro, involves planning on a massive scale. For this reason it cannot but delegate aspects of that planning to subordinate participants (Shapiro calls them interpreters in the quoted passage). Interpreters must make updates and adjustments as appropriate on an ongoing basis. Under these circumstances, the need to economise on trust becomes particularly urgent. It also becomes particularly acute, especially considering that the political societies that we are familiar with are characterised by a pluralism of values and interests. Can we really be confident that the many judges and other legal officials that administer the law in modern legal systems will act wisely, if we give them the power to act on their moral judgement, as Dworkin's theory recommends? Can we trust them to exercise this power competently, given that it arguably requires philosophical expertise that few of them are likely to possess? And even if all that could be granted for each individual judge, how can we nevertheless be sure that collectively they will come up with plans that mesh among themselves and resonate with the moral outlooks of legal subjects? Moral discourse is plagued by reasonable, deep-rooted and pervasive disagreement, even among moral experts. It should not surprise us, then, if the disagreement is replicated among judges following interpretivism's instructions and across society. Thus, argues Shapiro, the operation of the joint project of governing on interpretivist principles would require a prohibitively high investment of trust that is unlikely to be forthcoming in the societies with which we are familiar.[62] Law typically makes do with far less, and our theories of law must be attuned to this fact.

We should not exaggerate either the difficulties faced by modern legal systems or the limitations of legal officials. We should also not fail to note the affinity between Shapiro's view about the point of law and the positivist belief in its

---

[61] ibid 336.
[62] Shapiro does not rest content with this conceptual point. He seeks to enhance it by marshalling an actual example of a legal system, that of the US, where this condition has historically not been fulfilled. He recounts the arc of the young republic whose initial hopes to create a virtuous polity were frustrated and replaced by a more sombre view of human motives. He argues that the system of government it eventually opted for, with its strict separation of powers, reflects this view and therefore makes very modest demands on trust. ibid 312–24.

autonomy from morality. According to this belief, the law is there to settle moral questions for us, and in order to perform this function adequately it cannot throw us back to the same puzzles it was its job to resolve. Of course this is a belief that interpretivists need not and do not share. As we have already seen, the point of law for them is the justification of state coercion. Still, it would be a mistake to brush Shapiro's concern aside. If, as he claims, the implementation of interpretivism would seriously hamper the administration of the law, this would obviously tell against the theory. As I explain below, his objection bears particularly on the version of interpretivism advanced here. It is thus important to address it in some detail. Note that in doing so I shall not be talking about plans. The concept of a plan plays a crucial role in Shapiro's account but not in others, and at any rate it is completely alien to interpretivism. Furthermore, the objection makes sense without it. Its point is to cast doubt over interpretivism's ability to explain the reasoning and decision-making process of legal actors in a way that ensures the by and large efficient administration of the law. This does not presuppose that the administration of the law is an instance of planning.

In response to Shapiro's objection, it must first be noted that interpretivism primarily aims to answer the question of the grounds of law,[63] namely the metaphysical question about what makes something a legal right or duty. Accordingly, Dworkin's choice to spell out the interpretive test by reference to the deliberative process of an ideal judge appears to be an expository device more than anything else. From a metaphysical perspective, the issues raised by the objection do not seem especially threatening. The lack of agreement, trust and moral steadfastness may prevent us from finding out the correct answer but does not tell against there being such an answer, even in the most complex moral questions.

That being said, it is reasonable to ask the further question whether interpretivism offers us a plausible and workable epistemology that lines up with its metaphysics. Dworkin himself acknowledges that, despite its metaphysical focus, the interpretive account is not divorced from legal epistemology. Since 'legal reasoning presupposes a vast domain of justification, including very abstract principles of political morality',[64] the possibility that we will need to venture into moral theory to discover the content of the law is 'always there, on the cards'.[65] '"[O]rdinary" lawyers and judges . . . can set no a priori limit to the justificatory ascent into which a problem will draw them'.[66] It is at the level of

---

[63] R Dworkin, 'Legal Theory and the Problem of Sense' in R Gavison, *Issues in Contemporary Jurisprudence: The Influence of HLA Hart* (Oxford, Oxford University Press, 1987) 9; M Greenberg, 'How Facts Make Law' (2004) 10 *Legal Theory* 157.

[64] Dworkin, *Justice in Robes* (n 15) 49.

[65] ibid 56. Dworkin downplays the importance of this concession. Excursions into moral theory will be sporadic. For the most part, he insists, 'we tend to take [the argumentative structure of legal reasoning] as much for granted as the engineer takes most of what she knows for granted'. (ibid)

[66] ibid 68.

epistemology that Shapiro's objection has bite, for it contends that on the inter-pretivist picture legal officials are routinely charged with carrying out complex evaluations that make appeal to controversial moral standards. Some legal scholars are extremely sceptical about the competence of judges and other legal officials, taken individually, to perform this type of deliberation.[67] But how is the legal system supposed to work, if those who must administer and enforce the law cannot discover it or can only make judgements about the law that are endemically divisive? What good does it do to have an impeccable philosophical understanding of the grounds of legal duty, if those grounds are all but inscru-table to the ordinary judge or a matter of ineradicable controversy?[68]

These questions are pressing because they bear on the issue that exercises interpretivists, the justification of state coercion. Let's return to the account of legitimacy outlined a few sections ago. According to it, trust in legal institutions is necessary because it reinforces one's disposition to comply with the law. Thus, it is one of the structural features that the institutional apparatus of a political society must possess to an adequate degree so as to claim our allegiance. Without it, citizens lack the confidence that the agents of governance will duly use their legal powers. In addition, agents of governance who are epistemically disad-vantaged in carrying out their official duties are prone to making legal mistakes. A political regime that systemically directs its coercive force in an erroneous fashion, that is, in a way that the correct metaphysical account of the content of the law would condemn, has its moral warrant undermined, even if it has the best intentions.

The kinds of concern identified above can be and typically are addressed at the level of designing the joint project of governing. If a type of legal institution suffers from systemic epistemic shortcomings, separation of powers recom-mends that it not be assigned a task that requires the corresponding epistemic virtues. More generally, separation of powers recommends that the division of government power also be drawn on epistemic grounds. Something similar can be said about the way a legal system deals with moral disagreement. If, say, citi-zens are more likely to support decisions regarding contentious moral issues coming from a certain institution (for instance, one whose members are in a systematic way accountable to them) and if a high degree of support is impor-tant for political legitimacy, that consideration ought to inform institutional design. That is, it will count in favour of schemes of separation of powers that channel such contentious issues to the forum that will more satisfactorily deal with them.

---

[67] See eg J Waldron, 'Judges as Moral Reasoners' (2009) 7 *International Journal of Constitutional Law* 2.

[68] Shapiro's concern partially echoes Waldron's argument from disagreement that we discussed in ch 3. The points that I make below regarding the former buttress my case against the latter as well.

The channelling can be effected in a number of ways. Here I can only mention a few, without going into too much detail. The simplest is through a sharp division of substantive tasks, where no institution partakes in the carrying out of functions assigned to another, as when those who are good at protecting national security focus on national security and those who are good at upholding due process focus on due process. But even where there is an overlap in the substantive areas, as when courts are charged to try criminal charges in a context shaped by national security laws passed by the legislature, it is possible to maintain a workable division of labour, epistemic or otherwise. In such cases, courts may adopt doctrines that incorporate presumptions and rules of thumb or adjust the weights of various factors, such that they show due deference to the epistemic advantages of the legislature and to its other institutional credentials.[69] Or they may exercise the 'passive virtues', to use Alexander Bickel's famous term.[70] Finally, assuming that courts must unavoidably make judgement calls on divisive moral issues, they can do so to some extent on the basis of considerations which minimise the backlash. They can for instance adopt what Cass Sunstein has labelled minimalist justifications, by which he means those that do not engage deep differences of moral principle. These devices will not eliminate either the mistakes or the moral disagreements, but we must not forget that political legitimacy on the broader conception advanced here does not set the bar so high. Sometimes, a political regime can legitimately claim our compliance despite its having made a mistake and despite our disagreement, provided it has put in place separation of powers safeguards to the effect that its agents of governance are not set up for failure.

There is a common thread running through my response to Shapiro's objection, namely that we should shift our attention from individual officials to the joint project of governing as a whole. Remember, it is the latter that must be geared towards achieving justice, not necessarily the deliberative process of the former. It is one of the advantages of the project being collective that not all legal officials must discharge all government tasks. As long as the project as a whole inspires reasonable confidence that government power will be duly exercised and endemic legal mistakes will be avoided or rectified through internal checks, it is quite appropriate for individual legal officials to focus on their assigned role, which may well be a very partial one. To use Rawls' apt expression, neither the judge nor any other legal official for that matter possesses 'a plenitude of moral authority'.[71] The authority of each is limited, determined by

[69] See S Perry, 'Second Order Reasons, Uncertainty and Legal Theory' (1989) 62 *Southern California Law Review* 913; A Kavanagh, 'Deference or Defiance? The Limits of the Judicial Role in Constitutional Adjudication in G Huscroft (ed), *Expounding the Constitution: Essays in Constitutional Theory* (Cambridge, Cambridge University Press, 2008) 184.

[70] See A Bickel, *The Least Dangerous Branch: The Supreme Court at the Bar of Politics*, 2nd edn (New Haven CT, Yale University Press, 1986).

[71] J Rawls, 'Two Concepts of Rules' (1955) 64 *Philosophical Review* 3, 30.

his position or office in the joint project of governing. Hence, just because a mistake has been made somewhere in the joint project of governing or an opportunity presents itself to promote justice, this does not entail that any given official is under a duty to identify the mistake, provide redress for it or take the opportunity. Whether he does or not depends on his jurisdiction.[72] If it is too taxing or demanding to expect him to do so competently, institutional design recommends that he be relieved of the corresponding task or, in fact, that he be prohibited from performing it. This recommendation is still consistent with anti-positivism, since it is underpinned by considerations of political morality pertaining to institutional design.

How does the previous analysis bear on Shapiro's objection? It demonstrates, I hope, that although Shapiro is making a reasonable point, his mistake is to think that it is a conceptual rather than a substantive moral one. As such, natural lawyers should be more than happy to address it. Indeed the notion of moral considerations of institutional design informing a scheme of separation of powers gives them the resources to do so much more adequately than those whose self-professed value-neutrality pre-empts them from making any but the thinnest normative claims.

I shall conclude my comment on Shapiro's objection by noting an interesting implication of the account offered here regarding the methodology of jurisprudence. Remember that Hercules began his career as a heuristic device, only subsequently to rise to prominence in Dworkin's substantive theory of legality and political legitimacy. But just as the connection between political legitimacy and separation of powers challenged the moral component of Dworkin's focus on courts, my claim for the limited role of judges in the joint project of governing can be construed to undercut its heuristic value as well. The fact that individual officials are likely to have a very partial input in the project of governing opens the possibility that the point of that project will be partly opaque to them. As Rawls correctly notes, 'different sorts of arguments are suited to different offices'.[73] Accordingly, official decisions are bound to reflect the limitations, epistemic and argumentative, which attach to a specific official role. Hence, no matter how articulate they are, we are liable to be led astray, if we try to glean the point of the project from them. This applies to judges as much as other

---

[72] Dworkin himself sometimes opens this conceptual space. For instance, he writes: 'If the community says to a judge, "The Constitution is the highest law, and your job is to say what the Constitution means," then, as I have often tried to argue, that instruction will turn out to require a very considerable "excursion" into political morality. But we do not have to instruct our judges that way. It is perfectly intelligible to insist that our judges should not be charged with final and authoritative interpretation of the Constitution. If you fear too great judicial power, that is what you should say. It is a serious confusion to disguise your dislike of judges having great power, which can be remedied, in theory, by changing their jurisdictional power, as a false theory of legal reasoning'. (Dworkin, *Justice in Robes* (n 15) 56–57)

[73] See Rawls, 'Two Concepts' (n 71) 6.

officials. That is not to say that legal philosophers do not learn about the nature
of law from studying judicial decision-making and reasoning. For an interpretivist there is no sharp break between the principles of political morality that
explain and justify C-L legal systems as a whole and the determinants of judicial
duty. So in an important sense jurisprudence is still 'the silent prologue to any
decision at law'.[74] But legal philosophers must remain aware of the many steps
leading from the prologue to individual decisions. Each step brings into play
more specific principles of political morality that bear differently on different
state institutions. Generalising from the perspective of any one institution must
be carefully monitored and qualified.

VII. CONTINGENCY AND THE PROJECT OF GOVERNING

In the previous sections, I sought to add flesh to the idea that courts and the
legislature participate in a joint project of governing structured and justified by
separation of powers. The picture I painted of the joint project of governing is
highly moralised. I have claimed that when a project of governing is designed
such that it adheres to a reasonable scheme of separation of powers it is *pro tanto*
more legitimate. It is capable of generating trust among citizens and mitigating
the epistemic and other shortcomings of different state institutions so that collectively they will govern well. Accordingly, there is a moral reason for those
who participate in it to do their share, which crucially includes heeding the acts
and decisions of their fellow-participants.[75] I now want to juxtapose this picture
of the project of governing to two alternatives. Both have a positivist hue. I
should note that it is not the purpose of this chapter to evaluate the comparative
merits of legal positivism and anti-positivism. I discuss these two alternatives
only because I hope that the contrast will give us a clearer sense of the account
advanced here and will dispel some potential confusion about its scope and
ambition.

    As is well known, the idea that legal systems are joint activities of officials is a
central tenet of one of the main contemporary versions of legal positivism.

---

[74] Dworkin, *Law's Empire* (n 3) 90.
[75] The reason is not necessarily that state institutions *owe* a duty to one another. Whether this is
the case depends on the nature of the moral reasons that count in favour of doing one's share in
the joint activity. But it is quite unlikely that these reasons will give rise to such duties. It is much
more natural to talk of duties owed to citizens. Officials owe it to them to work together. Some legal
theorists take a different view. Building on Jules Coleman's theory of law, Kenneth Himma explains
the obligation of participants in the practice of officials in terms of mutual reliance. Such attitudes
arise primarily – if not exclusively – between officials. On Himma's view, then, the project of governing is to be understood as a 'closed' practice among officials. See K Himma, 'Inclusive Legal
Positivism' in J Coleman and S Shapiro (eds), *The Oxford Handbook of Jurisprudence and Legal Philosophy*
(Oxford, Oxford University Press, 2001) 125, 134. This is a crucial difference but I cannot discuss
it in any detail here. I revisit the issue in the following chapter.

This version, which has been championed by Jules Coleman, Kenneth Himma and Christopher Kutz, among others, has found a powerful recent statement in Shapiro's *Legality*. Theorists like Shapiro largely follow Bratman's influential analysis of joint action.[76] They argue that the activity of legal officials exhibits the characteristics of what Bratman has called a shared cooperative activity and maintain that the philosophical explanation of this activity can proceed without any reference to morality.[77] This is because for that activity to exist, all that is needed is that participants develop an appropriate set of interlocking intentions, namely a complex social fact. Shapiro argues that these intentions have shared plans as their objects. For Shapiro, plans are '"positive" entities – they are created via adoption and sustained through acceptance'. Applying this analysis to law, Shapiro concludes that 'if we want to discover the existence or content of the fundamental rules of a legal system, we must look only . . . to what officials think, intend, claim and do around here'.[78] Crucially, we do not need to look at considerations of political morality about what these fundamental rules must be.[79] Their existence, it is claimed, is independent of their moral merit. It depends principally on the social fact that a plan happens to have been adopted and acted upon by a certain group of officials.[80] In fact, the plan of our legal officials may well be a morally pernicious one. But that does not make it any less a plan, or indeed *the* plan that grounds law around here.

Planning has its own inner rationality. When one adopts a plan, one is rationally required to follow through with it. Furthermore, one is rationally required to flesh it out by adopting appropriate sub-plans. In the case of shared plans, one is also rationally required to 'mesh' one's plan-related conduct with that of one's fellow-participants. In large-scale projects this meshing is effected through higher-order plans that authorise some participants, the sub-planners, to plan for others. In these cases, rationality requires that one follow the sub-planners' lead. According to Shapiro, when we talk about the normativity of law, we need

---

[76] M Bratman, 'Shared Cooperative Activity' (1992) 101 *Philosophical Review* 327; M Bratman, 'Shared Intention' (1993) 104 *Ethics* 97.

[77] See characteristically J Coleman, *The Practice of Principle: In Defence of a Pragmatist Approach to Legal Theory* (Oxford, Oxford University Press, 2001) 74–102; Himma, 'Inclusive Legal Positivism' (n 75); C Kutz, 'The Judicial Community' (2001) 11 *Philosophical Issues* 442; S Shapiro, *Legality* (n 58). Shapiro and Kutz have argued that the joint activity of officials falls short of a fully cooperative joint activity in Bratman's sense and have offered thinned down versions of his model. In the text I focus on Shapiro's model for the sake of simplicity.

[78] Shapiro, *Legality* (n 58) 177.

[79] As already discussed, Shapiro thinks that such recourse to political morality is at odds with 'the logic of planning', which requires 'that plans are ascertainable by a method that does not resurrect the very questions that plans are designed to settle. Only social facts, not moral ones, can serve this function'. (ibid) This view has obvious resonance with Joseph Raz's theory of authority discussed in ch 2.

[80] In turn this requires that 'the plan was designed with a group in mind so that they may engage in a joint activity, it is publicly accessible and it is accepted by most members of the group in question'. (Shapiro, *Legality* (n 58) 177)

only commit ourselves to this very elementary form of rationality and nothing more. We need not think, for instance, that only a morally legitimate regime is legal, because unjust and illegitimate regimes do not generate a moral obligation to comply with the law.

Here, I cannot enter into an assessment of the pros and cons of this theory of law. It suffices to note the important differences with the account I have defended. My starting point is not anyone's intentions but the moral merit of the joint project of governing, the adequacy of the answer it gives to the problem of legitimacy. Needless to say, the considerations that shape the project will typically also be operative in the deliberation of the participants and will inform their intentions. Thus, insofar as members of constitutional assemblies are aware of the political capital that they possess, they are likely to have a certain perception of themselves as laying down the general framework of government for generations of officials to come. Likewise, insofar as officials of today take themselves to serve the political community, at whose birth stand the founding fathers, they are likely to develop a matching understanding of their role as one of continuing the project that the founding fathers had started. However, those intentions do not call the shots, normatively speaking. Only considerations of institutional design can give normative force to the division of power put in place by the constitutional assembly. The absence of such considerations cannot be compensated by the *folie de grandeur* of a dictator and the slavish reverence of his cronies.

It is true, of course, that given the anti-positivist character of my proposal many regimes which would come out as legal on Shapiro's view would not be so classed on the view defended here. That is not because I deny that there might be a philosophically interesting sense in which the dictator and his cronies have a plan to govern. But unless their plan gives an adequate answer to the problem of legitimacy, I contend it does not constitute law. Its being a plan is neither here nor there. Now, some think that it is natural to refer to tyrannical regimes as legal despite their perniciousness. Thus, it counts against anti-positivist accounts of law that they deny such regimes legal status. Whether this is so or not, it does not supply a knockdown argument against anti-positivism. As Mark Greenberg correctly notes, '[t]rue theories often have counterintuitive consequences – a great deal about what we now think about the world and about human beings would once have been thought to be absurd'.[81] A whole range of criteria will decide which one is the most successful theory. Once that happens, 'we then have to accept whatever counterintuitive consequences that theory has (at least until a better theory comes along)'.[82]

---

[81]   M Greenberg, 'The Moral Impact Theory of Law' (2014) 123 *Yale Law Journal* 1228.
[82]   ibid.

It may be countered that my response to Shapiro's parsimoniousness down-plays the problem. It is not just that the account offered here refuses to treat as law a whole host of bad projects of governing. More fundamentally, it fails because it assumes that law has a lot more structure and purpose than it actually does.[83] On this view, we do well to take seriously the contingent nature of exist-ing institutional arrangements. We may be excused for thinking otherwise in C-L legal systems with a formal constitution, which sets out the broad contours of the C-L relationship. In such legal systems it is tempting to regard that rela-tionship as the product of some kind of 'design'. But of course there are legal systems without a formal constitution. There, it could be argued, the C-L relationship has been shaped over time by various political forces that were less interested in laying down a lasting framework of government and more in creating an environment that will facilitate the promotion of their political agenda. The political history of C-L legal systems is littered with attempts at power-grabbing some of which are so successful that they become entrenched into the constitutional framework. Depending on political contingencies and the results of political struggles, pieces are added to that framework over time, defying any grand design. The result is more likely to be a hotchpotch than an institutional structure that follows some neat scheme of separation of powers. In addition, even where the C-L relationship is constitutionally regulated, it does not go without saying that its regulation tracks considerations of political morality. It may be – and often is – fuelled by political expediency.

These observations seem to reinforce the impression that what I am offering is a set of prescriptions for institutional reform rather than an explanation of the nature of existing institutions and of their interrelationship. Granted, some, maybe many, actual C-L legal systems do adhere to a defensible scheme of separation of powers, as enshrined perhaps in a constitutional text. Of those we may say that they fare better along the dimension of legitimacy. But we want to understand all C-L legal systems, including those whose creation and evolution is haphazard and piecemeal.

It is true that a theory of law would be seriously deficient if it edited away political 'noise' of the sort just described. Politics, messy as it is, makes a differ-ence to the law and we must be able to account for it. Nevertheless, upon closer inspection the proposal I have put forward does not ignore either the contin-gency of legal systems or the political realities that shape them. There is no doubt that political actors tend to have divergent and often ill thought out inten-tions and plans, and their acts in pursuit of those intentions and plans point in different directions. Unless you subscribe to a teleological view of history, you are unlikely to believe in an invisible hand capable of harmonising them all. Conflict and tension are thus likely to be rife. But on my account what ultimately

---

[83] I am grateful to Les Green for pressing this point.

determines the content of the joint project of governing – the roles assigned different state institutions participating in it – is not those intentions, plans and acts. Rather, whatever significance they have, they do only because and insofar as certain considerations of political morality give it to them. Likewise, the question my account seeks to answer is not factual but normative. It is not whether the intentions, plans and acts of political actors actually fit together, but what officials of today ought to do given that these intentions, plans and acts are part of the institutional history of their community. For the reasons I have rehearsed in this chapter, the answer to this question will also be given by the value of separation of powers. That's because, whether by design or by political circumstance, officials, at least in C-L legal systems, will find that they function alongside other officials who also assume a role in the governing of those systems and act in their name. So they have a duty to share the project of governing with them. This is why their official duty is sensitive to the intentions, plans and acts of political actors. Depending on your theory of separation of powers, these may count as contributions to the joint project of governing. Note also that, since political morality mediates their bearing on official duty, it will give us the resources to resolve any conflict and tension among them. It will direct us to prioritise, rank and weigh them and even disregard some of them.

Let me illustrate this with a couple of examples. In the last chapter I argued that institutional design has a diachronic as well as a synchronic element. In its diachronic dimension, it recommends that there be a relatively stable framework of government. It thus ascribes great weight to a founding moment or a formal constitution, inasmuch as they are capable of commanding broad support. It is such contingent political events – and not some ideal scheme of separation of powers – that will provide the blueprint of government. We can of course criticise that blueprint for falling short of the ideal. But until it is amended, legality dictates that officials of the system comply with it. In this sense, my account does not confuse what the law is and what it should be. Contingency shapes the former because political morality so requires.

Founding moments and formal constitutions are not the only things that can achieve stability of the right kind. In their absence other political events fill the void. They, too, should be viewed in light of separation of powers. That is to say, their impact on the content of the joint project of governing is determined by considerations about the political importance of the event and about the relative merit of structuring government one way or the other. For instance, a usurper does not have the moral licence of a representative constitutional assembly to alter the joint project of governing. On the other hand, even if a body has a popular mandate, it does not have the normative power to institute a tyrannical regime. Other institutional actors have no reason to play their part in it. Again, political morality checks the extent to which official duty is shaped by the intentions, plans and acts of political actors.

VIII. CONCLUSION

In this chapter I sought to question whether the theory of law should privilege the Herculean perspective over the perspectives of other institutional actors in the project of governing. I have argued that legality dictates that the project as a whole should be in good shape. That's because the problem of political legitimacy, to which legality is the answer, does not raise a retail issue but (crucially also) a systemic one. If that is so, then our theories of law must encompass those features of a political regime that help address its systemic dimension as well. To do that, we have to look beyond the judiciary. Separation of powers will be our guide. The subject matter of jurisprudence is thereby augmented. It does not only comprise the rights that are judicially enforceable, but also the powers and duties of all important state institutions – including courts – and their relationship with one another.

5

Institutions and Citizens

I. INTRODUCTION

THUS FAR, THIS book has largely remained within the confines of the official world. We have studied the duties of legal officials who occupy different institutional positions in a C-L legal system. I have argued that their relationship gives them special duties to assist and check one another.

Of course, the emphasis on courts and the legislature is a consequence of the book's institutional focus. But what does the account offered in the preceding chapters have to say about the impact of the C-L relationship *on legal subjects*? In this chapter I shall indicate how the shared nature of legal authority in C-L legal systems fuses, more generally, legal subjects' attitude toward and interaction with political institutions. It is not my purpose to produce a full map of the ways in which those principles make a practical difference to legal subjects, too. My interest is rather narrow. I shall present a strategy for insulating the official world from civil society inspired by Joseph Raz's theory of authority. I shall then test its adequacy in explaining the power that citizens have in some C-L legal systems to mount a constitutional challenge to a piece of legislation before a court. I shall juxtapose it to the explanation of this power provided by interpretivism. Interpretivism shows that recourse to the considerations that structure the C-L relationship is pervasive not only in the interaction among officials but also in the broader political culture. In fact, I argue, it crucially shapes and directs citizens' engagement with the law in those legal systems.

II. A BIZARRE AUTHORITY TRIANGLE

It is fair to say that citizens occupy an uneasy place in legal theory. This is nowhere as clear as in HLA Hart's theory of law. Hart is of course also a legal positivist. But although his view of the relationship between citizens and officials is unlikely to be completely independent of his commitment to legal positivism, I shall look at it in isolation. Besides, in this section my main aim is to identify a philosophical puzzle that is well exemplified in Hart's thought. I am not concerned to explore how a Hartian would best respond to it.

As is well known, Hart claims that the foundation of law is the rule of recognition, the practice of legal officials applying the same criteria for identifying valid law. Only where such a practice is in place can there be law. He further claims that legal officials must take the internal point of view towards that practice, in the sense that they must treat the common criteria of legal validity as furnishing a standard for their conduct.[1] This combination of convergent behaviour and attitude of acceptance is for him key to explaining the normativity of law. Hart contends that the presence of these two elements gives rise to a social rule. Since the official practice of identifying valid law manifests these two elements, those who take part in the practice thereby acquire a duty to apply the same criteria of legal validity as their fellow-participants. To be sure, this is not a moral duty. It belongs to what Ronald Dworkin called conventional morality. Still, it is genuine – a duty that officials have *qua* participants. It does not simply explain the fact that, say, other officials criticise deviations from the practice or demand conformity and acknowledge such criticisms and demands;[2] it justifies it.[3]

Who counts as an official in Hart's account? In *The Concept of Law* Hart does not give a systematic and unequivocal answer to this question. Often, he seems to talk indiscriminately about legislators and judges. Other times he distinguishes judges from other officials but treats them collectively as participants in the rule of recognition.[4] Elsewhere he refers exclusively to courts, without going as far as to claim explicitly that judges are somehow more important than other officials in determining the content of the rule of recognition.[5] In the Postscript Hart revisits the issue by saying that the rule of recognition 'is in effect a form of *judicial* customary rule existing only if it is accepted and practiced in the law-identifying and law-applying operations of the courts'.[6]

I do not claim that Hart fails to recognize the complexity of the official world. Quite the opposite is the case. Typically, the rule of recognition identifies who has law-making power and under what conditions this power can effectively be exercised. For Hart, the office of the lawmaker is different from that of the judge whose institutional duty is to decide according to the law that has been thus created. In effect, it is because of this division of labour that it becomes plausible to closely associate the rule of recognition with judicial practice. Since courts are characteristically charged with 'law-identifying and law-applying operations', the criteria of the rule of recognition are most clearly manifested in what *they* do as opposed to other legal officials such as legislators.

---

[1] HLA Hart, *The Concept of Law*, 2nd edn with a new Postscript (Oxford, Oxford University Press, 1994) 114–17.

[2] ibid 56–57.

[3] For a different view, see J Dickson, 'Is the Rule of Recognition Really a Conventional Rule?' (2007) 27 *Oxford Journal of Legal Studies* 373.

[4] See eg Hart, *Concept of Law* (n 1) 114–15.

[5] ibid 101–02

[6] ibid 256 [emphasis added].

On this view, the principles of institutional design that structure the C-L relationship play either a preliminary or an auxiliary role in Hart's explanation of the rule of recognition. Their role is preliminary insofar as such principles distinguish between law-making and law-applying organs and thus help us identify those officials whose practice constitutes the rule of recognition. Alternatively their role may be auxiliary, as some of Hart's followers have insisted. The space for the latter role is opened by the thought that participants in conventional practices like the rule of recognition need not be driven solely by the fact of behavioural uniformity.[7] The argument goes like this: in legal systems where the rule of recognition tracks principles of institutional design, this fact will arguably furnish a crucial part of the motivation of those who take part in the practice of officials. Maybe it can also be said to partly constitute the relevant rule. Here, I do not want to take issue with this view. Clearly, though, there remains a difference. The difference is brought out when we consider wicked legal systems, say, legal systems without robust checks and balances systems or ruled by an unelected oligarchy. Despite the failure of those systems to live up to the ideal of separation of powers, officials may still be said to practise a rule of recognition on Hart's account provided that they accept the oligarchs' decisions as law.[8] This suggests that it is the conventional aspect of the practice that drives the cart, with reasons of institutional design, where they exist, playing an ancillary part.

This way of conceiving of the rule of recognition relegates legal subjects to the periphery of the legal enterprise. As far as they are concerned, Hart claims that the existence of a legal system only requires that they by and large comply with the law for whatever reason. Fear of sanction suffices. In other words, legal subjects need not –though they may – adopt the internal point of view towards the law. And even if they do, it seems that they cannot see themselves as under a conventional duty to follow the law, as legal officials do. After all, they are not participants in the practice of officials. Thus, Hart drives a wedge between the official world and civil society. The explanation of law's normativity, restricted to the former, is independent of its impact to the latter. Needless to say, the considerations that make the practice of officials morally appealing, if they exist, may also give legal subjects moral reasons for compliance. If judges have a practice of treating the enactments of a democratically constituted legislature as a source of law, the value of democracy supplies citizens a *pro tanto* moral reason to obey the law created by the legislature. Still, this value performs a different function for officials and citizens. In the case of legal officials, it supports their conventional rule of applying one set of criteria of legal validity and not

---

[7] See generally A Marmor, *Social Conventions: From Language to Law* (Princeton NJ, Princeton University Press, 2009) 155–75.

[8] Andrei Marmor, among others, claims that this is compatible with saying that official practice does not generate a genuine obligation in such a case. ibid.

others, whereas for citizens it partly grounds their moral duty to obey the law. Once again, the difference becomes obvious if we consider a wicked legal system. Because of its wickedness, citizens lack a moral reason to obey it. At least they have no such reason, just because it is the law. On the other hand, the wickedness of the legal system does not bear on the existence of the rule of recognition among officials. For Hart, there is nothing stopping them from following a rule that upholds the law of that wicked legal system. But the mere existence of such a rule on the part of officials does not supply a reason for citizens to comply with the law, any more than the practices of a religious community give outsiders reason to follow them.[9] At least in this type of situation, the rule applies to officials only but has no appeal for ordinary citizens.

We are now left with a puzzle. It seems that citizens are not to be counted as participants in the rule of recognition, although they may take the internal point of view towards the law validated by the rule of recognition and although they may have a *pro tanto* moral reason to do so when the operation of the rule helps realise democracy or other values of political morality. At the same time, it is reasonable to think that, as the law is primarily addressed to citizens, the reasons that would make the law morally appealing to them should govern the behaviour of officials as well. However, as we have noted, such reasons appear to play, at best, an ancillary role in grounding their practice. The puzzle becomes particularly acute if we take the view advocated in previous chapters, because according to it principles of political morality do not play an ancillary role; rather they structure the C-L relationship and define the duties of judges vis-à-vis the legislature. On this view, unless a decision by the legislature is supported by the proper combination of reasons of content and institutional design, judges have no duty to further it. But if official practice is governed by the same principles of political morality that have sway over citizens and loses its normative character without them, it appears doubtful that we can keep officialdom and citizenry entirely separate.

The aforementioned puzzle resonates in the elaborations of Hart's accounts offered by his followers. On the one hand, there are those who take the rule of recognition to be rather esoteric, an official practice isolated from the broader political culture. Jules Coleman has put the point especially forcefully:

> Even if a rule of recognition is authoritative, its authority is unrelated to the reasons for acting that ordinary citizens might have. After all, the rule of recognition is a normative social practice among relevant officials – especially judges. It is a characterization of *their* behaviour, an interpretation of description of what they do. In particular, it describes the standards they employ and the practices they follow in determining the legal validity of the official actions of other, e.g. legislation or

---

[9] Outsiders may of course have other reasons to comply, say out of respect towards the members' religious sensibilities.

executive orders. The rule of recognition is a guide for officials, not ordinary citizens. Whereas validity is truth-preserving; it is not authority preserving.[10]

In the same vein, Coleman further argues that judges could be seen to be involved in a joint project of 'making possible the existence of a durable legal practice'.[11] Plausibly, participants in a project with this aim are more interested in keeping in step with other judges than with citizens, provided of course that the latter are by and large compliant. (Even if they are not, they only pose a problem for law's efficacy.) Individual officials themselves are of course not totally insulated from the political culture. For one thing, their involvement in the rule of recognition is often fuelled by broader political considerations. Nevertheless, it need not be; the primary underpinning of their practice is not supplied by such outward-looking considerations as much as an inward-looking concern for what fellow-participants do. Go back to Coleman's view of official practice. A durable legal practice is not necessarily one effectively governed by principles of political morality. If this is what judges aim to sustain with the rule of recognition, they can do so without necessarily heeding such principles. Kenneth Himma buttresses this view with the suggestion that the basis of the obligation generated by participation in the rule of recognition could be mutual reliance among officials.[12] Once again, citizens drop out of the picture. Although judges of a wicked legal system may be thought to rely on each other to carry on their evil joint intentions, their conduct obviously fails to create normative expectations beyond the official world.

By contrast, other theorists such as Gerald Postema are sceptical about any sharp distinction between the official world and legal subjects.[13] Postema argues that 'the law directs action to its ends (whatever they may be) *in its characteristic fashion* only insofar as its standards find a place in the patterns of practical reasoning of those subject to them'.[14] Law is supposed to furnish normative standards for citizens; citizens are expected to use their practical reasoning so as to bring their conduct in line with them. Also, the law operates against the background of shared understandings among those who are supposed to have their conduct governed by it. Clearly, officials impact on the practical deliberations

[10] J Coleman, 'Authority and Reason' in R George, *The Autonomy of Law: Essays on Legal Positivism* (Oxford, Clarendon Press, 1996) 287, 298.

[11] J Coleman, *The Practice of Principle: In Defence of a Pragmatist Approach to Legal Theory* (Oxford, Oxford University Press, 2001) 97. Scott Shapiro also defends such a 'parsimonious' account of official practice. See S Shapiro, *Legality* (Cambridge MA, Harvard University Press, 2011).

[12] K Himma, 'Inclusive Legal Positivism' in J Coleman and S Shapiro (eds), *The Oxford Handbook of Jurisprudence and Legal Philosophy* (Oxford, Oxford University Press, 2002) 125, 134.

[13] See G Postema, 'Coordination and Convention at the Foundations of Law' (1982) 11 *Journal of Legal Studies* 164, 186–93.

[14] ibid 187. Elsewhere Postema writes: 'If officials are to undertake to guide. . .action in a legal manner, they must do so in a way that acknowledge and engage [citizens' capacities] of rational self-direction'. See G Postema, 'Philosophy of the Common Law' in Coleman and Shapiro (eds), *Oxford Handbook* (n 12) 588.

of citizens, but in order to do so effectively they must heed the 'beliefs, attitudes and expectations'[15] of the latter. Plausibly, one can include here value-laden beliefs, attitudes and expectations about what is a proper exercise of official power. In these two ways, Postema contends, there is interdependence between citizens and officials. Without it, law would be unintelligible as a distinctive social activity.

How can we resolve the puzzle I have just sketched? In the next two sections I shall present two solutions. The first one vindicates Hart's insulation of the official world from civil society. While it accepts that the reasons that make official practice morally appealing are crucial in determining whether citizens have an obligation to obey the law, they do not pertain to its status as law. Following on from this it claims that whatever interdependence there is between officials and citizens is external to law. The second solution, by contrast, opens up official practice to civil society. It maintains that not only do citizens and officials heed the same kinds of moral considerations, but citizens may also come to play an integral role in the project of governing.

III. FUSSY PEOPLE AND THE LIMITS OF AUTHORITY

A. The Theory of Authority as a Strategy of Insulation

As a general matter, Hart and his followers do not advocate that citizens must adopt a passive or deferential attitude to law. Being a social construct, law is for them neither sacrosanct nor infallible. So citizens should not feel inhibited to criticise the law and judge its merits.[16] In a democracy, they can do more than that. With their vote citizens influence legislative decision-making in the sense that legislators thereby have a standing reason to heed and incorporate in a vision of the just and well-ordered polity the views and interests of their constituents. Perhaps more importantly, citizens have the power to vote out of office the legislators with whose record they disagree.[17] In this way they also assume

---

[15] Postema, 'Coordination and Convention' (n 13) 192.

[16] In fact, Hart claims that his theory of law fosters such an active stance on the part of citizens. Unlike natural law, legal positivism demystifies law. Stripped of any metaphysical aura, the law thus becomes more amenable to criticism. In addition, legal positivism avoids confusing what the law is and what it should be and in this way makes the target of critique clearer. See HLA Hart, 'Positivism and the Separation of Law and Morals' (1958) 71 *Harvard Law Review* 593. At the same time, Hart cautioned, nothing guarantees that citizens will be critical, let alone defiant, in their engagement with the law. In a famous passage he warns that a society is no less governed by law, even if its citizens are reduced to a 'sheeplike' state, unprotestingly letting themselves be led to the 'slaughterhouse'. See Hart, *Concept of Law* (n 1) 117.

[17] To be precise, they have the power to vote another candidate in. Bernard Manin rightly stresses that this and other features of democratic elections make them essentially a forward-looking institution. Voters choose those candidates with whose platform for the new term they

supervisory powers over the workings of the legal system. Because they face periodic elections, legislators ought to think twice before they pass this or that piece of legislation. At the very minimum, they ought to come up with a persuasive justification why they decided the way they did, perhaps contrary to the express wishes of the electorate.[18]

However, all this seems to belong to the realm of politics, not law. The influence political participation exerts operates at the stage where a legal reform is debated, prior to its being decided upon. At some point, though, the votes are counted and an institutional decision is made one way or the other. At this point, the active citizen recedes in the background; one might say she then becomes a legal subject. Arguably, even if she has been instrumental in the making of the decision as a causal matter, it is the decision, once made, that produces the change in the law as a constitutive matter. This division between politics and law is well captured in Jeremy Bentham's famous view of the good citizen: 'Under a government of Laws, what is the motto of a good citizen? To obey punctually; to censure freely'.[19] If a private citizen thinks a government policy is bad or counter-productive, she campaigns to have it repealed. If she thinks a new policy is needed, she campaigns to have it enacted. But until she succeeds, she must put up with the law as she finds it.

This line of reasoning suggests that to the distinction between politics and the law there corresponds a difference in attitude on the part of citizens: free censure on the one hand and punctual obedience on the other. In this section I want to consider how this difference can be fleshed out so as to insulate the official world from civil society. To do this, I shall revisit Raz's conception of authoritative guidance. We discussed this theory in chapter two. There we challenged its adequacy as an explanation of the C-L relationship. But it may be that it has more traction if it is applied to the relationship between citizens and institutions. More specifically it may be that its value-free criterion of legal validity serves to effect the switch from free censure to punctual obedience. Against Raz, I shall argue that it is not always possible to pre-empt citizens' recourse to moral principles in the identification of the law. I shall begin the task of establishing this negative claim in this section. But we will only be able to conclude our inquiry after we have compared the Razian strategy to the interpretive alternative and we have tested them both in the context of the relationship between courts and the legislature.

agree. But past behaviour will more often than not function as a reliable indicator of future performance. See B Manin, *Principles of Representative Government* (Cambridge, Cambridge University Press, 1997). Relatedly, see D Kyritsis, 'Constitutional Review in Representative Democracy' (2012) 32 *Oxford Journal of Legal Studies* 297.

[18] H Pitkin, *The Concept of Representation* (Berkeley CA, University of Berkeley Press, 1967).

[19] J Bentham, *Comment on the Commentaries and A Fragment on Government* (JH Burns and HLA Hart eds, London, Athlone Press, 1977) 398–99.

One can find elements of Raz's view regarding the attitude of legal subjects towards the law in his writings on a number of topics. It shines through his discussion of the rule of law,[20] respect for law,[21] and the obligation to obey the law,[22] to name a few examples. In what follows, it is not my purpose to cover all this ground. I shall focus on what Raz's account of legal validity tells us about legal subjects and the law. Recall that according to Raz it must be possible to identify a norm as valid law just by appeal to its provenance from a de facto authority, without reference to the moral considerations that the authority was supposed to take into account when creating the norm (the dependent reasons in Razian terminology). Those considerations may bear on the authority's legitimacy but they do not furnish conditions for the legal validity of its norms. This feature of authoritative directives follows from the exclusionary force that they are claimed as having and is encapsulated in the sources thesis.

Critics of Raz's notion of authority have argued that it is untenable because the exclusionary force of authoritative directives involves a suspension of judgement, a violation of practical rationality. It seems to them remarkable that a reason can exclude other reasons bearing on a situation.[23] I think this criticism misses the mark. There are, it can be argued, a number of ways that Raz's theory can meet it. To begin with, exclusionary reasons *need not* neutralise judgement. Nothing in the structure of exclusionary reasons prevents us from considering the merits of the authoritative directive. What we cannot do is *act on* the merits. To do so would be at odds with its authoritative status. Secondly, arguably the exclusionary force of authoritative directives is itself grounded in reason. According to the normal justification thesis the justification for someone's being a practical authority is that it is more likely for us to do the right thing if we follow the authority's directives than if we try to figure out the right course of action ourselves. For instance, you and I have reason to resort to an arbitrator to resolve our dispute because we cannot work out a solution ourselves and we trust that she will balance the conflicting interests more carefully and equitably than ourselves. Furthermore, in order for us to do the right thing, we need not act *for* the right reasons, that is, treat *them* as our reasons for

---

[20] See J Raz, *The Authority of Law: Essays on Law and Morality* (Oxford, Oxford University Press, 1979) ch 11.

[21] ibid ch 13.

[22] ibid ch 12. See also J Raz, *Ethics in the Public Domain* (Oxford, Clarendon Press, 1994) ch 14.

[23] For a version of this criticism, see M Moore, 'Authority, Law and Razian Reasons' (1989) 62 *Southern California Law Review* 827; and H Hurd, 'Challenging Authority' (1991) 100 *Yale Law Journal* 1611. A similar point has been pressed by Larry Alexander in a number of publications. See among others L Alexander, 'Law and Exclusionary Reasons' 18 *Philosophical Topics* (1990) 5; L Alexander, 'Can Law Survive the Asymmetry of Authority?' in L Meyer (ed), *Rules and Reasoning: Essays in Honour of Fred Schauer* (Oxford, Hart Publishing, 1999) 39; and L Alexander and E Sherwin, *The Rule of Rules: Morality, Rules and the Dilemmas of Law* (Durham and London, Duke University Press, 2001) 73.

action.[24] Suffice it that we merely conform to them. So, if we follow the arbitrator's decision because she has made it and its content coincides with the right course of action, we have done all that is rationally required of us.

Still, the normal justification of practical authorities does not eliminate what Raz calls the normative gap between the reason we have for treating the arbitrator as a practical authority over us and the reason for following her directive. As Raz has succinctly summarised it, taking the example of a rule by a club committee,

> [t]hat it is good to uphold the authority of the committee is a reason for the validity of its rules, including the rule that one may not bring more than three guests to social functions of the club. But the desirability of upholding the authority of the committee is not a reason for not bringing more than three guests (not, that is, under this description).[25]

The suggestion seems to be this. Take a complete statement of the course of action that the committee rule requires: bring no more than three guests to club functions. The reasons we normally have for relying on the authority of a club committee is, let's say, coordination, finality, superior expertise etc. Arguably it is not entailed by these reasons that we have a duty not to bring more than three guests to club functions. Neither can this duty be grounded in the reasons we have anyway not to bring more than three guests, if we do. Finality, coordination and superior expertise are the reasons why we treat the club committee as an authority (normative fact). But the reason why we ought to bring no more than three guests is that an authority has said so (social fact).

We can see now how this view of authoritative guidance offers a solution to the puzzle we encountered in our discussion of Hart's theory. Raz will readily acknowledge that the considerations on which the moral appeal of official practice depends are relevant to the legitimacy of the law. These considerations therefore ought to be taken into account by officials when they deliberate what to instruct citizens, and by citizens themselves in their censuring capacity, that is, when they assess whether their officials have done a good job. But these considerations do not furnish the grounds of the law. The logic of authoritative guidance dictates that the law is grounded in a different reason, namely that a directive has been issued by an authority. When faced with an authoritative directive, citizens are expected to treat the fact of its being issued as reason for complying with it that replaces the first order reasons that the authority adjudicated. Here punctual obedience reigns.

---

[24] J Raz, *Practical Reason and Norms*, 2nd edn with new postscript (Oxford, Oxford University Press, 1990) 178–86.

[25] J Raz, 'Reasoning with Rules' (2001) *Current Legal Problems* 1, 12 reprinted as J Raz, *Between Authority and Interpretation* (Oxford, Oxford University Press, 2009) ch 7.

Authoritative guidance, on this view, puts officials and citizens on a different footing by reference to the normative predicament of each. In order to discharge their duty, officials are tasked to act on certain moral reasons and issue directives on their basis. In turn the directives, once issued, elicit a practical attitude on the part of citizens which is not directly justified by those reasons; accordingly, the obedient citizen ought not to act on them if in the presence of a directive that adjudicates on them. This division of deliberative labour neatly distinguishes officialdom and citizenry[26] and thus dissolves Hart's puzzle. Note also that, delineated this way, officialdom encompasses all officials regardless of their position in the project of governing. Whatever their relationship to one another, judges and legislators are all authorities vis-à-vis legal subjects.

B. Enter the Fussy People

In the rest of this section I shall raise some doubts about the plausibility of this insulation strategy by showing how values can come to pervade the identification of authoritative directives. Once again, my critique will trade on the idea of *jurisdiction*, that is, the idea that there must be limits in the scope of law's authority. Its upshot will be that because of those limits it is not possible to identify an authoritative directive without resort to moral considerations, as the sources thesis requires. This moral exercise must be factored into our accounts of the practical difference authorities make in the reasoning of ordinary citizens. I shall start by analysing subjects' attitude towards de facto authorities in general. I shall then move on to see whether the situation is different in the case of law.

As in chapter two I shall accept for the sake of the negative argument I am mounting that non-jurisdictional moral considerations are covered by the exclusionary force of an authoritative directive. Nonetheless, I shall suggest that moral considerations that determine an authority's jurisdiction are sometimes not pre-empted in the reasoning of legal subjects; in fact, legal subjects appeal to them to identify some standard as part of the law.[27] To bring out this point, I shall focus on the deliberation of *fussy people*, as I shall call them. While perhaps others prefer to adopt a rather uncritical attitude on the issue, fussy people want to think the matter through before they follow someone else's directives. This does not make them any more upright than their non-fussy neighbours. For, they are not so interested in the question: 'Which course of action is best supported by reason?' Their slogan is rather: 'Who are you to tell me how to lead

---

[26] More accurately, what is being distinguished are the two corresponding capacities. Clearly, the same person can have both.

[27] Note however that I do not intend to show that such appeal is a necessary component of their attitude towards the law.

my life?' This is not to say that they are particularly anti-authoritarian either. They accept various practical authorities in their lives and do not deny that the decisions of such authorities have a significant impact on their normative situation. They are merely fussy about what it takes for someone to be an authority in the first place.

How does their fussiness play out? Take the club example introduced earlier to illuminate the normative gap. Suppose the members of a golf club generally acknowledge that the club committee has the power to determine their rights and duties in respect of the life of the club. That makes the committee a de facto authority. It may even be a legitimate one when it comes to issues like the use of club facilities. Imagine now that the club committee decrees that members ought to go to Blackpool for the summer. But this matter clearly falls outside those over which it justifiably has authority. Fussy people are particularly vexed by this failure. They take seriously the fact that the authority of the committee is limited to adjudicating on certain reasons only, say, reasons concerning how many guests to bring along to club functions. In chapter two we called those j-reasons and we called non-j issues all the reasons for which this is not the case, like the reasons members have to go to Blackpool or Bournemouth for the holidays. I shall stick to this terminology here. It follows from the fact that fussy members take the distinction between j-reasons and non-j reasons seriously that, whenever they are faced with a decision from the club committee, they will try to ascertain that the decision purports to adjudicate on the right sort of reason. This exercise is of special significance. When the committee decrees all club members must go to Blackpool for the summer, fussy club members will not simply lobby to change the decree. They will be disinclined to treat it as an authoritative directive in the first place (provided they spot the jurisdictional error).

It is no good saying that fussy people have rebelled against the committee's authority. The jurisdictional limits that fussy people fuss over do not in any way affect its authority in the exercise of its regular role. It is assumed that, once a directive passes the test of jurisdiction, fussy people are bound by it and cannot consider the matter afresh as if there were no authoritative intervention. Neither will it do to retort that fussy people are merely assessing the merits of the decision. They are not. As was stressed in chapter two, an authority can stay intra vires and still reach a mistaken decision. Fussy people tolerate that state of affairs. It is the unwarranted expansion of the committee's power they get worked up about. The question they do ask – who are you to tell me? – is independent from the question whether the decision prescribes the right course of action. On the other hand, their fussiness is intimately linked with authoritative guidance. It reflects the moral concern that we identified towards the end of chapter two. Being an authority over someone is an immense power, and it should not be granted lightly. Once granted, it should be kept within its proper bounds. Fussy people are fixed on policing those bounds.

Given that fussiness is a response to a moral concern, it is to be expected that being fussy involves moral reasoning. But it is not necessary to make such a strong claim at this point. For the aim of critiquing the sources thesis, it suffices to say that fussiness involves recourse to the dependent reasons, the reasons that the de facto authority in question is meant to adjudicate on. To repeat, this exercise is required for each and every decision coming from the de facto authority. Its purpose is to identify the reasons the decision aims to regulate and establish whether they fall in the category of j-reasons or non-j reasons. I hasten to add that fussy people need not have a fully worked out theory of those matters. Perhaps they are overly suspicious or fascinated by conspiracy theories, and their reasoning simplistic and rudimentary. What is crucial is that for them the identification of a decision with authoritative force involves more than the social fact that it has come from a de facto authority.

Could it be countered that, even if it carries the day, my argument captures the attitude of only a small and perhaps eccentric type of authority subject? This suggestion misses the point. The sources thesis must apply across the board, not just to the many unfussy. Cutting the losses to leave fussy subjects out will not save it. Quite the opposite, fussy people compel us to reconsider the attitude that the unfussy have towards authority as well. When fussy people protest against the ultra vires decision of the club committee, they do not speak only for themselves. The club committee has no business making holiday plans for any club member.

C. The Fussy People before the Law

Does the argument work in the case of our attitudes towards the law? Arguably, the club committee is different from law because the former has limited authority, whereas the latter claims according to Raz unlimited authority. 'In most contemporary societies', he writes, 'law is the only human institution claiming unlimited authority'.[28] 'Any conditional or qualified recognition of legitimacy', he goes on, 'will deny law the authority it claims for itself'.[29] Does this mean that there is no room for fussy *legal subjects*? It would seem that what was possible in the case of the club committee, namely the reconciliation of fussiness and submission to authority, is impossible in the case of law. Presumably, fussiness signals defiance in the face of law's claim to unlimited authority.

One familiar line of response trades on the idea of fundamental rights. Unsurprisingly, people can be fussy about such rights, too. Fussy liberals, so to speak, insist that, whatever else the law has the power to do, it may not dictate

[28] J Raz, *The Morality of Freedom* (Oxford, Clarendon Press, 1986) 76.
[29] ibid.

whom legal subjects must marry (if at all) or which books they must read (if any). It just does not have authority to balance the relevant reasons. Coordination-based considerations may reduce the scope of possible limitations, without totally eliminating them. So for instance, it cannot plausibly be maintained that a rule that decrees which books legal subjects must read is supposed to solve a coordination problem. Here there seems to be a discrepancy between legal subjects' attitude towards the law and its putatively unlimited claim to authority. For fussy liberals, matters pertaining to the exercise of their fundamental rights lie outside law's authority. On the other hand, just like fussy club members, fussy liberals are no anarchists. They are prepared to accept law's authority on other matters.

How could Raz account for fussy liberals? He might say that they also accept that the law can regulate issues of fundamental rights, though only in one way, namely by permitting persons to do as they please with regard to these issues. Compare the parallel contention he makes with regard to law's claim to authority:

> [E]very legal system claims authority to regulate behavior in some way but not necessarily in every way. Therefore, the test is satisfied by those legal systems, which contain, e.g., liberties granted by constitutional provisions which cannot be changed by any legal means. Such systems may not claim authority to regulate the permitted behavior in any other way, but they regulate it in one way by permitting it.[30]

So what from one angle appears to be a jurisdictional error Raz would recast as an error regarding the directive's merit. It is quite appropriate, he would say, for a legal directive to adjudicate my reasons to marry Daisy or Sue. It will be intra vires, whichever course it prescribes in the matter. But unless it permits me to make that decision for myself, it is mistaken in substance. At first blush Raz's alternative description seems plausible. If so, it could put to rest the jurisdictional concerns of fussy liberals. It would bring in line their expectations about law's limits and the claim to authority it makes.

In order fully to evaluate that description, I would have to delve into broader questions of political authority. I would have to compare different accounts of the relationship between the individual and her political community.[31] However, such a task would fall outside the scope of this book. For this reason I do not intend to press the argument from fussy liberals any further. What I propose to do instead is connect the discussion of fussy legal subjects with the overarching theme of this book, the shared authority of courts and the legislature in C-L legal systems. After all, it is institutions like them that make decisions in the

---

[30] J Raz, *Authority of Law* (n 20) 117.

[31] For a nice contrast between two extreme positions on this issue, see R Dworkin, *Freedom's Law: The Moral Reading of the American Constitution* (Oxford, Oxford University Press, 1999) 139; and J Waldron, 'A Majority in the Lifeboat' (2010) 90 *Boston University Law Review* 1043.

name of the law. It is their decisions that fussy legal subjects subject to the test of jurisdiction. I shall show that, once we disaggregate the different contributions of courts and the legislature in this way, there is as much scope for fussiness in one's attitude towards the law as there is towards limited authorities like the golf club. But first I need to introduce an alternative to Raz's insulation strategy. This is the task of the next section.

IV. THE PROTESTANT ATTITUDE

The crux of Raz's solution to Hart's puzzle is to insulate legal officials from citizens by reference to the reasons that guide each. Only officials are meant to be guided by the dependent reasons, leaving citizens with a different reason (at least in their capacity as authority subjects): that an authoritative directive has been issued. Needless to say, there is a correlation between this view of citizens' attitude towards the law and Raz's general theory of law with its value-free notion of legal validity. Both are supported by the same conception of authoritative guidance.

How is the relationship between citizens and officials conceived by an anti-positivist theory of law that, unlike Raz's, espouses that moral considerations are among the determinants of legal duty? In previous chapters we elaborated a version of anti-positivism based on Dworkin's interpretive theory of law, and it is on this theory that I shall rely here as well. Interpretivism is not solely a theory about state institutions and their impact on the content of law. For Dworkin, citizens in a vigorous legal system are also supposed to assume what he calls a protestant attitude towards legal practice. In fact, despite his focus on courts he places considerable emphasis on this attitude taking hold among citizens. He writes:

> We studied that attitude mainly in appellate courts, where it is dressed for inspection, but it must be pervasive in our ordinary lives if it is to serve us well even in court . . . It is a protestant attitude that makes each citizen responsible for imagining what his society's public commitments to principle are, and what these commitments require in new circumstances.[32]

In order to discharge their responsibility, citizens must try to come up with a set of principles of political morality that they think best explain and justify this practice, principles that are both morally attractive and explanatorily adequate. Part of this task will be to identify what the roles of the different institutional actors in the legal system are, what powers they have, what limits are set to these powers and what mechanisms of checks and balances are there to police those limits. Citizens' account of the roles of the various state institutions is

---

[32] R Dworkin, *Law's Empire* (Oxford, Hart Publishing, 1998) 413.

answerable to the value of separation of powers. More precisely, it must articulate a plausible elaboration of that value that can be said to underlie the set-up of those institutions and the distribution of government tasks among them.

This kind of deliberation is the mirror image of the reasoning that, as argued in previous chapters, judges and other legal officials ought to engage in to determine their institutional duty. It is also the hallmark of fussy people. The judgement that an exercise of power fits into a morally defensible scheme of separation of powers puts to rest their concern for jurisdiction, because it gives them reason, if there is such a reason, for submitting to this or that institution; it answers the question that exercises them: Who are you to tell me? When a legal subject in a C-L legal system asks this question of a legislator or a judge, the legislator or judge must be able to show that his decision is a legitimate exercise of his institutional role within the joint project of governing. In large part, this means that he must show either that his decision adjudicates on an issue that the legislator or judge is there to regulate according to the scheme of division of labour that underlies the enterprise or that it checks the decision of another institution on the basis of the system of checks and balances that the enterprise includes. Legal subjects have good reason to entrust the regulation of their conduct to those who are well suited to regulate it, as the principle of division of labour dictates. They also have good reason to follow the law's determinations, when the law includes mechanisms to oversee the use of power by the various state agents as the principle of checks and balances dictates. Therefore, a legal system that institutes a scheme of division of labour and a mechanism of checks and balances makes a *pro tanto* stronger claim to have authority over legal subjects. No wonder, then, that such considerations will be active in the deliberations of citizens adopting the protestant attitude.

It is easy to get carried away by the image of legal subjects demanding a warrant for official action and legal officials, either judges or legislators, responding by citing considerations of institutional design. One could even imagine such a response being offered in an actual exchange between officials and citizens. Undoubtedly this will often be the case, even more so in a liberal culture where the duty of justification presumably follows from a heightened sense of respect for the individual. Administrative law offers us plenty of examples of such a special duty of justification. Nevertheless, as administrative lawyers know all too well, it does not follow from its being good to give reasons that reasons must be offered. Still, the protestant attitude is independent of whether legal officials have any special duty to justify their decisions or whether they actually undertake such a task. The need for a justification of the sort outlined above stems from the nature of legal duty. In fact, even when no explicit justification has been offered for a certain political decision along these lines, every legal subject on his own can assess what, if any, contribution that decision makes to their legal rights and duties. To do that, she will need to judge whether it is supported by the proper combination of substantive and institutional reasons.

Notice how this account differs from Raz's. Whereas for Raz the official world is insulated from citizens by way of a sharp division of deliberative labour between authorities and authority subjects, for Dworkin no such division of labour exists. The principles that govern the relationship between officials and determine official duty are also among the principles that determine citizens' attitude towards the law, at least when the latter are in protestant mode. Both sides speak the same language and respond to the same concerns. Interpretivism therefore holds out the possibility of a different solution to Hart's puzzle. According to it, the practice of officials is not esoteric and inward-looking but porous, assigning a crucial role to citizens. But what does this mean, more precisely? And what are the implications for the theory of law, if it is true?

V. ENGAGING WITH THE LAW

A. From Ideal to Practice

Can we bring the two options I have just sketched from the lofty heights of abstraction and aspiration down to the real world? To do this, we need to examine concrete examples of citizens engaging with the law. 'Engaging with the law' is a deliberately vague expression that aims to capture the diverse forms of interaction between ordinary citizens and the legal system without committing to one or the other explanation of this interaction. Clearly, no side denies that citizens engage with the law in various ways. They may be said to do so when they participate in democratic politics, or when they censure freely and obey punctually. Earlier I suggested that these forms of interaction can easily fit into the Hartian scheme. But, as I shall argue in this section, there are hard cases that challenge that scheme.

As my point of focus, I shall use the form of interaction involved in constitutional review of legislation and assess which option best accounts for it. Many systems of constitutional review give citizens the power to challenge decisions made by the legislature,[33] but they can only do so on certain specified grounds. It is often objected that in legal systems with constitutional review the side that has lost out at the legislative stage gets a free second chance to defeat its opponents in court. This is said in a derogatory manner, because it is thought to contradict the spirit of the good citizen encapsulated in Bentham's statement.[34]

---

[33] Importantly, not all do. The analysis that follows does not apply to those that do not.

[34] It is no wonder that Bentham also wanted to minimise the role of the judiciary in the development of the law. On this aspect of Bentham's philosophy, see G Postema, *Bentham and the Common Law Tradition* (Oxford, Clarendon Press, 1986) ch 12.

But perhaps such an arrangement is not as bad as this objection makes it out to be. To begin with, on the face of it, constitutional challenges do not question the authority of the legislature. Neither do they seem to be revolutionary. Their upshot is not that a piece of legislation must be repealed by judicial fiat but that it is not an exercise of the legal authority bestowed upon the legislature.[35] Accordingly, the role of courts when they review legislative decisions is typically just that, namely to exercise a circumscribed review, not to decide *de novo*.

What does constitutional review teach us about citizens' attitudes to law? Not much, Raz might argue. Recall that Raz has a way of accommodating within his theory of authority claims that a piece of legislation must be struck down because it does not conform to constitutional norms guaranteeing fundamental rights. He can say that these norms enshrine not limits of the legislature's jurisdiction but substantive standards by which we will measure whether the legislature has used its power well. On this view, the striking down of a statute by the reviewing court amounts to the repeal of a valid law on the ground that the legislature got the balance of dependent reasons wrong. So, for Raz systems of constitutional review are not a counter-example to Bentham's view of the good citizen. Rather, they are merely another institutional channel for legal reform. Granted, citizens may only use a narrower set of resources to make the case for reform before the reviewing court than they would if the matter were to be revisited by the legislature. But that does not warrant the conclusion that in mounting a constitutional challenge they are questioning that the original decision created valid law to begin with. Until it is struck down, they are supposed to obey it punctually as befits an authoritative directive claiming unlimited authority.

It is doubtful that all constitutional challenges fit into this mould.[36] Federalism cases are a good illustration. It would be quite a stretch to say that, when a court polices the division of labour between the federal legislature and the state, it does so on the basis of a substantive judgement about, say, how inter-state commerce should be regulated. Here, it makes much more sense to speak in terms of the jurisdiction of the respective authorities, of *who* should regulate inter-state commerce. Therefore, the citizens who argue that the federal legislature

---

[35] I am using this terminology because it resonates with the discussion of Raz's theory of authority in the previous section and in ch 2 but also because I want to cut through the variety of remedies afforded by different systems of constitutional review. In some cases, the reviewing court is said to set aside the unconstitutional statute, in others refuse to enforce it or render it unenforceable, and in others invalidate it. Reasonably, some remedies seem to vindicate the idea that due to the unconstitutionality there was no valid law *ab initio*, while others sit more comfortably with the view that the original validity of the law remains unaffected by the judicial decision. By translating constitutional review into the language of the theory of authority, we forestall similar appeals to legal phenomenology.

[36] For a sophisticated attempt to reconcile constitutional challenges with Raz's theory of authority, see M Giudice, 'Unconstitutionality, Invalidity, and Charter Challenges' (2002) 15 *Canadian Journal of Law and Jurisprudence* 69.

has regulated a matter – or adjudicated on a dependent reason – that falls within the jurisdiction of states are best understood as contesting the vires of the federal legislature, not the merits of its decision. Needless to say, they cannot make this argument unless they have recourse to the dependent reasons to ascertain which reasons the federal legislature has adjudicated. Once again, the argument that law is not subject to a jurisdictional test, because it claims unlimited authority, is neutralised by shifting our attention from the authority *law* claims to the authority *legal institutions* claim on law's behalf. The latter claim leaves room for fussiness and thus vitiates Raz's insulation strategy.

Instead of trying to amend Raz's theory to solve this problem, I shall juxtapose how Dworkin's alternative can explain the active role that constitutional review often assigns citizens in legal practice. In saying that their role is active, I do not only mean that constitutional review gives citizens the *initiative* to bring a constitutional challenge. I also mean that the vitality of constitutional review depends on it being possible for them to view official decisions in a critical way. In legal systems where they can bring such a challenge, they are expected to appreciate that the making of an official decision is not the end of the matter, legally speaking. They ought to be watchful, not just about the direction of one's political community, as one must be who censures freely, but also about what legal rights and duties one has as a consequence of a legislative decision. The views public officials form about the legal rights and duties created by a legislative decision may well be mistaken, and citizens are expected to understand that they have a role to play in correcting them. This is a very different stance towards legal institutions from the one Raz has in mind. With their notion of a protestant attitude interpretivists offer a more convincing account of it. Interpretivists would insist that citizens are active in the sense that they are expected to have recourse to the principles of political morality that determine legal duty. Besides, figuring out how these principles bear on legal duty requires the exercise of difficult, controversial moral judgements. Legal officials can get these judgements wrong as much as citizens. All the more reason, then, for the latter to remain vigilant.

At the same time, interpretivists can vindicate the thought that citizens who are making a constitutional complaint are not merely calling for the reform of a bad but perfectly valid law; rather, they are pointing to a legal mistake. As noted, the protestant attitude is sensitive to the same principles of political morality that determine the duty of legal officials. Among them, principles of institutional design will direct citizens to give weight to the decisions of this or that state institution, just as they direct judges. So, protestant interpretation preserves the distinction between what the law is and what it should be. It is not an exercise in utopian politics any more than judicial interpretation. In challenging the constitutionality of a statute, citizens accept that, were it not for its constitutional defect, the statute would be legally binding.

Now, suppose we conclude that the notion of the protestant attitude better captures the spirit in which citizens engage with the law when they mount a constitutional challenge. It still would not automatically follow that the Hartian view of the relationship between officials and citizens is vitiated. The difficulty arises from the fact that, even when a piece of legislation is invalidated, this is brought about by a judicial decision, that is, the decision of another authority. Though it might be citizens setting in motion the process that leads to its invalidation, the process itself takes place entirely in the official sphere. Correspondingly, we could grant that citizens sometimes develop a protestant attitude towards legal practice, one perhaps strongly informed by moral considerations, and still doubt that this makes any difference to the theory of law. Citizens adopting this attitude will come to form their own views about their legal rights and duties or about the powers of institutions charged with the task of governing. But those views are devoid of any institutional significance. They may of course have persuasive force and thereby sway official judgement. However, given that they do not *replace* official judgement, we think they are *about* legal rights and duties rather than *determinative of* legal rights and duties. Of course, one should not rush to conclude from this that citizens' views are no better than idle talk. Nevertheless, it is crucial to bear in mind that they must go through official channels to be at all effective. There then comes a point at which what would otherwise be mere private opinion acquires jurisprudential significance. Arguably, the sharp distinction between citizenry and officialdom is in this way preserved.

To begin with, it is a mistake to exaggerate the thrust of the interpretivist account of citizens' engagement with the law. It does not aim to eliminate the distinction between citizens and officials. Quite plainly, the distinction itself is supported by weighty reasons of institutional design; it is good to have officials rule upon constitutional challenges. But interpretivism denies that the distinction can be drawn in deliberative terms, as Raz suggests. Citizens and officials are partners in the same project at least in the sense that they are guided by the same considerations, when they reflect on their rights and duties under the law. Interpretivism also maintains that the practice of officials is porous to inputs from citizens. Since the latter develop a protestant attitude regarding their legal rights and duties, this is only to be expected. From this perspective, it is not without importance that constitutional review gives the protestant attitude institutional expression and edge. There, the input leaves a trail and has a noticeable effect.

Furthermore, we should not be distracted by the fact that constitutional review pits one state institution against another. One can imagine a legal system where constitutional challenges were directed to the legislature. Clearly, it is possible for someone to own up to their mistake, once it is pointed out to them, and mend their ways by themselves. On the other hand, there are good – though not always overriding – reasons counting in favour of subjecting legislative performance to an external check,[37] and more specifically in favour of assigning the task to judges.[38] I shall not rehearse these reasons. What matters for present purposes is the content of the complaint and the normative resources it draws on, not the forum in which it is raised. So, maybe citizens mounting a constitutional challenge *are* playing one state institution against the other. But they do so *not* in the name of utopian justice but in the name of the law.

The point of the last paragraphs helps us address a related objection. This one trades on the notion of finality. It proceeds from the observation that even if the legislature does not have the final say in legal systems with a practice of constitutional review, some court does, against whose decision no appeal lies. Maybe with regard to decisions of that authority having a protestant attitude is pointless. The same can be said about legislative decisions in legal systems without a practice of constitutional review. As a result, the argument goes on, in every legal system there will be some final authority whose decisions are law just because the authority has said so. But finality, too, is a red herring. No doubt, it makes sense from the perspective of institutional design to grant one organ the last word. Citizens adopting the protestant attitude will have no problem appreciating the force of this consideration. But final arbiters can also make mistakes. So, although their decision may be the end of the matter, practically speaking, it is not the end of the conversation. There is still scope and use for the protestant attitude after the decision has been handed down even if there is a sense in which it can no longer be challenged. It is perfectly conceivable for citizens to assert not simply that this is a bad decision, but that it is a bad decision in law.

That is not to downplay the fact that partisan groups have sometimes invited courts to exercise a power that is not properly theirs and replace the view of the just and well-ordered polity duly expressed by the legislature with another view that was more favourable to them (although not in these words). Neither should we forget that courts have often succumbed to the temptation of imposing their views on issues that it was the legislature's job to address under the guise of review. But these are risks inherent in a system of checks and balances. They have to be balanced against the risk of leaving the legislature unchecked coupled with the benefits from a system of review of legislation specifically by courts. At any rate, our focus here is not on the merits and demerits of constitutional review but on the kinds of institutional moves and claims it permits and the attitude of citizens towards state institutions it elicits.

---

[37] Unsurprisingly, in looking for such reasons we will once again encounter separation of powers. Separation of powers recommends checks and balances arrangements of this type.

[38] It has also been suggested that constitutional review has the potential to bolster popular deliberation. See R Dworkin, *Freedom's Law* (Oxford, Oxford University Press, 1999) 30–31. An account that acknowledges the participatory aspect of judicial review can be found in S Fredman, 'Judging Democracy: The Role of the Judiciary under the HRA 1998' (2000) *Current Legal Problems* 99.

B. A Two-way Street

It is fair to say that the alternative understanding of citizen engagement with the law that I am sketching was pioneered by Lon Fuller. Fuller famously resists thinking of law as a 'one-way projection of authority, emanating from an authorised source and imposing itself on the citizen'.[39] Law, he insists, should not be equated with the mere 'manifested fact of social authority or power'.[40] Instead, being a purposeful social enterprise, the law must be understood in light of its purpose. Fuller thinks that law's purpose is to subject human conduct to the governance of rules. This assumes that a legal subject 'is, or can become, a responsible agent, capable of understanding and following rules, and answerable for his defaults'.[41] Hence, the study of law cannot stop at the point where a legally significant decision has been made. It has to examine both the way it is administered by officials and the way it is being engaged with by citizens. In this chapter, I have sought to make Fuller's vision of law more tractable by identifying a real-life situation where it can be shown to be at work. In legal systems with a practice of constitutional review, citizens do not simply evaluate official conduct against the purposes and values governing the joint project of governing; they can also call out and effectively challenge legal mistakes in official conduct. I also hope to have more closely defined the considerations that guide citizens' attitude towards the law and their engagement with it and with its officials. In such systems we can agree with the thesis encapsulated in this passage from *Law's Empire*:

> Law is not exhausted by any catalogue of rules or principles, each with its own dominion over some discrete theater of behavior. Nor by any roster of officials and their powers. Law's empire is defined by attitude, not territory or power or process.[42]

So far, so good. But what about other legal systems? Needless to say, constitutional review is far from a universal feature of all law. It may of course be a sign of health of a legal system if it incorporates mechanisms that foster a protestant attitude, but their presence does not seem to be among the conditions for law's existence. You do not have to be a legal positivist to harbour this kind of scepticism. Even a natural lawyer might say that the existence of legal standards depends on moral conditions as a metaphysical matter, whether or not citizens see this. In fact, he might take the view that citizens rarely do see it. Those of a more Finnisian bent would perhaps add that the legal systems characterised by citizen indifference towards the law are peripheral instances of the concept of

---

[39]   L Fuller, *The Morality of Law*, 2nd edn with a reply to critics (New Haven CT, Yale University Press, 1969) 192.
[40]   ibid 145.
[41]   ibid 162.
[42]   Dworkin *Law's Empire* (n 32) 413.

law, with the central case being that of a legal system with an active and inquis-itive populace.[43] But this does not change the fact that the former are also legal systems.

I should make clear that it is not my purpose to generalise my discussion to all legal systems or even all C-L legal systems. True to the exercise in particular jurisprudence I am conducting, I remain agnostic about whether there can be law without protestant interpretation. I have primarily sought to show how con-stitutional review involves a form of citizen engagement with the law that can better be captured by interpretivism than by Raz's insulation strategy. That being said, I do not want to preclude that the lessons drawn from this compari-son radiate out to legal systems without practices of constitutional review. Recall one of those lessons: though constitutional review brings the protestant attitude into sharp relief and renders it obviously consequential, taking it up makes sense even where there is no ready institutional avenue to challenge the legal mistakes of officials. If that is so, it merits further investigation to consider how citizens of such legal systems engage with the law and how officials interact with them. It may be that the philosophical similarities in citizens' engagement with the law between legal systems with and without constitutional review are at least as interesting as their differences.

VI. CONCLUSION

On the account I have been defending in previous chapters the considerations that ground official duty also bear on the moral legitimacy of the law vis-à-vis legal subjects. When a state institution decides in a way that is supported by such considerations, it makes a better moral claim to shape the legal rights and duties of the latter. But even if we accept that these considerations matter to legal subjects as well as officials, we can still ask the further question how they matter. In this chapter I suggested that the attitude of citizens toward legal institutions, at least in C-L legal systems equipped with a system of constitutional review, is not one of unquestioned obedience. By contrast, it has as a necessary compo-nent resort to moral argument of a certain form – the form that befits authorita-tive guidance. The purpose of this argument is to ascertain that an exercise of power by this or that legal institution merits their allegiance. In other words, citizens' engagement with the law in this sub-category of legal systems is in an important sense active. It is the attitude of someone who stands ready to challenge the power that the state claims to exercise upon him. I have used the notion of protestant interpretation as a model for that attitude and I have

---

[43] On the distinction between peripheral and central instances of a concept, see J Finnis, *Natural Law and Natural Rights*, 2nd edn (Oxford, Oxford University Press, 2011) 9–11.

juxtaposed it to a conception of citizens' attitude towards the law drawn from the theory of Joseph Raz. Raz distinguishes officials and legal subjects on the basis of the kinds of reasons that each may appropriately act on in systems of authoritative guidance. But systems of constitutional review are difficult to square with this conception.

6

Broadening the Canvas

A. A Moralised Account of Institutional Cooperation

IN THIS BOOK I sought to develop the institutional component of interpretivism. Central to this exercise was the idea of institutional cooperation,
which I tried to spell out by appeal to the value of separation of powers. I
defined separation of powers as the value of coordinated institutional effort for
the purpose of creating and maintaining a just and well-ordered society. Because
the different state institutions are involved in a coordinated institutional effort,
a joint project of governing, as I called it, they have a duty to respect the contributions made to this effort by other participants. That is to say, they have a duty
to assist in the implementation of the decisions of the other participants and
build upon them in the exercise of their own role. But this is not a duty of
unquestioned deference. They ought to respect these contributions only insofar
as they merit it, that is, only insofar as these contributions can be shown to be in
line with the relevant principles of political morality, which include separation
of powers.

I identified two broad categories of separation of powers reasons that determine (in part) the kind of respect owed one state institution by another. These
are division of labour reasons and checks and balances reasons. Division of
-labour reasons count in favour of a certain state institution deciding a given
political issue on the basis that it is well suited to do so. Checks and balances
reasons on the other hand justify one state institution interfering with and perhaps also overriding the decisions of another, in order to avert misuse of power.

I also argued that this account of institutional cooperation is not outlandish.
Legal systems with courts and a legislature, I claimed, are best understood in
these terms. I suggested that with the help of the value of separation of powers
we can make better sense of the Janus-like relationship that courts bear to legislatures. That is to say, we can make better sense both of the way that courts and
legislatures are interdependent – in particular the way that courts are receptive
vis-à-vis the legislature –, and of the supervisory powers over the legislature that
courts very often assume.

According to this suggestion, separation of powers tells us that it is part of being a good judge that he ought to decide cases in accordance with prior legislative decisions. It also tells us what deciding *in accordance with* prior legislative decisions entails in each case facing the court. More specifically a judge ought to respect and further a legislative decision if it is supported by the proper combination of two sorts of reasons: first, reasons that pertain to the desirability of having a certain authoritative structure in place and, secondly, reasons that pertain to the substance of the decision. I called the former reasons of institutional design and the latter reasons of content. Hence, the fact that a decision has the right content does not suffice to justify its having an impact on our rights and duties under the law. There must also be good moral reasons to assign a certain individual or institution to a position of power over us in order for the decisions emanating from that individual or institution to have that impact. It is reasons of the latter sort that the analysis of the value of separation of powers rehearsed in the previous chapters was meant to articulate.

B. Legal Theory from the Perspective of the C-L Relationship

I have not said much in this book about how to combine content and institutional design more precisely. This is partly due to the fact that the proper combination varies from one C-L legal system to another and across sub-domains of legal practice, and it would take a more particularised analysis to define it further. The range of options is very wide indeed. Thus, we should not exclude the possibility that in some cases considerations of institutional design all but pre-empt recourse to content. Proceduralist theories of democracy famously propound such a view. They claim, for instance, that the only morally satisfactory solution to the reasonable disagreement that afflicts political decision-making is to ground the moral authority of a political settlement exclusively on considerations pertaining to the procedure that led to the settlement rather than on considerations about its justice. The account of the joint project of governing offered here makes sense of this claim, but of course its plausibility ultimately rests on its substantive appeal. Conversely, one promising way to delineate the proper scope and intensity of the power of courts to review legislation for its conformity with constitutional principles is by charting the circumstances under which considerations of content (in conjunction with checks and balances considerations) may on occasion outweigh the institutional warrant of the legislature to shape our rights and duties through its decisions. Again, it is a substantive issue whether there are any such circumstances. (Proceduralists will insist that there are none.) There is little that an abstract inquiry into the structure of the C-L relationship can contribute to this issue. What it can do, though, is help pose it in a way that makes it more tractable, that is, as an issue pertaining to the allocation of government power among different state institutions.

More importantly, I have omitted a detailed analysis of the nature of the interplay between institutional design and content because my primary aim has been different. I sought to show that interpretivism, when properly understood and elaborated, gives a convincing philosophical explanation of the C-L relationship. In particular, I used the example of C-L legal systems to illustrate the way an interpretivist can account for the normative impact of the acts and decisions of one political institution, the legislature on the official duty of another institution of the same legal system, the judiciary. To this end, it is sufficient to establish that they can *in principle* have that impact. The idea that there is an interplay between considerations of content and institutional design is key to doing this. The interplay checks the extent to which judges may have recourse to considerations of content. This is because it is morally desirable that 1) political decisions be taken according to a scheme of division of labour that includes checks and balances mechanisms and 2) participants in the joint project of governing respect and give effect to those decisions. Because of this, I have suggested, it is possible that a judge must decide a case before her in a way that is sub-optimal, as judged from the standpoint of ideal justice.

I have added that it is not arbitrary to measure the C-L relationship against separation of powers standards and determine the roles of the two partners in it according to them. These are the standards that the C-L relationship properly aspires to. In this book, I have offered the following rationale for this proposition: I have claimed that adherence to separation of powers furnishes a standing guarantee that public power will be exercised properly. Hence conformity with separation of powers gives the exercise of power by courts and the legislature moral authority over citizens. It supplies the right kind of warrant for the impact that their project of governing has on the rights and duties of legal subjects.

I have maintained that this elaboration of interpretivism enhances both our understanding of it and its philosophical appeal. Let me highlight two ways in which it achieves this. First, it dislodges courts and the accompanying notion of judicial enforceability from the privileged position that they occupy in Ronald Dworkin's work. The law is meant to rule in ways other than by enforcing certain rights and duties upon individual demand, and legality suffers unless those further ways also adhere to the right principles of political morality. The same applies to the C-L relationship. We want that relationship to include some standing guarantees that power will not be misused, and the judicial enforceability of certain moral rights of citizens is only one of them. There are others, captured by the broader concept of separation of powers I have relied on. If you think that the point of law is to justify the coercive force of the state, you must be interested in them, too.

Secondly, the elaboration of interpretivism advanced here staves off the criticism that interpretivism collapses law and morality. According to it, the two are distinct because the former is sensitive to principles of institutional design that the latter is not. Assuming that I have been successful in this task, it is unnecessary to spell out in detail how the two types of moral consideration are combined in legal interpretation. Now, there is no denying that the version of interpretivism I have defended only provides a *moral reason* why legislative decisions ought to matter to the way judges decide cases. So, the distinction between law and morality that it puts forward may strike many as inadequate. However, interpretivism seems to fare better than its adversaries on this score. Thus, I have shown that an influential alternative based on Joseph Raz's theory of authority is vulnerable to serious criticisms. Specifically, with its insistence on a view of authoritative guidance that pre-empts recourse to moral considerations it fails to account for the limited authority claimed by different state institutions in the name of the law. The C-L relationship helps bring out this failure. As I have claimed, the legal status of the contributions of the two partners depends on the moral considerations that delimit their authority. This is an insight that is better accommodated by the idea of a joint project of governing structured by the relevant principles of political morality.

In my critique of Raz's theory and my presentation of the interpretivist alternative, I have for the most part relied on examples where one state institution of a C-L legal system makes a decision that either merits the respect of the other or not. But I have warned against generalising from this type of example and supposing that I am subscribing to something like the following view: 'We have a legal duty to *x* if and only if there is a decision to that effect made by the competent organ and there are no overriding substantive considerations that we not *x*'. This view may be thought to undermine interpretivism's status as a genuine alternative to legal positivism, for it contends that the making of a decision by a competent organ is a necessary condition for the existence of a legal duty. Presumably, what makes this condition essential is the logic of authoritative guidance, whereby the issuing of an authoritative decision constitutes a special method for bringing about norms. According to this view, the ground of legal norms – as of all authoritative norms – is a social, not a moral, fact. Positivist theories of law that argue for a value-free criterion of legal validity predictably zero in on this kind of explanation. This explanation is not fundamentally shaken by adding that, for a legal duty to exist – perhaps in a full-bloodied way –, other conditions, including moral ones, must be met as well. Arguably, the breaking up of the inquiry into two stages might just reflect two distinct philosophical concerns, one about legal validity and the other about the moral legitimacy of law.

However, the view sketched in the previous paragraph is different from the one I propound in at least two respects. First, it seems to suggest that all moral considerations come in at a second wave, after a norm has been created by virtue of a social fact alone. By contrast, I have claimed that the ground of a legal right or duty is a *combination* of moral considerations of content and institutional design. Both considerations determine the moral weight to be assigned social facts such as the making of a legislative decision. In addition, the two types of considerations interact with each other. Thus, it is likely that some social issues raise serious content-related moral concerns that can only be set aside by the weightiest considerations of institutional design. This complexity is hidden from view when we look solely at the fact that a decision has been made, even if the body that made it is generally accepted as a legal authority.

Second and related, for a legal right or duty to exist on my account it is not necessary that it be explicitly decreed. This is a common case but not the only possibility. In fact, the approach adopted in this book provides us with a vantage point from which to challenge the view that the law necessarily comprises norms that are grounded in official say-so. In the context of the C-L relationship, this view would have us think that judges are there to give effect to norms created by legislative say-so. Contrariwise, I have argued that legislative decisions must be located within the joint project of governing in which courts and the legislature take part. This shift in the locus of law's authority enables us to downplay the jurisprudential significance of the social fact that a certain decision has been made by a recognised source. A judge can be said to be under a legal duty, even if no single decision specifically provides for it, provided that having such a duty flows from the principles of political morality that underpin the project of governing. This is most obviously so in legal systems where courts are assigned supervisory power over the legislature. There, it is possible that they have a duty to defy or even act contrary to a legislative decision. This, we have seen, is compatible with viewing them as cooperating with the legislature under a scheme of separation of powers that is also sensitive to checks and balances considerations.

C. Limited Authority and Citizen Engagement with the Law

I said earlier that separation of powers is crucial for the legitimacy of the legal order. Judges and legislators make a better claim to the allegiance of legal subjects when their relationship is structured by this value. In this book I further argued that this view of law's authority in C-L legal systems also changes our understanding of the role of citizens in the workings of the law. Focusing on C-L legal systems with a practice of constitutional review I contrasted two positions regarding citizens' attitude toward the law. One, associated with a legal positivist conception of law, is more comfortable with a clear separation between officials and citizens and seeks to effect this separation by means of a deliberative division of labour. However, this division is unworkable. By contrast, on the alternative position that draws on the version of interpretivism developed in this book officialdom and citizenry interweave: citizens are supposed actively to assess whether officials have made good use of their power. In addition, they are assigned a crucial institutional role in correcting official mistakes, a role which promotes legality, not justice. This form of engagement with the law transforms their relationship with officials. It is not necessarily a sharply vertical relationship between ruler and ruled. Endowed with the power to contest the legality of official action, citizens are placed on a level footing with those who govern them.

II. WHERE DO WE GO FROM HERE?

The aspiration of philosophical theories of law is, quite rightly, to articulate necessary truths about legal practice that explain its enduring characteristics. Although it is entirely possible and, as I have maintained in this book, philosophically illuminating to discover truths of this kind by examining a sub-domain of legal practice, the parochial character of this approach perhaps restricts the appeal of its conclusions. There clearly is a lot of law outside the C-L relationship, so our philosophical interests overshoot the scope of my analysis. Therefore, the question naturally arises whether the version of interpretivism defended here can be applied more broadly. In this section, I want to briefly outline two possible avenues for its extension to other types of institutional interaction and interdependence.

In a sense my focus on the C-L relationship has been a safe choice: the two partners in the relationship have already been the object of sustained philosophical study. Thus, talking about them helps connect my claims with some standing concerns and debates in jurisprudence. But, as already noted, C-L legal systems comprise other institutions apart from these two. Hence, a more comprehensive theory will factor in this further complexity. Crucially, it will make room for the executive. There is a reason why the executive has not been as prominent in our most influential theories of law. Of the branches of government it is the one that is most sprawling, most resistant to generalisations, and whose functions are most difficult to categorise. In light of this, it is small wonder that courts and the legislature are more appealing focal points for those whose ambition is to produce a theory that applies to all law. On the other hand, if your inquiry is primarily driven by the normative question under what conditions state power is legitimate, it is imperative that you examine how the project of governing is structured to monitor the use of executive power. For, in the legal systems that we are most familiar with, the executive is the steam engine of government and the branch that has the most interaction with citizens.

This expanded jurisprudential inquiry necessitates a closer engagement with constitutional theory. In this book I have sought to avoid it by focusing on just one aspect of institutional cooperation, namely that the acts and decisions of one participant make a difference to the duties of another in principle. This aspect is particularly intuitive in the C-L relationship. But it becomes less so once the executive enters the picture. Besides, since the executive is so diverse, we cannot position it in the joint project of governing unless we have some kind of map of the different forms it takes. With this map we can then match functions to forms. To do all this we need to develop more fine-grained theories of separation of powers, which will incorporate a broad gamut of lower level principles or will flesh out higher level principles in a way that varies from one institutional actor to the other.

In the last two paragraphs I indicated how the account defended here needs to be elaborated to encompass all the main agents of governance in the nation-state. But we should not stop there. In some quarters, the nation-state and its institutions are considered outdated. Or, perhaps more accurately, it is considered outdated to look at domestic legal institutions in isolation from the many legal regimes, international, supranational and transnational, of which nation-states are today also part. In choosing to focus on the relationship between two domestic legal institutions, I did not intend to disparage or downplay such concerns. On the contrary, I think it is very likely that the account of institutional cooperation can be used as a template for the relationship among institutions and governance regimes beyond the nation-state. Here I can do no more than prefigure this wider inquiry.

When one looks at the multitude of legal institutions that exist outside the national constitutional order today, one cannot but be struck. Institutions of this sort are not only many but also powerful and of increasing importance for governments, corporations and individuals. Predictably, then, they have attracted the attention of legal philosophers.[1] In fact, many claim that their proliferation in recent years throws up a particularly serious threat for mainstream theories of law. The point is typically put in the following way: we often say that such institutions belong to separate legal systems. For instance, we speak of national legal systems as opposed to the international or the European Union legal system. Surely, it is argued, the theory of law must be able to account for their interrelation. It is here that the problem arguably arises. As each legal system is thought to have its own independent criteria for a standard's membership in it, it becomes a contingent matter whether one legal system will acknowledge the

---

[1] See eg with reference to the European Union, J Dickson, 'How Many Legal Systems? Some Puzzles Regarding the Identity Conditions of, and Relations between, Legal Systems in the European Union' (2008) 2 *Problema* 9. See also generally K Culver and M Giudice, *Legality's Borders: An Essay in General Jurisprudence* (Oxford, Oxford University Press, 2010) and N Roughan, *Authorities: Conflicts, Cooperation, and Transnational Legal Theory* (Oxford, Oxford University Press, 2013).

validity of norms belonging to another. Even if it does, it can acknowledge them on its own terms and subject to conditions that are alien to the legal system to which they primarily belong. This will inevitably generate incongruence and conflict. For instance, the same type of conduct will be viewed as contrary to the law from one perspective and in conformity with it from another. Given how intrusive these various legal systems are today, incongruence and conflict is likely to be endemic. Besides, due to the lack of an overarching legal framework the resolution of such conflict will require recourse to extra-legal, political means. Why is this a threat for mainstream theories of law? At the very least, the argument goes, these phenomena tell against accounts that stress the law's putative systematic character. More strongly, they show that the ability of law, and especially state law, to guide behaviour in conditions of pluralism is seriously hampered.

I do not purport to evaluate either the perceived threat or the cogency of the responses to it. I sketched this trend in legal theory to juxtapose to it the approach I favour. I start from the observation that, at the most general level, our moral concerns about international or supranational institutions are the same as about domestic institutions. The former are also agents of governance, so we want them to govern us in ways that they are suited to do and to be subject to checks against misuse of power. Therefore, institutional cooperation makes as much moral sense beyond the state as it does within it. Supranational and international institutions will need to rely on other institutions to carry out the tasks that they are not well equipped to perform. Likewise, they can more effectively be kept in check if they are supervised by an independent institution, operating either at the same or a different level. All these forms of interaction are mediated by principles of political morality which respond to the basic moral concerns about the proper exercise of power. In turn, these principles also guide the attitude of other institutions vis-à-vis the decisions of, say, the Court of Justice of the European Union. If its decisions are supported by the right principles, then they merit a measure of institutional respect and assistance.

Needless to say, it is possible that in this exercise national courts and legislatures will reappear as agents of international or supranational governance. They will then need to be drawn into a wider network of institutional cooperation and their role will accordingly become more intricate. We should not expect that the fit between the different elements of that role will always be unproblematic. More often than not, institutions are structured to respond to a specific set of political demands. When an already established institution is called upon to deal with novel issues, it may find it difficult to adjust and harmonise the old and new tasks.

We can view the controversy regarding the relationship between EU law and the constitutional law of Member States as an example of this kind of difficulty. Equipped with the account advanced here, we have a way of resolving similar difficulties that does away with the formalism that so often plagues them. We do not need to conceive of the corresponding legal systems as insular chains of validity, each producing a distinct set of norms, answerable only to its own criteria. Rather, we can be guided by a moral question: How ought the joint effort of different institutional actors to be structured so that they collectively make a better claim to moral legitimacy? Each of them, within and beyond the nation-state, makes a contribution to the joint effort. However, the bearing of that contribution is determined by the principles of political morality that govern it. These may be different for national and supranational institutions. But, being *moral* principles, they can in principle be brought under one master account. Sure enough, their combined effect will likely leave areas of indeterminacy. But, as we have noted earlier, such indeterminacy is going to be weak and bear no resemblance to the radical conflict that pluralists make so much of.

Many legal theorists will object that a solution that recommends recourse to moral considerations – on this scale – is no solution at all. I accept that such recourse is not unproblematic and I have examined some of the problems that might attend it in chapter four. There I also discussed the resources of the joint project of governing to resolve them by channelling and coordinating the deliberative and other capacities of various institutional actors. There is no reason why similar resources should not be available at the international and supranational level, at least in principle.

It must be stressed, though, that the aforementioned approach will at best provide a partial account of the range of international and supranational regimes. Agents of governance are not the be-all and end-all of such regimes, especially given that they are nowhere near as advanced as the agents of governance of the nation-state. Besides, the broadening of the jurisprudential canvass that I am proposing comes with theoretical risks. To begin with, the coexistence of multiple agents of governance should not immediately be equated with cooperation. This equation, we have seen, is much more natural in the domestic context, where more often than not the roles of different state institutions are the outcome of an overarching constitutional arrangement. Even when no such arrangement was actually agreed in a constitutional moment, we tend to assume that the evolution of their respective roles has been shaped by the regulative ideal that they are engaged in a joint project of governing; and, in any case, this is how we view things given the highly systematic and centralised character of the national legal systems with which we are most familiar. But it does not go without saying that we can make a similar assumption in other institutional contexts. We must allow for the possibility that, although two institutions regulate the same domain of social life, perhaps in the same territory, and although coordination and even cooperation between them would be desirable, as things stand they have no duty to respect each other's decisions. In other words, it is possible that they can be indifferent towards one another. The task of jurisprudence is to come up with principles of political morality that justify this attitude of indifference, not turn it willy-nilly into one of cooperation. It may be, of course, that because they interact de facto, they will be forced to pick up the pieces, if the other one makes a blunder. At a minimum, it may be that each has a moral reason to take into account decisions made by the other because these decisions causally affect the persons and relationships that they too ought to regulate. But we should be wary to call this form of interaction cooperation. We should not be surprised to find that the legal world is a fragmented place, with discontinuities and tensions, just as the moral world is – at least on a plausible view – fragmented, fraught with discontinuities and tensions.

Another, not unrelated, mistake that extensions of the account must avoid is to interpret what inter- or supranational cooperation there is by appeal to principles of political morality suited primarily for the domestic context. Not all political communities have the same purposes and are guided by the same values. Even if it is true that justice is the first virtue of national political communities,[2] it may not be so of others. Accordingly, the institutions that govern each political community are subject to different standards. This applies both to content and institutional design. To refer to an example widely discussed in the literature, democratic legitimacy is a crucial principle of institutional design in the nation-state, but it is doubtful that many important international regimes should track democratic legitimacy in the same way as C-L legal systems. Therefore, we must work our way outwards from the C-L relationship with caution. Our inquiry must be alert to the moral complexity of various institutional arrangements and their impact on one another. This is the leitmotif of particular jurisprudence, even while it strives towards greater generality.

[2] J Rawls, *A Theory of Justice* (Cambridge MA, Harvard University Press, 1971) 3.

Bibliography

Addler, M and Himma, K, *The Rule of Recognition and the US Constitution* (Oxford, Oxford University Press, 2009)

Alexander, L, 'Law and Exclusionary Reasons' 18 *Philosophical Topics* (1990) 5

—— 'Can Law Survive the Asymmetry of Authority?' in L Meyer (ed), *Rules and Reasoning: Essays in Honour of Fred Schauer* (Oxford, Hart Publishing, 1999) 39

—— and Sherwin, E, *The Rule of Rules: Morality, Rules and the Dilemmas of Law* (Durham and London, Duke University Press, 2001)

Allan, TRS, 'Human Rights and Judicial Review: A Critique of "Due Deference"' (2006) 65 *Cambridge Law Journal* 671

Bentham, J, *Comment on the Commentaries and A Fragment on Government* edited by JH Burns and HLA Hart (London, Athlone Press, 1977)

Bickel, A, T*he Least Dangerous Branch: The Supreme Court at the Bar of Politics*, 2nd edn (New Haven, Yale University Press, 1986)

Bix, B, 'Legal Positivism' in MP Golding and WA Edmundson (eds), *The Blackwell Guide to the Philosophy of Law and Legal Theory* (Oxford, Blackwell Publishing, 2005) 29

Bratman, M, 'Shared Cooperative Activity' (1992) 101 *Philosophical Review* 327

—— 'Shared Intention' (1993) 104 *Ethics* 97

Cane, P, 'Public Law in The Concept of Law' (2013) 33 *Oxford Journal of Legal Studies* 649

Chang, R, 'Introduction' in R Chang (ed), *Incommensurability, Incomparability and Practical Reason* (Cambridge MA, Harvard University Press, 1997) 1

Choper, J, *Judicial Review and the National Political Process* (Chicago, The University of Chicago Press, 1980)

Claus, L, 'Montesquieu's Mistakes and the True Meaning of Separation' (2005) 25 *Oxford Journal of Legal Studies* 419

Coleman, J, 'Authority and Reason' in R George, *The Autonomy of Law: Essays on legal positivism* (Oxford, Clarendon Press, 1996) 287

—— 'Negative and Positive Positivism' (1982) 11 *Journal of Legal Studies* 139

—— *The Practice of Principle: In Defence of a Pragmatist Approach to Legal Theory* (Oxford, Oxford University Press, 2001)

Cooke JE (ed), *The Federalist* (Middletown CT, Wesleyan University Press, 1961)

Culver, K and Giudice, M, *Legality's Borders: An Essay in General Jurisprudence* (Oxford, Oxford University Press, 2010)

Dickson, J, 'Is the Rule of Recognition Really a Conventional Rule?' (2007) 27 *Oxford Journal of Legal Studies* 373

—— 'How Many Legal Systems? Some Puzzles Regarding the Identity Conditions of, and Relations between, Legal Systems in the European Union' (2008) 2 *Problema* 9

Duxbury, N, *Elements of Legislation* (Cambridge, Cambridge University Press, 2012)

Dworkin, R, *Taking Rights Seriously* (London, Duckworth, 1978)

—— *A Matter of Principle* (Cambridge MA, Harvard University Press, 1985)

Dworkin, R, 'Legal Theory and the Problem of Sense' in R Gavison, *Issues in Contemporary Jurisprudence: The Influence of HLA Hart* (Oxford, Oxford University Press, 1987) 9
—— 'Objectivity and Truth: You'd Better Believe it' (1996) 25 *Philosophy and Public Affairs* 87
—— *Law's Empire* (Oxford, Hart Publishing, 1998)
—— *Freedom's Law* (Oxford, Oxford University Press, 1999)
—— *Justice in Robes* (Cambridge MA, Harvard University Press, 2006)
—— *Justice for Hedgehogs* (Cambridge MA, Harvard University Press, 2011)
—— 'A New Philosophy of International Law' (2013) 41 *Philosophy and Public Affairs* 2
Ekins, R, *The Nature of Legislative Intent* (Oxford, Oxford University Press, 2012)
Eliot, TS, 'Tradition and Individual Talent' in TS Eliot, *Selected Essays* (New York, Harcourt, 1950)
Endicott, T, *Vagueness in Law* (Oxford, Oxford University Press, 2000)
—— 'Raz on Gaps: The Surprising Part' in L Meyer, S Paulson and T Pogge (eds), *Rights, Culture and the Law: Themes from the Legal and Political Philosophy of Joseph Raz* (Oxford, Oxford University Press, 2003) 99
—— 'Interpretation, Jurisdiction and the Authority of Law' (2007) 6 *APA Newsletter* 14–19.
Enoch, D, 'Reason-Giving and the Law' in L Green and B Leiter (eds), *Oxford Studies in Philosophy of Law* vol 1 (Oxford, Oxford University Press, 2011) 1
—— 'Authority and Reason-Giving' (2014) 89 *Philosophy and Phenomenological Research* 296
Finnis, J, 'On Reason and Authority in *Law's Empire*' (1987) 6 *Law and Philosophy* 357
—— *Natural Law and Natural Rights*, 2nd edn (Oxford, Oxford University Press, 2011)
Fredman, S, 'Judging Democracy: The Role of the Judiciary under the HRA 1998' (2000) *Current Legal Problems* 99
Fuller, L, 'Positivism and Fidelity to Law: A Reply to Professor Hart' (1958) 71 *Harvard Law Review* 630
—— *The Morality of Law*, 2nd edn with a reply to critics (New Haven and London, Yale University Press, 1969)
Gardner, J, '5 1/2 Positivist Myths' (2001) 46 *American Journal of Jurisprudence* 199
Giudice, M, 'Unconstitutionality, Invalidity, and Charter Challenges' (2002) 15 *Canadian Journal of Law and Jurisprudence* 69
Green, L, *The Authority of the State* (Oxford, Oxford University Press, 1988)
—— 'Positivism and the Inseparability of Law and Morals' (2008) 83 *New York University Law Review* 1035
Greenberg, M, 'How Facts Make Law' (2004) 10 *Legal Theory* 157
—— 'The Standard Picture and Its Discontents' in L Green and B Leiter (eds), *Oxford Studies in Philosophy of Law: Volume 1* (Oxford, Oxford University Press, 2011) 39
—— 'The Moral Impact Theory of Law' (2014) 123 *Yale Law Journal* 1118
Halpin, A, 'The Methodology of Jurisprudence: Thirty Years Off the Point' (2006) 19 *Canadian Journal of Law and Jurisprudence* 67
Hart, HLA, 'Positivism and the Separation of Law and Morals' (1958) 71 *Harvard Law Review* 593
The Concept of Law, 2nd edn with a new Postscript (Oxford, Oxford University Press, 1994)
Hershovitz, S, 'Legitimacy, Democracy and Razian Authority' (2003) 9 *Legal Theory* 219
—— 'Integrity and *Stare Decisis*' in S Hershovitz (ed), *Exploring Law's Empire* (Oxford, Oxford University Press, 2006) 103.
Himma, K, 'Inclusive Legal Positivism' in J Coleman and S Shapiro (eds), *The Oxford Handbook of Jurisprudence and Legal Philosophy* (Oxford, Oxford University Press, 2002) 125

—— 'Law's Claim to Legitimate Authority' in J Coleman (ed), *Hart's Postscript: Essays on the Postscript to the* Concept of Law (Oxford, Oxford University Press, 2001) 271

Hurd, H, 'Challenging *Authority*' (1991) 100 *Yale Law Journal* 1611

Kavanagh, A, 'Deference or Defiance? The Limits of the Judicial Role in Constitutional Adjudication' in G Huscroft (ed), *Expounding the Constitution: Essays in Constitutional Theory* (Cambridge, Cambridge University Press, 2008) 184

Kornhauser, L and Sager, L, 'The Many as One: Integrity and Group Choice in Paradoxical Cases' (2004) 32 *Philosophy and Public Affairs* 249

Kripke, S, *Wittgenstein on Rules and Private Language* (Oxford, Basil Blackwell, 1982)

Kutz, C, 'The Judicial Community' (2001) 11 *Philosophical Issues* 442

Kyritsis, D, 'Representation and Waldron's Objection to Judicial Review' (2006) 26 *Oxford Journal of Legal Studies* 733

—— 'Principles, Policies and the Power of Courts' (2007) 20 *Canadian Journal of Law and Jurisprudence* 379

—— 'What is Good about Legal Conventionalism?' (2008) 14 *Legal Theory* 135

—— 'The Normativity of The Practice of Officials' in S Bertea and G Pavlakos (eds), *New Essays on the Normativity of Law* (Oxford, Hart Publishing, 2011) 177

—— 'Constitutional Review in Representative Democracy' (2012) 32 *Oxford Journal of Legal Studies* 297

—— 'The Persistent Significance of Jurisdiction' (2012) 25 *Ratio Juris* 343

—— 'Law's Province in the Domain of Value' (forthcoming *Jurisprudence*)

MacCormick, N, *Institutions of Law: An Essay in Legal Theory* (Oxford, Oxford University Press, 2007)

Manin, B, *Principles of Representative Government* (Cambridge, Cambridge University Press, 1997)

Markwick, P, 'Law and Content-Independent Reasons' (2000) 20 *Oxford Journal of Legal Studies* 579

Marmor, A, 'Authority, Equality and Democracy' (2005) 18 *Ratio Juris* 315

—— *Social Conventions: From Language to Law* (Princeton NJ, Princeton University Press, 2009)

Montesquieu, CL de Secondat, Baron de, *The Spirit of the Laws*, rev edn of the Nugent translation (1873, first published 1748)

Moore, M, 'Authority, Law and Razian Reasons' (1989) 62 *Southern California Law Review* 827

Nagel, T, 'The Problem of Global Justice' (2005) 33 *Philosophy and Public Affairs* 113

Owens, D, *Shaping the Normative Landscape* (Oxford, Oxford University Press, 2012)

Pitkin, H,

The Concept of Representation (Berkeley CA, University of Berkeley Press, 1967)

Perry, S, 'Second Order Reasons, Uncertainty and Legal Theory' (1989) 62 *Southern California Law Review* 913

Postema, G, 'Coordination and Convention at the Foundations of Law' (1982) 11 *Journal of Legal Studies* 164

—— *Bentham and the Common Law Tradition* (Oxford, Clarendon Press, 1986)

—— '"Protestant" Interpretation and Social Practices' (1987) 6 *Law and Philosophy* 283

—— 'Integrity: Justice in Workclothes' (1997) 82 *Iowa Law Review* 821

—— 'Philosophy of the Common Law' in J Coleman and S Shapiro (eds), *The Oxford Handbook of Jurisprudence and Legal Philosophy* (Oxford, Oxford University Press, 2001)

Rawls, J, *A Theory of Justice* (Cambridge MA, Belknap Press, 1971)

Rawls, J, 'Two Concepts of Rules' (1955) 64 *Philosophical Review* 3

Raz, J, *The Concept of a Legal System* (Oxford, Oxford University Press, 1975)

—— 'The Institutional Nature of Law' (1975) 38 *Modern Law Review* 489

—— *The Authority of Law: Essays on Law and Morality* (Oxford, Oxford University Press, 1979)

—— *The Morality of Freedom* (Oxford, Clarendon Press, 1986)

—— 'Dworkin: A New Link in the Chain' (1986) 74 *California Law Review* 1103

—— *Practical Reason and Norms*, 2nd edn with postscript (Oxford, Oxford University Press, 1990)

—— *Ethics in the Public Domain* (Oxford, Clarendon Press, 1994)

—— 'Intention in Interpretation' in R George (ed), *The Autonomy of Law* (Oxford, Oxford University Press, 1996) 249

—— 'On the Authority and Interpretation of Constitutions' in L Alexander (ed), *Constitutionalism: Philosophical Foundations* (Cambridge, Cambridge University Press, 2001) 152

—— 'Disagreement in Politics' (1998) 43 *American Jurisprudence of Jurisprudence* 25

—— 'Reasoning with Rules' (2001) *Current Legal Problems* 1

—— 'About Morality and the Nature of Law' (2003) 48 *American Journal of Jurisprudence* 1

—— 'Incorporation by Law' (2004) 10 *Legal Theory* 1

—— 'The Problem of Authority: Revisiting the Service Conception' (2006) 90 *Minnesota Law Review* 1003

—— *Between Authority and Interpretation* (Oxford, Oxford University Press, 2009)

Réaume, D, 'Is Integrity a Value? Dworkin's Theory of Legal Obligation' (1989) 39 *University of Toronto Law Journal* 380

Rehnquist, WM, 'The Idea of a Living Constitution' (1976) 54 *Texas Law Review* 693

Roughan, N, *Authorities: Conflicts, Cooperation, and Transnational Legal Theory* (Oxford, Oxford University Press, 2013)

Sager, L, *Justice in Plainclothes* (New Haven CT, Yale University Press, 2004)

—— 'Material Rights, Underenforcement, and the Adjudication Thesis' (2010) 90 *Boston University Law Review* 579

Sartori, G, 'Constitutionalism: A Preliminary Discussion' (1962) 56 *American Political Science Review* 853

Schauer, F, 'The Best Laid Plans' (2010) 120 *Yale Law Journal* 586

Schmitt, C, *Der Hüter der Verfassung* (Munich and Leipzig, Dunkler/Humblot, 1926)

Shapiro, S, 'Law, Plans and Practical Reason' (2002) 8 *Legal Theory* 387

—— *Legality* (Cambridge MA, Harvard University Press, 2011)

Simmons, AJ, 'Justification and Legitimacy' (1999) 109 *Ethics* 739

Smith, 'The Many Faces of Political Integrity' in S Hershovitz (ed), *Exploring Law's Empire: The Jurisprudence of Ronald Dworkin* (Oxford, Oxford University Press, 2006) 119

Stavropoulos, N, 'Hart's Semantics' in J Coleman (ed), *Hart's Postscript: Essays on the Postscript to the* Concept of Law (Oxford, Oxford University Press, 2001) 59

—— 'Interpretivist Theories of Law' in E Zalta (ed), *Stanford Encyclopedia of Philosophy (Winter 2003)* available at http://plato.stanford.edu/archives/win2003/entries/law-interpretivist

—— 'The Relevance of Coercion: Some Preliminaries' (2009) 22 *Ratio Juris* 339

—— 'Obligations, Interpretivism and the Legal Point of View' in A Marmor, *The Routledge Companion to Philosophy of Law* (New York, Routledge, 2012) 76

Tamanaha, B, *A General Jurisprudence of Law and Society* (Oxford, Oxford University Press, 2001)

Vile, MJC, *Constitutionalism and the Separation of Powers*, 2nd edn (Indianapolis, Liberty Fund, 1998)

Waldron, J, 'The Circumstances of Integrity' (1997) 3 *Legal Theory* 1

—— *Law and Disagreement* (Oxford, Oxford University Press, 1999)

—— 'Authority for Officials' in L Meyer, S Paulson and T Pogge (eds), *Rights, Culture and the Law: Themes from the Legal and Political Philosophy of Joseph Raz* (Oxford, Oxford University Press, 2003) 45

—— 'Did Dworkin Ever Answer the Crits?' in S Hershovitz (ed), *Exploring Law's Empire* (Oxford, Oxford University Press, 2006) 155

—— 'Can There Be a Democratic Jurisprudence?' (2009) 58 *Emory Law Journal* 675

—— 'Judges as Moral Reasoners' (2009) 7 *International Journal of Constitutional Law* 2

—— 'A Majority in the Lifeboat' (2010) 90 *Boston University Law Review* 1043

Waluchow, W, *Inclusive Legal Positivism* (Oxford, Oxford University Press, 1994)

Williams, B, *In the Beginning was the Deed* edited by G Hawthorn (Princeton and Oxford, Princeton University Press, 2005)

Wittgenstein, L, *Philosophical Investigations* (Oxford, Blackwell Publishers, 2000)

Index

adjudication, theory of, 12, 44, 65, 85–86, 81, 99

agents of governance, 4, 71–72, 109, 160–61, 163

anti-positivism, 1–2, 7–8, 9–10, 12–13, 19, 125, 128–30

authority
  and authority subjects, 9–10, 30, 32–33, 38–39, 53–54, 139–45, 147, 159–60
  and jurisdiction, 31–33, 40–41, 48–51, 54–55, 140–45
  and pre-emption, 27–28, 34–35, 45–46, 51–52, 139–40
  political, 96, 108, 145
  transnational, 21–22, 161–64

Bentham, J, 138
Bickel, A, 124
Bratman, M, 127

Cane, P, 5, 23
Chang, R, 76
checks-and-balances
  and constitutional review, 13
  and separation of powers, 15–17, 104–07, 118–19

coercion, 23, 56, 96, 101, 105, 108
constitutional review
  and citizens, 147–53
  and democracy, 78–80, 113–14
  and fundamental rights, 38, 42–43
  and Razian authority, 38, 40–43, 144, 148–49

convention, 38, 82–84
conventionalism, 13–14, 128
coordination, 47, 87

Dickson, J, 161
disagreement, 59, 77–78, 108–09, 112, 118, 120–21

division of labour, 42–43, 82, 109, 123–24, 133, 140–41, 145–47, 155–56

Dworkin, R, 1–2, 11–12, 56–60, 62, 69–71, 91, 95–105, 122, 125, 145–47, 151–52

Endicott, T, 48–51, 77

enforceability, judicial, 15, 93–97, 102, 114–16

Enoch, D, 84–89

Finnis, J, 62, 77
fit
  and justification, 59–60, 91–92
  holistic conception of, 62–63, 65–68
  threshold conception of, 61

Fuller, L, 1, 152

Gardner, J, 8, 51–53
Green, L, 25, 35
Greenberg, M, 20, 56, 128

Hart, HLA, 1–2, 10, 81, 132–35, 137
Hershovitz, S, 46, 111, 117
Hurd, H, 32, 36

incommensurability, 76–77
institutional design
  and content, 70–75, 81–84, 110–12, 151–59
  and justice, 70–71, 73–74
  and separation of powers, 13, 110, 119, 129–30
  as constraint on interpretation, 73–77, 84
  beyond the state, 162–64

institutional history, 15, 56–57, 74–75, 82–84, 99–102, 129–30

institutional settlement, 9, 77–80
integrity 98–104
  and justice, 16–17, 103, 116,
  in legislation, 99–102

intentions
  and joint activity, 126–28
  of founding fathers, 127
  of legislators, 89, 117–19

internal point of view, 133–35
interpretation
  and protestant attitude, 145–47, 149–50, 151–53
  collaborative, 58, 70, 91–92
  conceptual, 58
  constructive, 57–58
  explanatory, 58, 92
  fit and justification, 59–63

www.ingramcontent.com/pod-product-compliance
Lightning Source LLC
Chambersburg PA
CBHW050515280326
41932CB00014B/2330